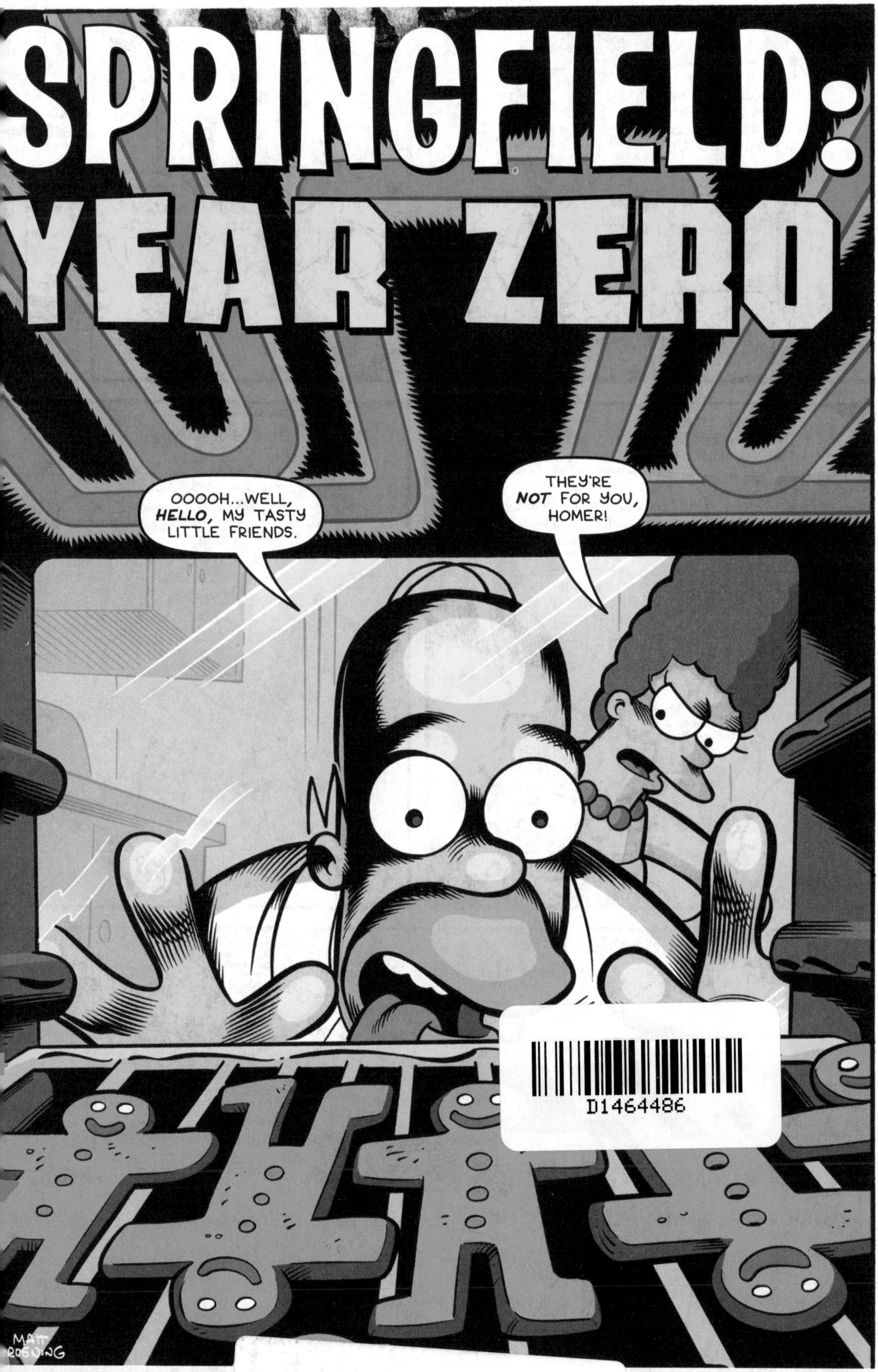
SPRINGFIELD: YEAR ZERO
OOOOH...WELL, HELLO, MY TASTY LITTLE FRIENDS.
THEY'RE NOT FOR YOU, HOMER!

HUCK DIXON BLACKBURN SCRIPT

JOH DELA PENC

KAREN BATES LETTERS

NATHAN KANE EDITOR

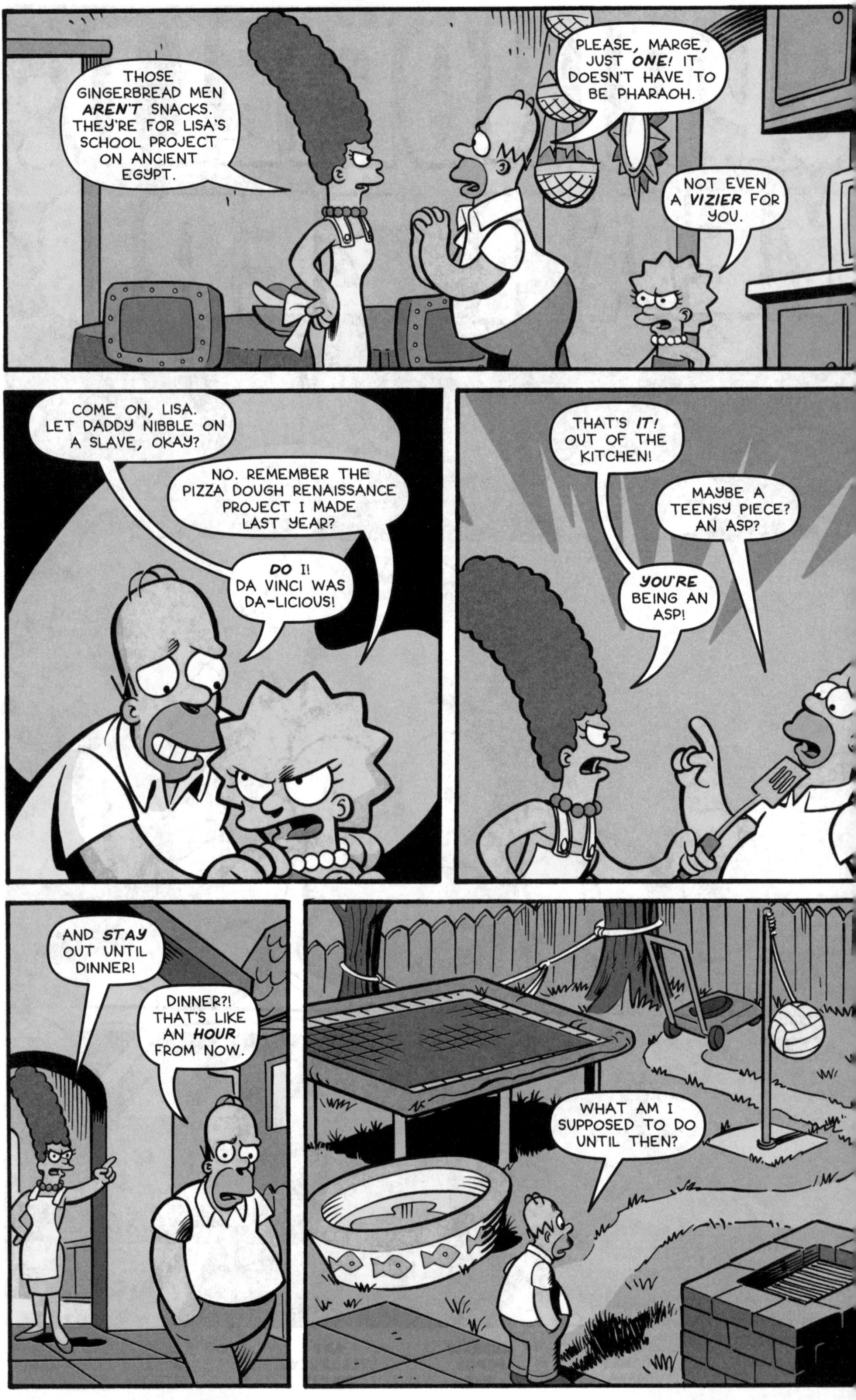

THOSE GINGERBREAD MEN **AREN'T** SNACKS. THEY'RE FOR LISA'S SCHOOL PROJECT ON ANCIENT EGYPT.
PLEASE, MARGE, JUST **ONE!** IT DOESN'T HAVE TO BE PHARAOH.
NOT EVEN A **VIZIER** FOR YOU.
COME ON, LISA. LET DADDY NIBBLE ON A SLAVE, OKAY?
NO. REMEMBER THE PIZZA DOUGH RENAISSANCE PROJECT I MADE LAST YEAR?
DO I! DA VINCI WAS DA-LICIOUS!
THAT'S **IT!** OUT OF THE KITCHEN!
MAYBE A TEENSY PIECE? AN ASP?
YOU'RE BEING AN ASP!
AND **STAY** OUT UNTIL DINNER!
DINNER?! THAT'S LIKE AN **HOUR** FROM NOW.
WHAT AM I SUPPOSED TO DO UNTIL THEN?

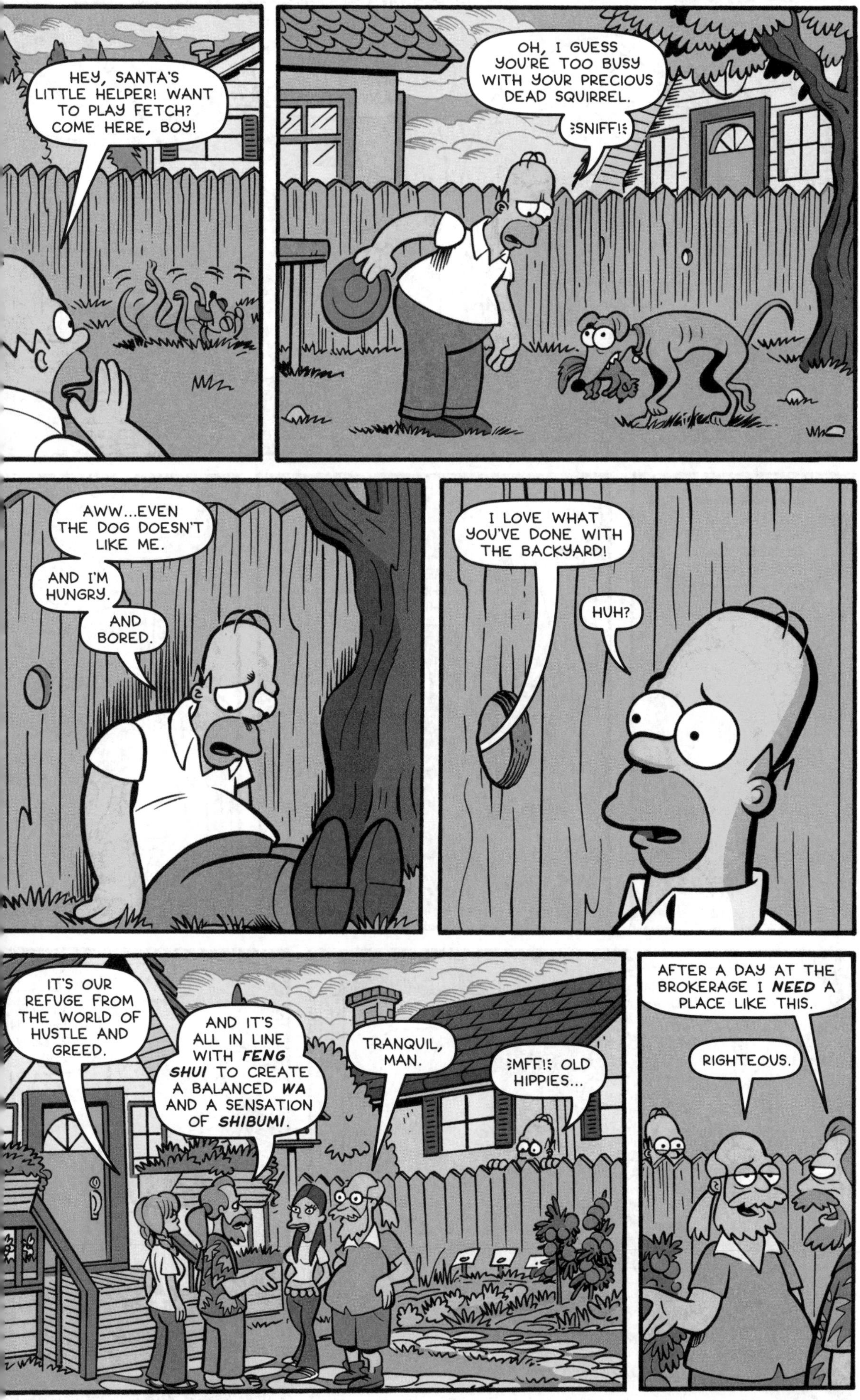
HEY, SANTA'S LITTLE HELPER! WANT TO PLAY FETCH? COME HERE, BOY!
OH, I GUESS YOU'RE TOO BUSY WITH YOUR PRECIOUS DEAD SQUIRREL.
SNIFF!
AWW...EVEN THE DOG DOESN'T LIKE ME.
AND I'M HUNGRY.
AND BORED.
I LOVE WHAT YOU'VE DONE WITH THE BACKYARD!
HUH?
IT'S OUR REFUGE FROM THE WORLD OF HUSTLE AND GREED.
AND IT'S ALL IN LINE WITH FENG SHUI TO CREATE A BALANCED WA AND A SENSATION OF SHIBUMI.
TRANQUIL, MAN.
MFF! OLD HIPPIES...
AFTER A DAY AT THE BROKERAGE I NEED A PLACE LIKE THIS.
RIGHTEOUS.

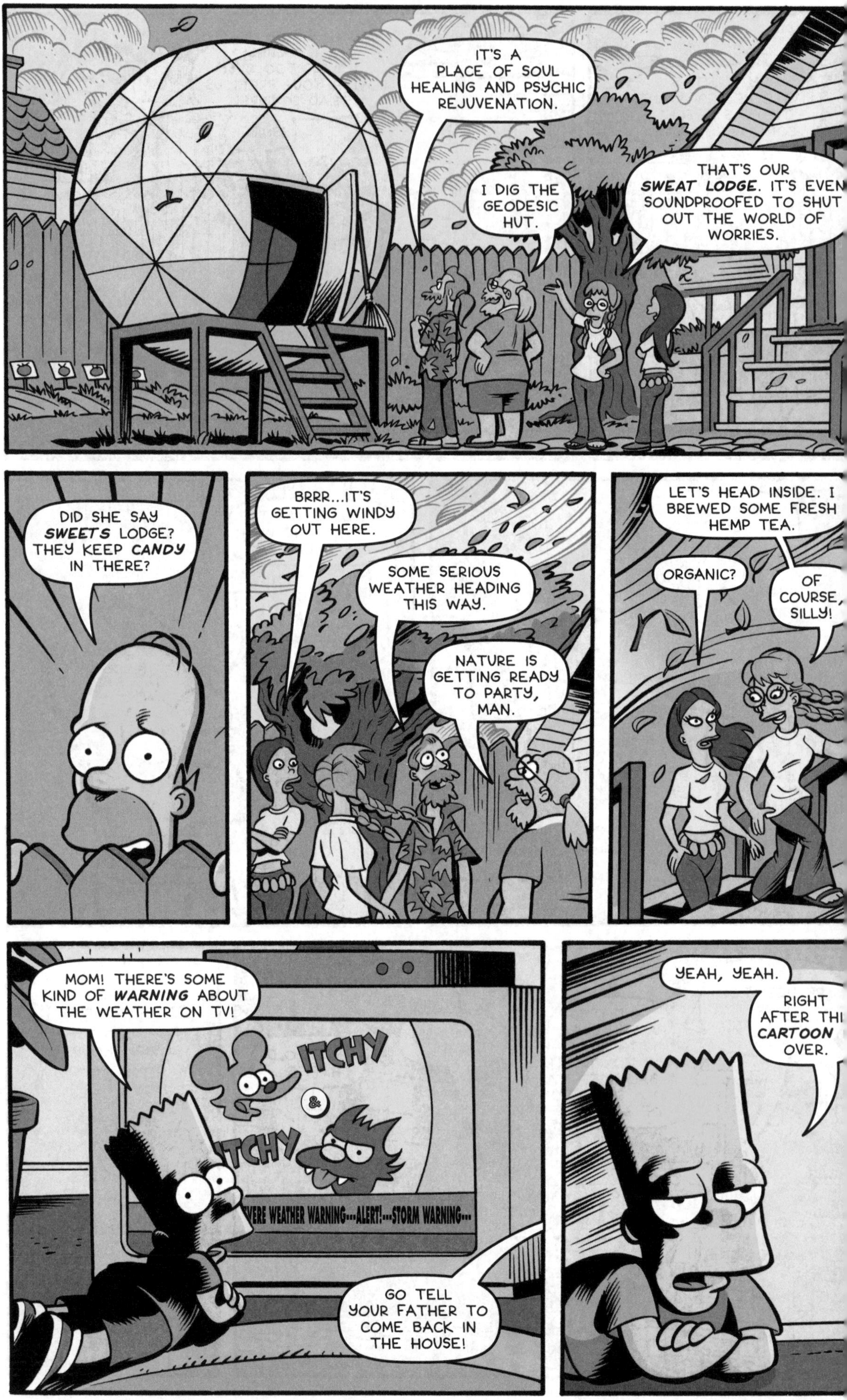
IT'S A PLACE OF SOUL HEALING AND PSYCHIC REJUVENATION.
I DIG THE GEODESIC HUT.
THAT'S OUR SWEAT LODGE. IT'S EVEN SOUNDPROOFED TO SHUT OUT THE WORLD OF WORRIES.
DID SHE SAY SWEETS LODGE? THEY KEEP CANDY IN THERE?
BRRR...IT'S GETTING WINDY OUT HERE.
SOME SERIOUS WEATHER HEADING THIS WAY.
NATURE IS GETTING READY TO PARTY, MAN.
LET'S HEAD INSIDE. I BREWED SOME FRESH HEMP TEA.
ORGANIC?
OF COURSE, SILLY!
MOM! THERE'S SOME KIND OF WARNING ABOUT THE WEATHER ON TV!
ITCHY
&
ERE WEATHER WARNING---ALERT!---STORM WARNING---
GO TELL YOUR FATHER TO COME BACK IN THE HOUSE!
YEAH, YEAH.
RIGHT AFTER THI CARTOON OVER.

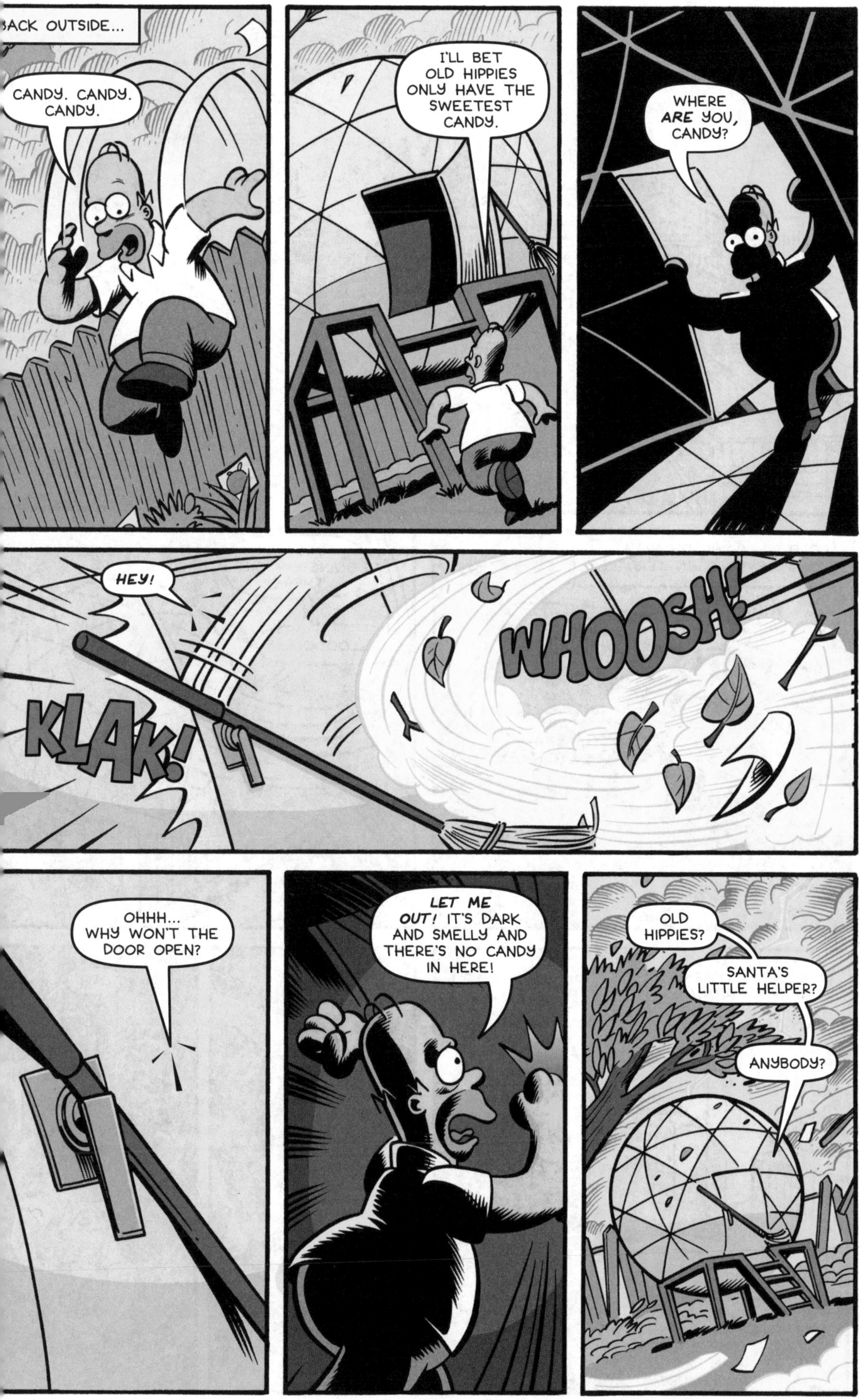
BACK OUTSIDE...
CANDY. CANDY. CANDY.
I'LL BET OLD HIPPIES ONLY HAVE THE SWEETEST CANDY.
WHERE ARE YOU, CANDY?
HEY!
KLAK!
WHOOSH!
OHHH... WHY WON'T THE DOOR OPEN?
LET ME OUT! IT'S DARK AND SMELLY AND THERE'S NO CANDY IN HERE!
OLD HIPPIES?
SANTA'S LITTLE HELPER?
ANYBODY?

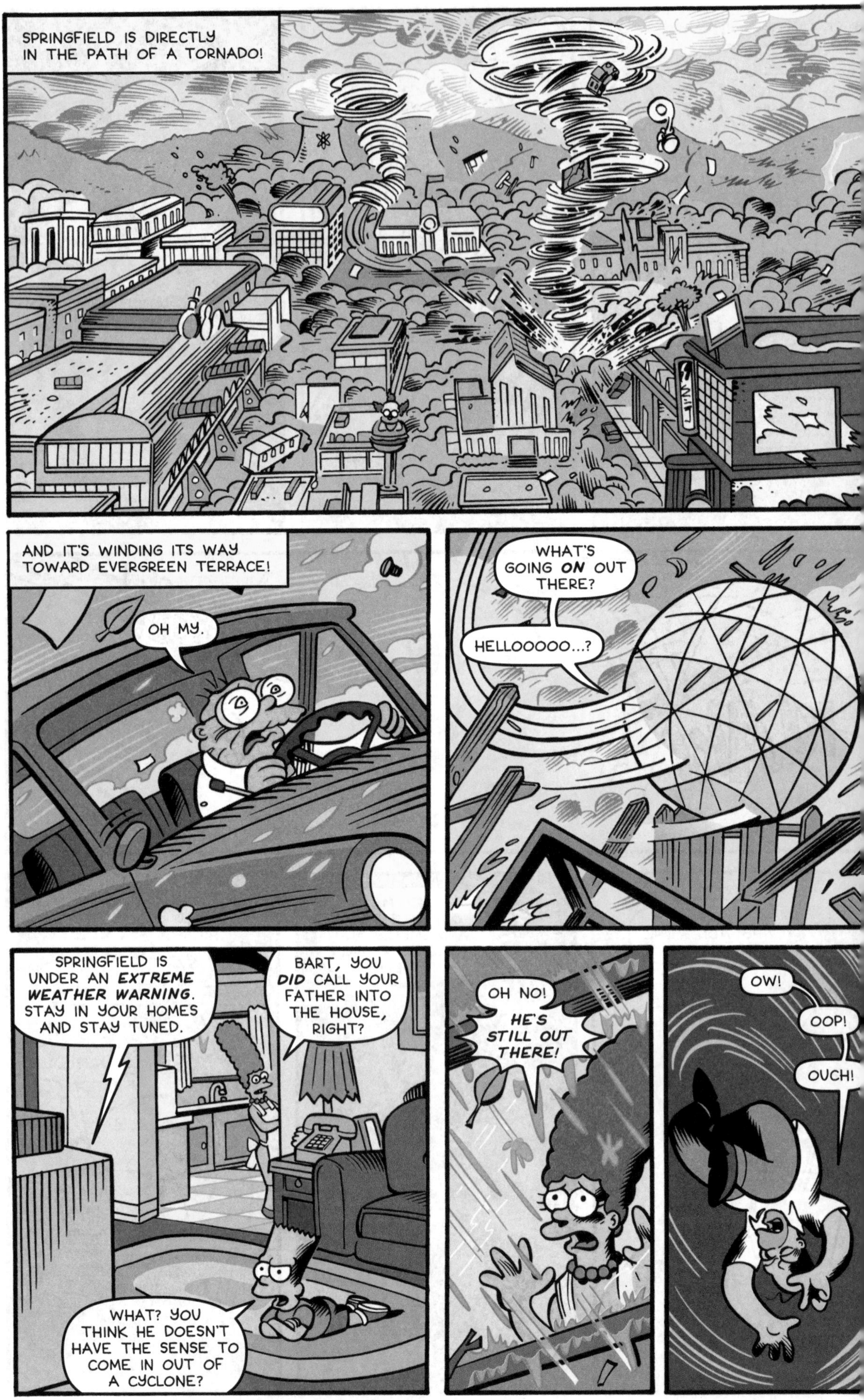
SPRINGFIELD IS DIRECTLY IN THE PATH OF A TORNADO!
AND IT'S WINDING ITS WAY TOWARD EVERGREEN TERRACE!
OH MY.
WHAT'S GOING ON OUT THERE?
HELLOOOOO...?
SPRINGFIELD IS UNDER AN EXTREME WEATHER WARNING. STAY IN YOUR HOMES AND STAY TUNED.
BART, YOU DID CALL YOUR FATHER INTO THE HOUSE, RIGHT?
WHAT? YOU THINK HE DOESN'T HAVE THE SENSE TO COME IN OUT OF A CYCLONE?
OH NO!
HE'S STILL OUT THERE!
OW!
OOP!
OUCH!

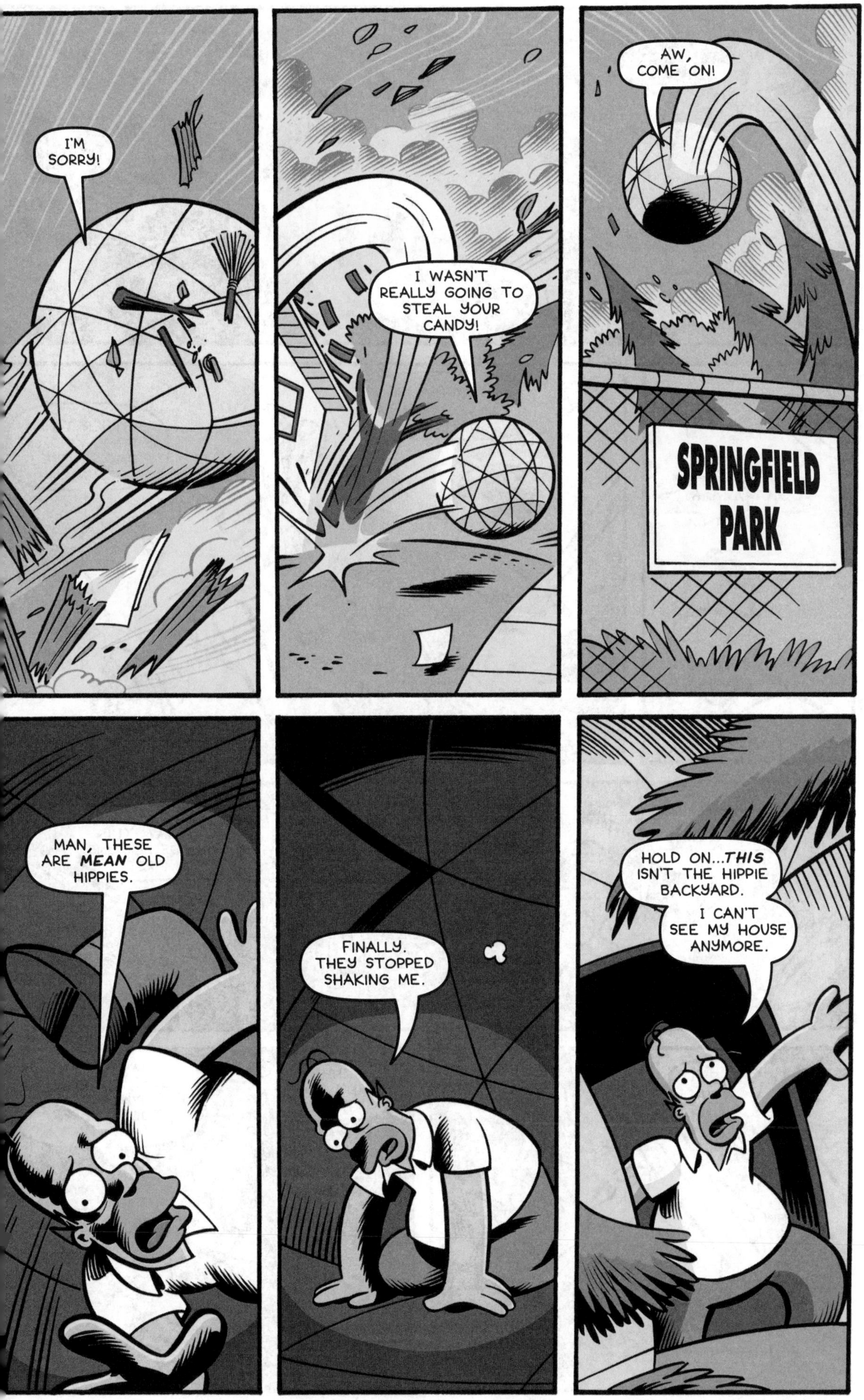
I'M SORRY!
I WASN'T REALLY GOING TO STEAL YOUR CANDY!
AW, COME ON!
SPRINGFIELD PARK
MAN, THESE ARE **MEAN** OLD HIPPIES.
FINALLY. THEY STOPPED SHAKING ME.
HOLD ON...**THIS** ISN'T THE HIPPIE BACKYARD.
I CAN'T SEE MY HOUSE ANYMORE.

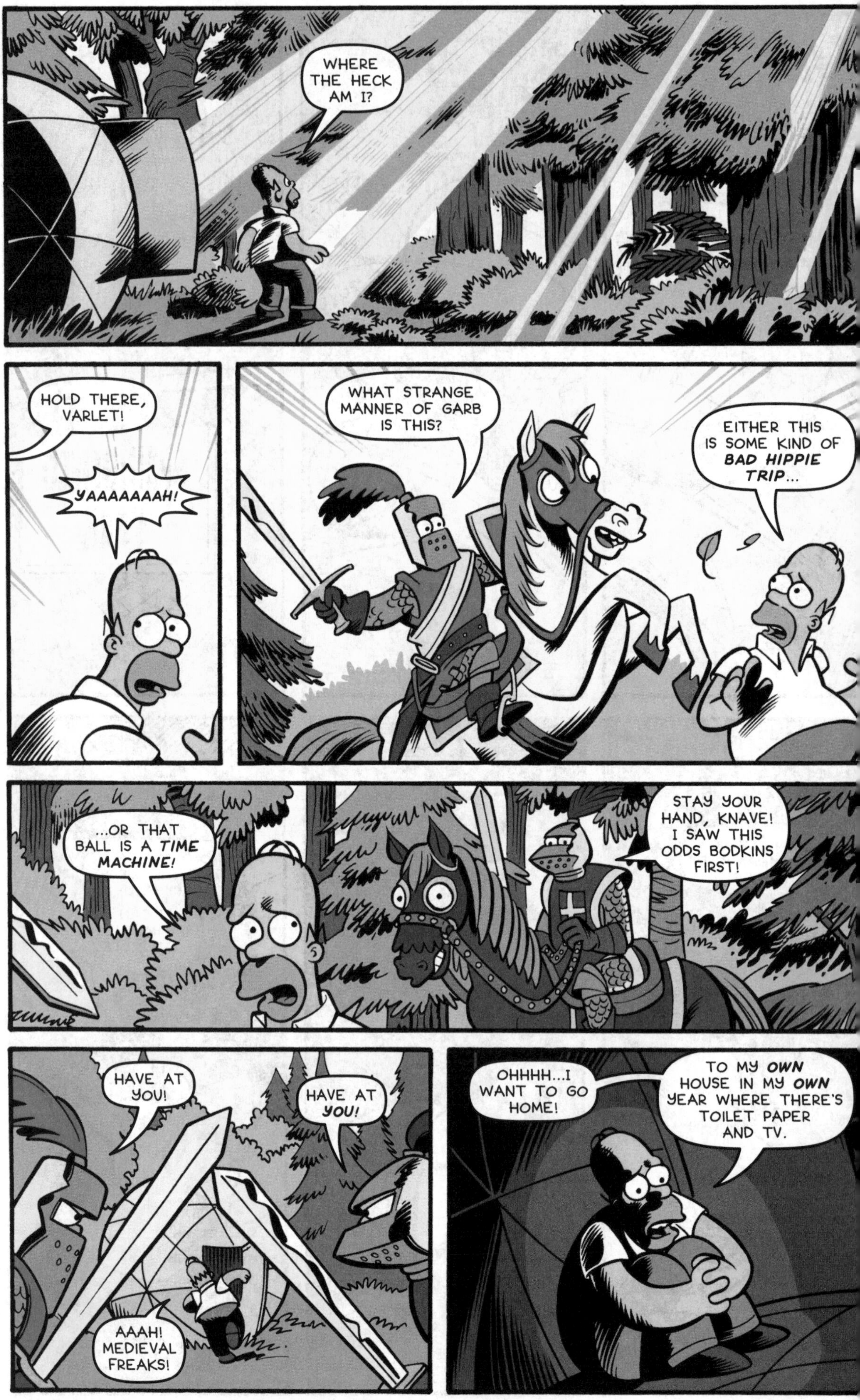
WHERE THE HECK AM I?
HOLD THERE, VARLET!
YAAAAAAAH!
WHAT STRANGE MANNER OF GARB IS THIS?
EITHER THIS IS SOME KIND OF BAD HIPPIE TRIP...
...OR THAT BALL IS A TIME MACHINE!
STAY YOUR HAND, KNAVE! I SAW THIS ODDS BODKINS FIRST!
HAVE AT YOU!
HAVE AT YOU!
AAAH! MEDIEVAL FREAKS!
OHHHH...I WANT TO GO HOME!
TO MY OWN HOUSE IN MY OWN YEAR WHERE THERE'S TOILET PAPER AND TV.

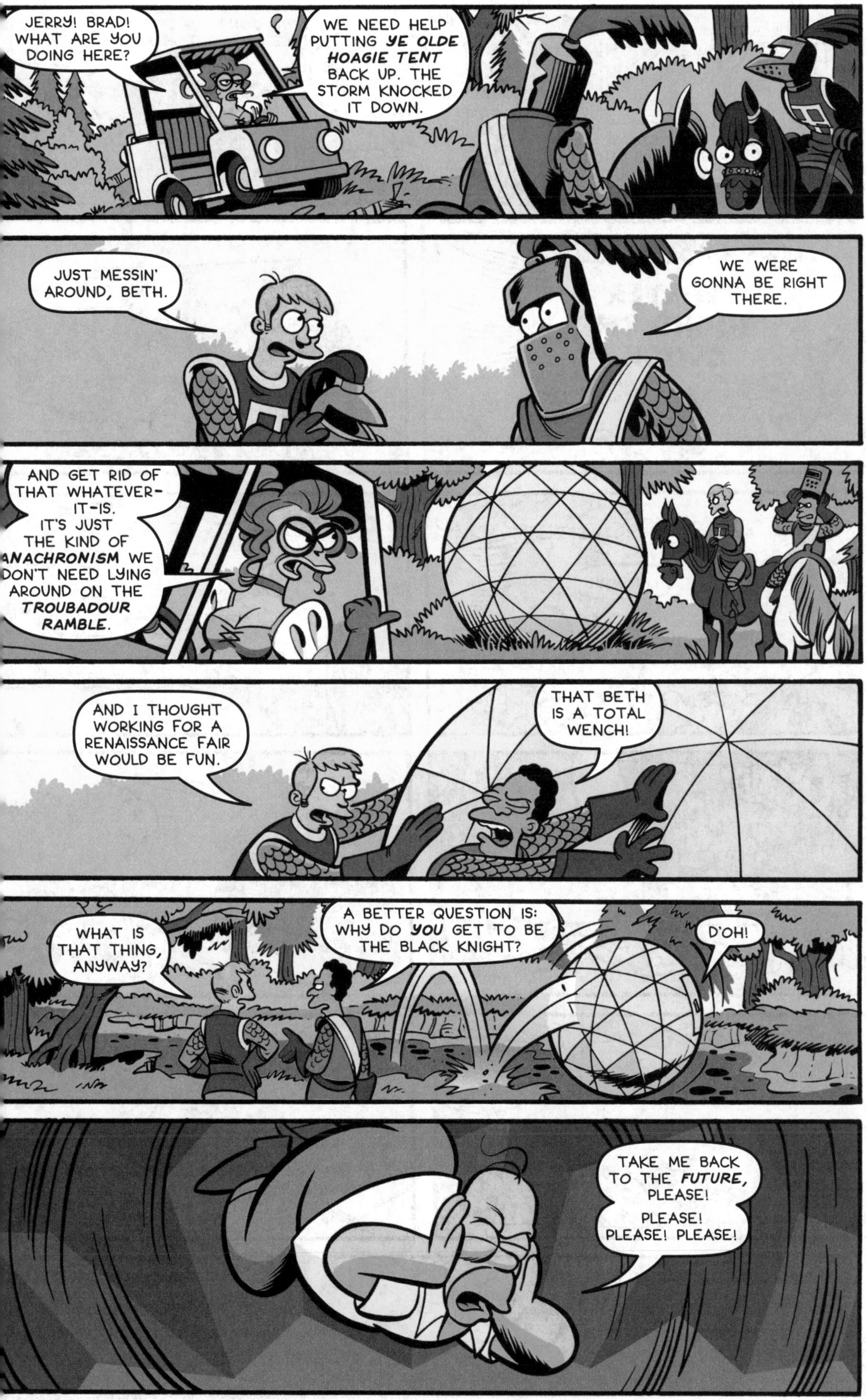
JERRY! BRAD! WHAT ARE YOU DOING HERE?
WE NEED HELP PUTTING *YE OLDE HOAGIE TENT* BACK UP. THE STORM KNOCKED IT DOWN.
JUST MESSIN' AROUND, BETH.
WE WERE GONNA BE RIGHT THERE.
AND GET RID OF THAT WHATEVER-IT-IS. IT'S JUST THE KIND OF *ANACHRONISM* WE DON'T NEED LYING AROUND ON THE *TROUBADOUR RAMBLE*.
AND I THOUGHT WORKING FOR A RENAISSANCE FAIR WOULD BE FUN.
THAT BETH IS A TOTAL WENCH!
WHAT IS THAT THING, ANYWAY?
A BETTER QUESTION IS: WHY DO *YOU* GET TO BE THE BLACK KNIGHT?
D'OH!
TAKE ME BACK TO THE *FUTURE,* PLEASE!
PLEASE! PLEASE! PLEASE!

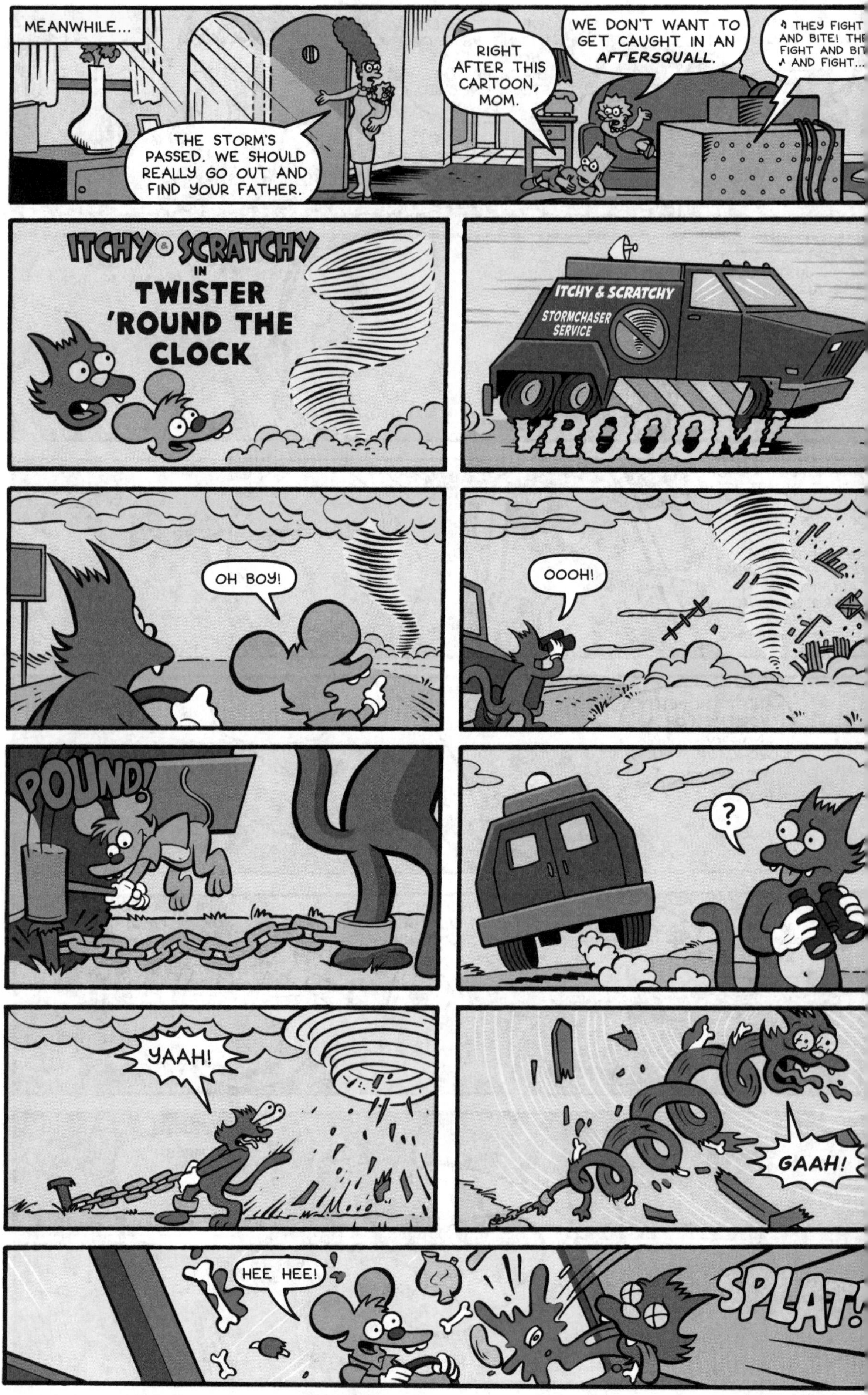
MEANWHILE...
THE STORM'S PASSED. WE SHOULD REALLY GO OUT AND FIND YOUR FATHER.
RIGHT AFTER THIS CARTOON, MOM.
WE DON'T WANT TO GET CAUGHT IN AN AFTERSQUALL.
♪ THEY FIGHT AND BITE! THE FIGHT AND BIT ♪ AND FIGHT...
ITCHY & SCRATCHY IN TWISTER 'ROUND THE CLOCK
ITCHY & SCRATCHY STORMCHASER SERVICE
VROOOM!
OH BOY!
OOOH!
POUND!
?
YAAH!
GAAH!
HEE HEE!
SPLAT!

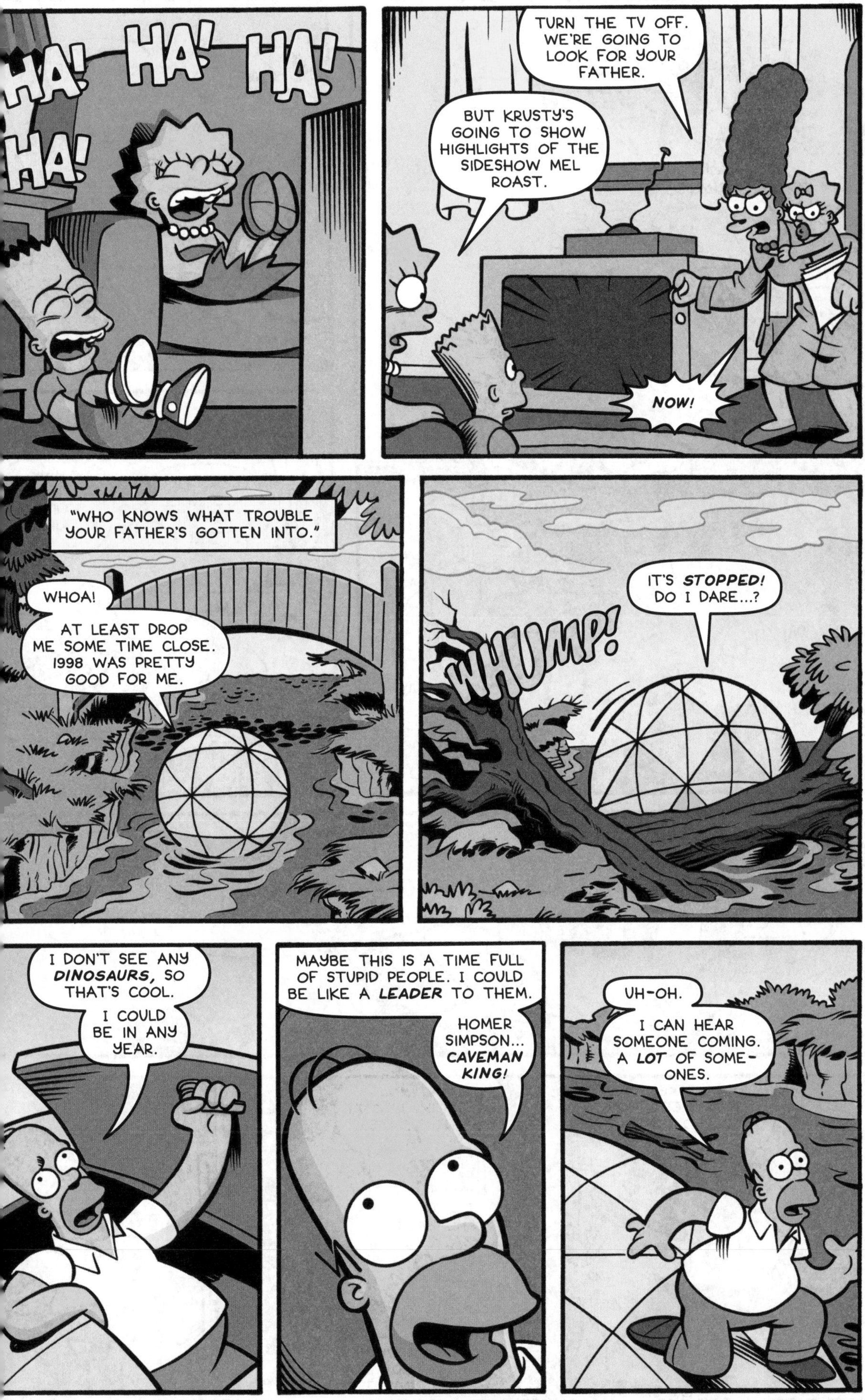
HA! HA! HA!
HA!
TURN THE TV OFF. WE'RE GOING TO LOOK FOR YOUR FATHER.
BUT KRUSTY'S GOING TO SHOW HIGHLIGHTS OF THE SIDESHOW MEL ROAST.
NOW!
"WHO KNOWS WHAT TROUBLE YOUR FATHER'S GOTTEN INTO."
WHOA!
AT LEAST DROP ME SOME TIME CLOSE. 1998 WAS PRETTY GOOD FOR ME.
WHUMP!
IT'S STOPPED! DO I DARE...?
I DON'T SEE ANY DINOSAURS, SO THAT'S COOL.
I COULD BE IN ANY YEAR.
MAYBE THIS IS A TIME FULL OF STUPID PEOPLE. I COULD BE LIKE A LEADER TO THEM.
HOMER SIMPSON... CAVEMAN KING!
UH-OH.
I CAN HEAR SOMEONE COMING. A LOT OF SOME-ONES.

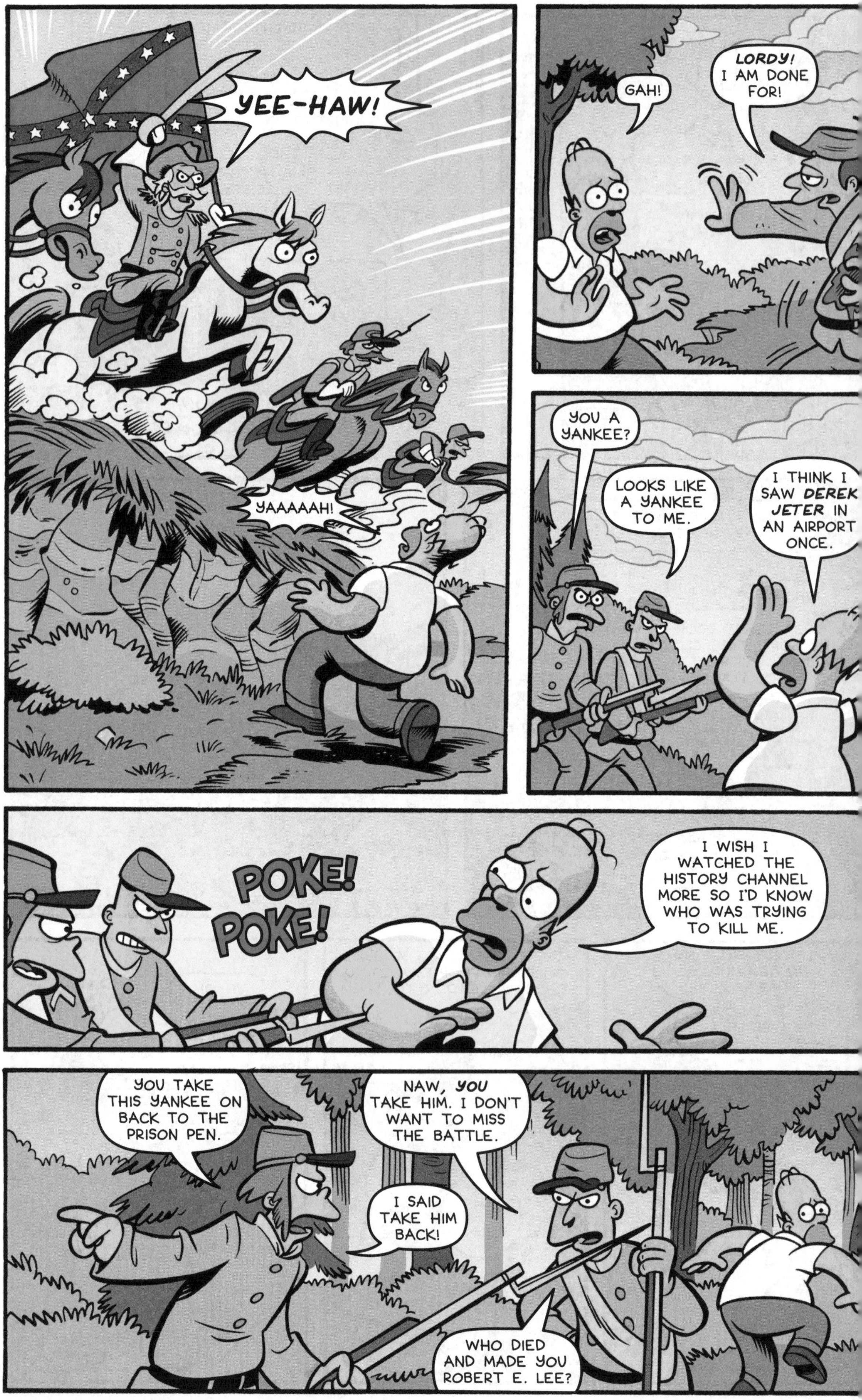
YEE-HAW!
YAAAAAH!
GAH!
LORDY! I AM DONE FOR!
YOU A YANKEE?
LOOKS LIKE A YANKEE TO ME.
I THINK I SAW DEREK JETER IN AN AIRPORT ONCE.
POKE! POKE!
I WISH I WATCHED THE HISTORY CHANNEL MORE SO I'D KNOW WHO WAS TRYING TO KILL ME.
YOU TAKE THIS YANKEE ON BACK TO THE PRISON PEN.
NAW, YOU TAKE HIM. I DON'T WANT TO MISS THE BATTLE.
I SAID TAKE HIM BACK!
WHO DIED AND MADE YOU ROBERT E. LEE?

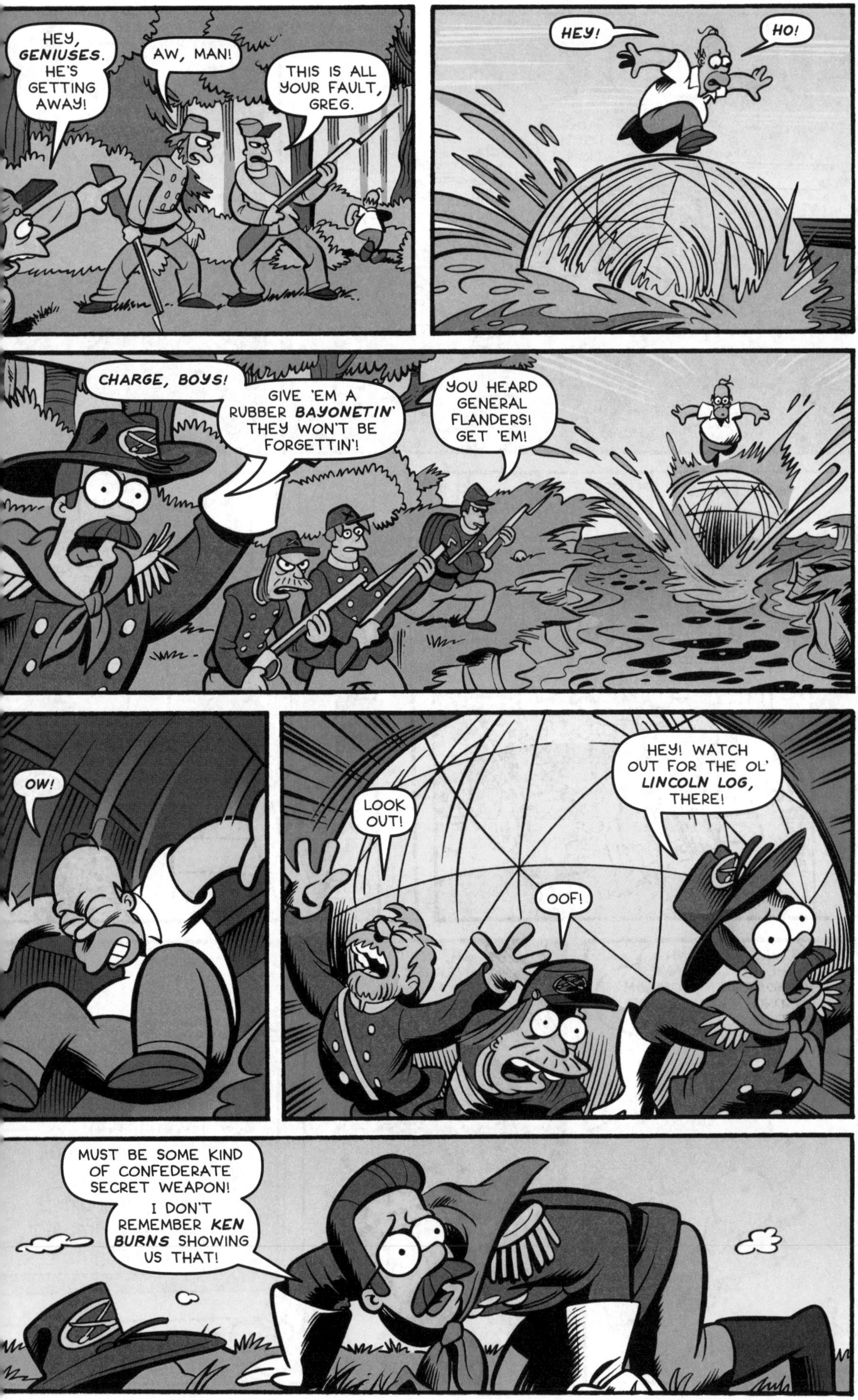
HEY, GENIUSES. HE'S GETTING AWAY!
AW, MAN!
THIS IS ALL YOUR FAULT, GREG.
HEY!
HO!
CHARGE, BOYS!
GIVE 'EM A RUBBER BAYONETIN' THEY WON'T BE FORGETTIN'!
YOU HEARD GENERAL FLANDERS! GET 'EM!
OW!
LOOK OUT!
HEY! WATCH OUT FOR THE OL' LINCOLN LOG, THERE!
OOF!
MUST BE SOME KIND OF CONFEDERATE SECRET WEAPON!
I DON'T REMEMBER KEN BURNS SHOWING US THAT!

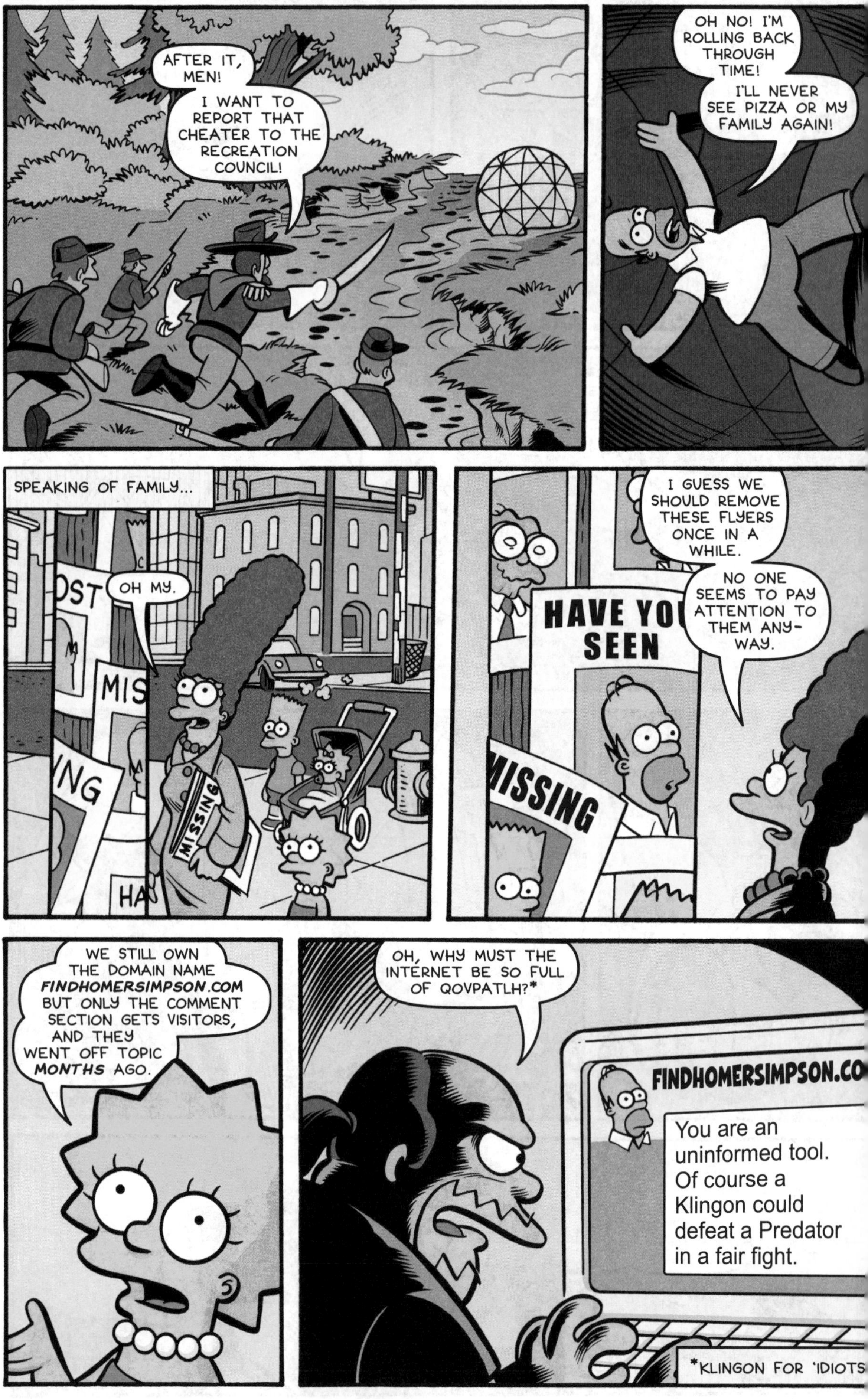
AFTER IT, MEN!
I WANT TO REPORT THAT CHEATER TO THE RECREATION COUNCIL!
OH NO! I'M ROLLING BACK THROUGH TIME!
I'LL NEVER SEE PIZZA OR MY FAMILY AGAIN!
SPEAKING OF FAMILY...
OH MY.
MISSING
I GUESS WE SHOULD REMOVE THESE FLYERS ONCE IN A WHILE.
NO ONE SEEMS TO PAY ATTENTION TO THEM ANYWAY.
HAVE YOU SEEN
MISSING
WE STILL OWN THE DOMAIN NAME FINDHOMERSIMPSON.COM BUT ONLY THE COMMENT SECTION GETS VISITORS, AND THEY WENT OFF TOPIC MONTHS AGO.
OH, WHY MUST THE INTERNET BE SO FULL OF QOVPATLH?*
FINDHOMERSIMPSON.CO
You are an uninformed tool. Of course a Klingon could defeat a Predator in a fair fight.
*KLINGON FOR 'IDIOTS

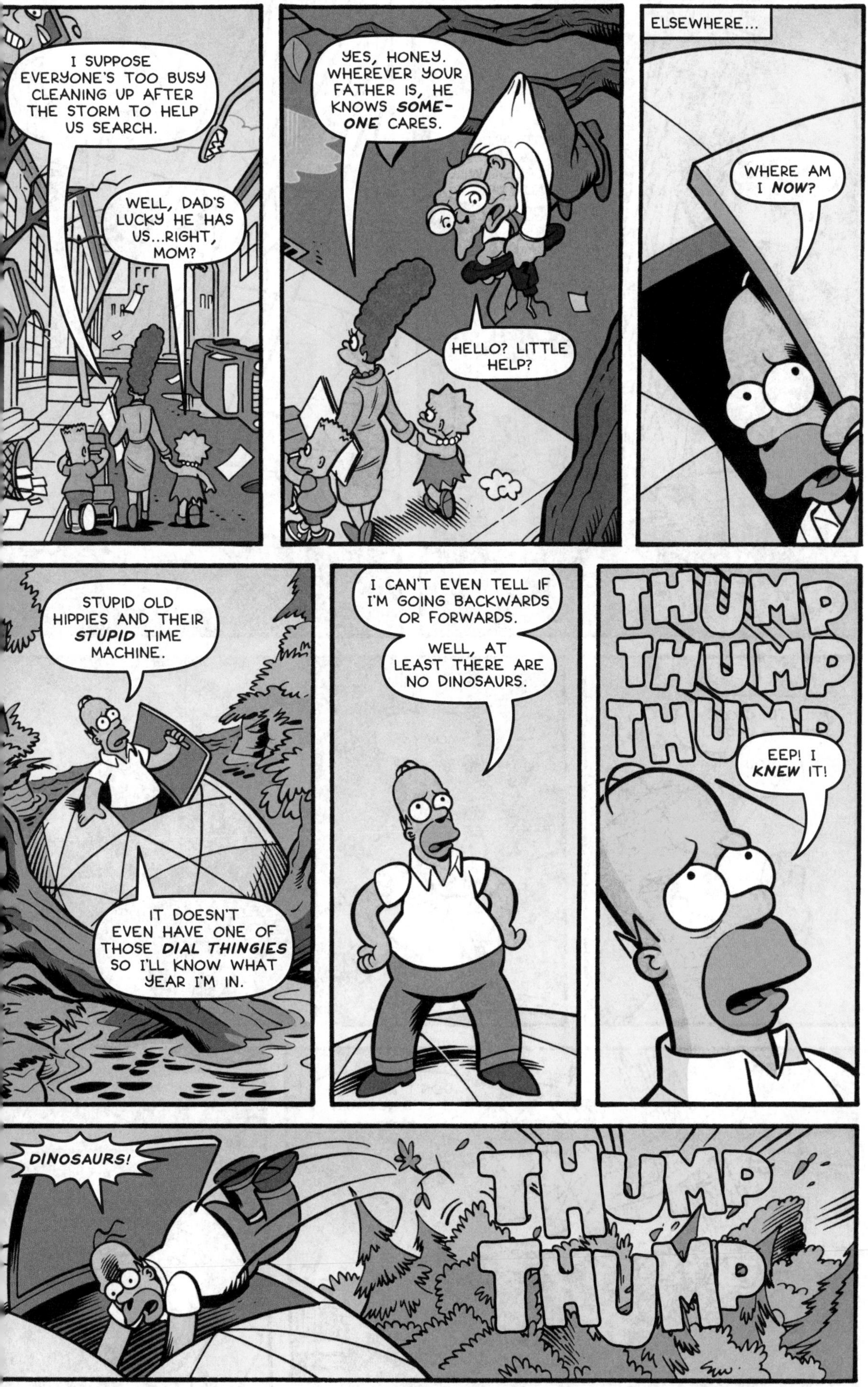
I SUPPOSE EVERYONE'S TOO BUSY CLEANING UP AFTER THE STORM TO HELP US SEARCH.
WELL, DAD'S LUCKY HE HAS US...RIGHT, MOM?
YES, HONEY. WHEREVER YOUR FATHER IS, HE KNOWS *SOME-ONE* CARES.
HELLO? LITTLE HELP?
ELSEWHERE...
WHERE AM I *NOW?*
STUPID OLD HIPPIES AND THEIR *STUPID* TIME MACHINE.
IT DOESN'T EVEN HAVE ONE OF THOSE *DIAL THINGIES* SO I'LL KNOW WHAT YEAR I'M IN.
I CAN'T EVEN TELL IF I'M GOING BACKWARDS OR FORWARDS.
WELL, AT LEAST THERE ARE NO DINOSAURS.
THUMP THUMP THUMP
EEP! I *KNEW* IT!
DINOSAURS!
THUMP THUMP

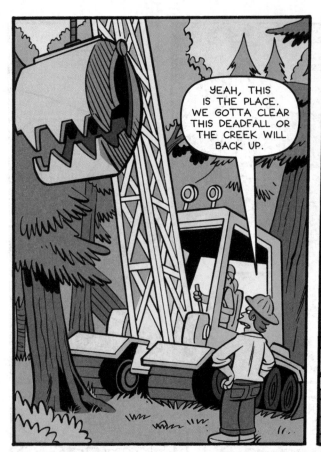

YEAH, THIS IS THE PLACE. WE GOTTA CLEAR THIS DEADFALL OR THE CREEK WILL BACK UP.

WHAT THE HECK'S *THAT*?

WHO KNOWS? IT'S GOTTA GO.

LITTLE MORE... LITTLE MORE...

YOU GOT IT!

MOMMY!

DON'T *EAT* ME, MR. DINOSAUR!

UNNH!

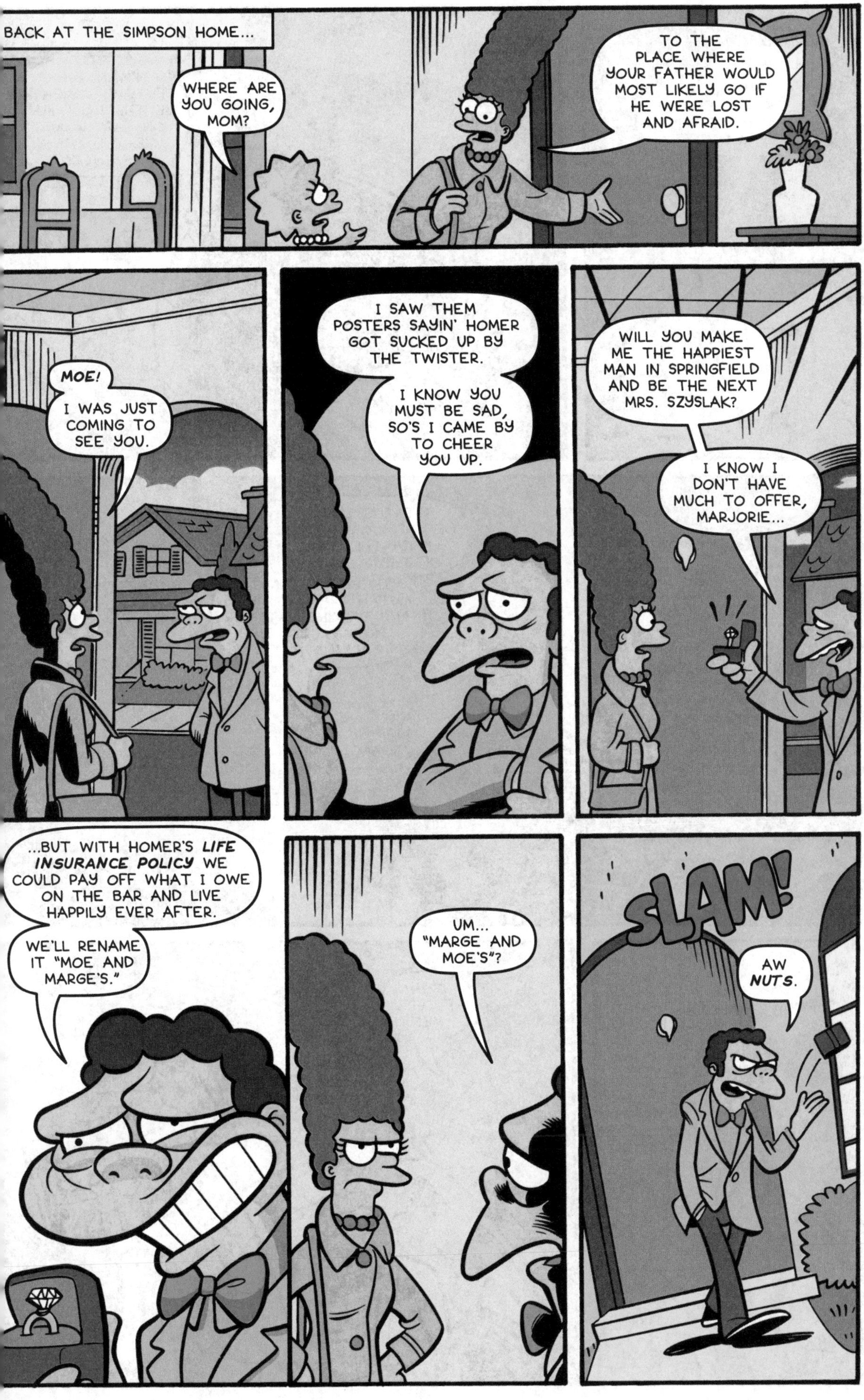

BACK AT THE SIMPSON HOME...
WHERE ARE YOU GOING, MOM?
TO THE PLACE WHERE YOUR FATHER WOULD MOST LIKELY GO IF HE WERE LOST AND AFRAID.
MOE!
I WAS JUST COMING TO SEE YOU.
I SAW THEM POSTERS SAYIN' HOMER GOT SUCKED UP BY THE TWISTER.
I KNOW YOU MUST BE SAD, SO'S I CAME BY TO CHEER YOU UP.
WILL YOU MAKE ME THE HAPPIEST MAN IN SPRINGFIELD AND BE THE NEXT MRS. SZYSLAK?
I KNOW I DON'T HAVE MUCH TO OFFER, MARJORIE...
...BUT WITH HOMER'S **LIFE INSURANCE POLICY** WE COULD PAY OFF WHAT I OWE ON THE BAR AND LIVE HAPPILY EVER AFTER.
WE'LL RENAME IT "MOE AND MARGE'S."
UM... "MARGE AND MOE'S"?
SLAM!
AW **NUTS**.

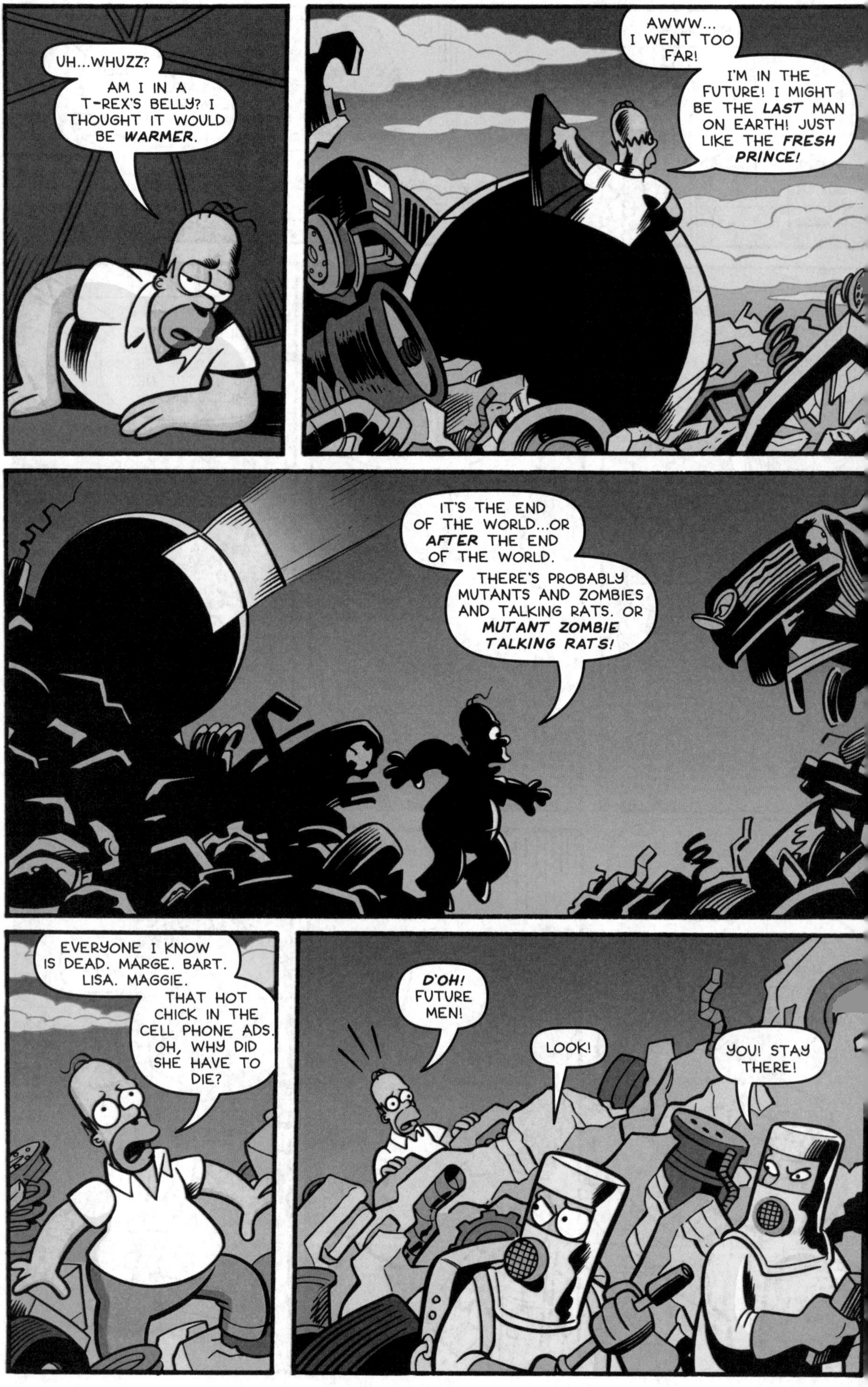
UH...WHUZZ?
AM I IN A T-REX'S BELLY? I THOUGHT IT WOULD BE **WARMER**.
AWWW... I WENT TOO FAR!
I'M IN THE FUTURE! I MIGHT BE THE **LAST** MAN ON EARTH! JUST LIKE THE **FRESH PRINCE**!
IT'S THE END OF THE WORLD...OR **AFTER** THE END OF THE WORLD.
THERE'S PROBABLY MUTANTS AND ZOMBIES AND TALKING RATS. OR **MUTANT ZOMBIE TALKING RATS**!
EVERYONE I KNOW IS DEAD. MARGE. BART. LISA. MAGGIE.
THAT HOT CHICK IN THE CELL PHONE ADS. OH, WHY DID SHE HAVE TO DIE?
D'OH! FUTURE MEN!
LOOK!
YOU! STAY THERE!

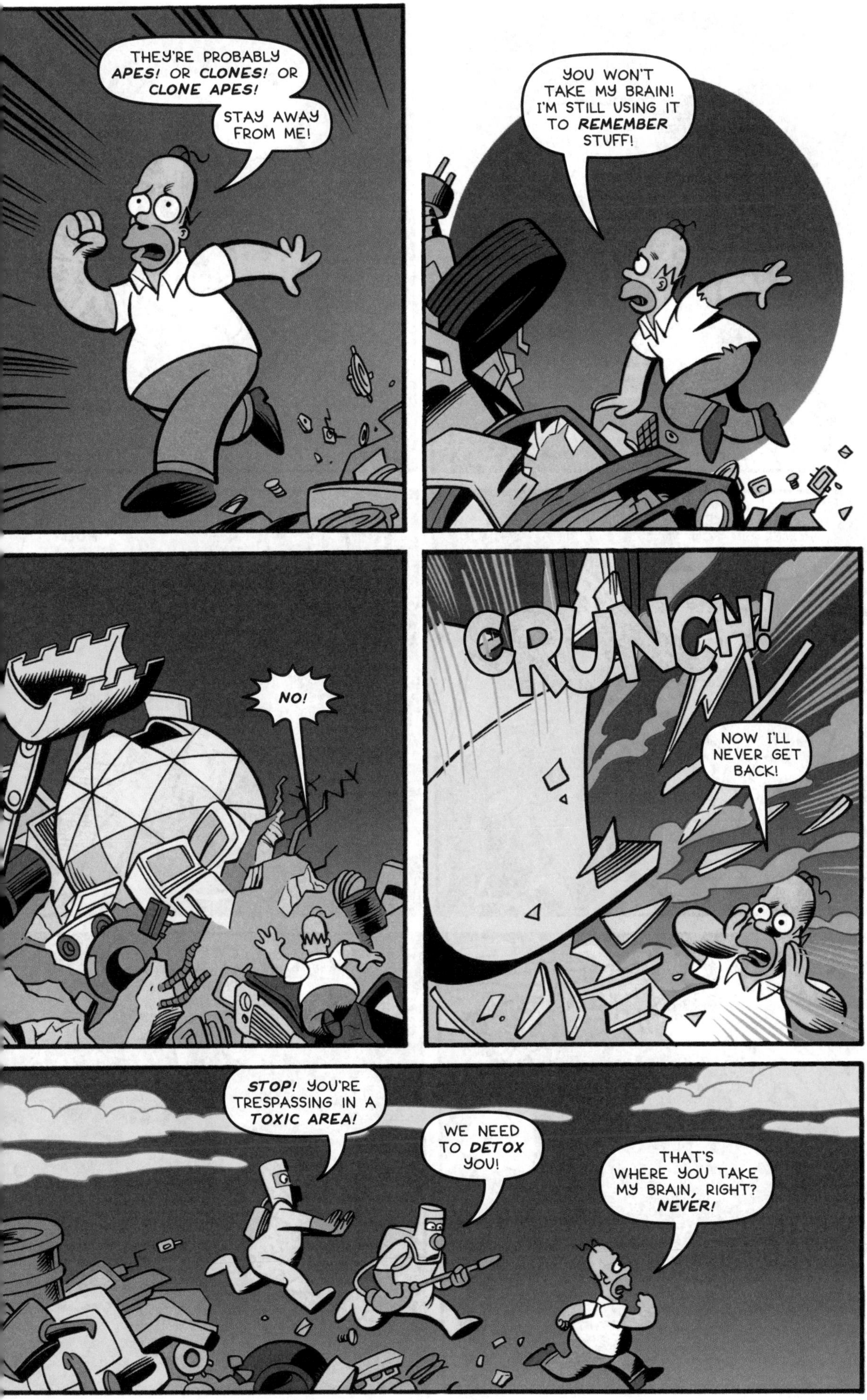
THEY'RE PROBABLY **APES!** OR **CLONES!** OR **CLONE APES!**
STAY AWAY FROM ME!
YOU WON'T TAKE MY BRAIN! I'M STILL USING IT TO **REMEMBER** STUFF!
NO!
CRUNCH!
NOW I'LL NEVER GET BACK!
STOP! YOU'RE TRESPASSING IN A **TOXIC AREA!**
WE NEED TO **DETOX** YOU!
THAT'S WHERE YOU TAKE MY BRAIN, RIGHT? **NEVER!**

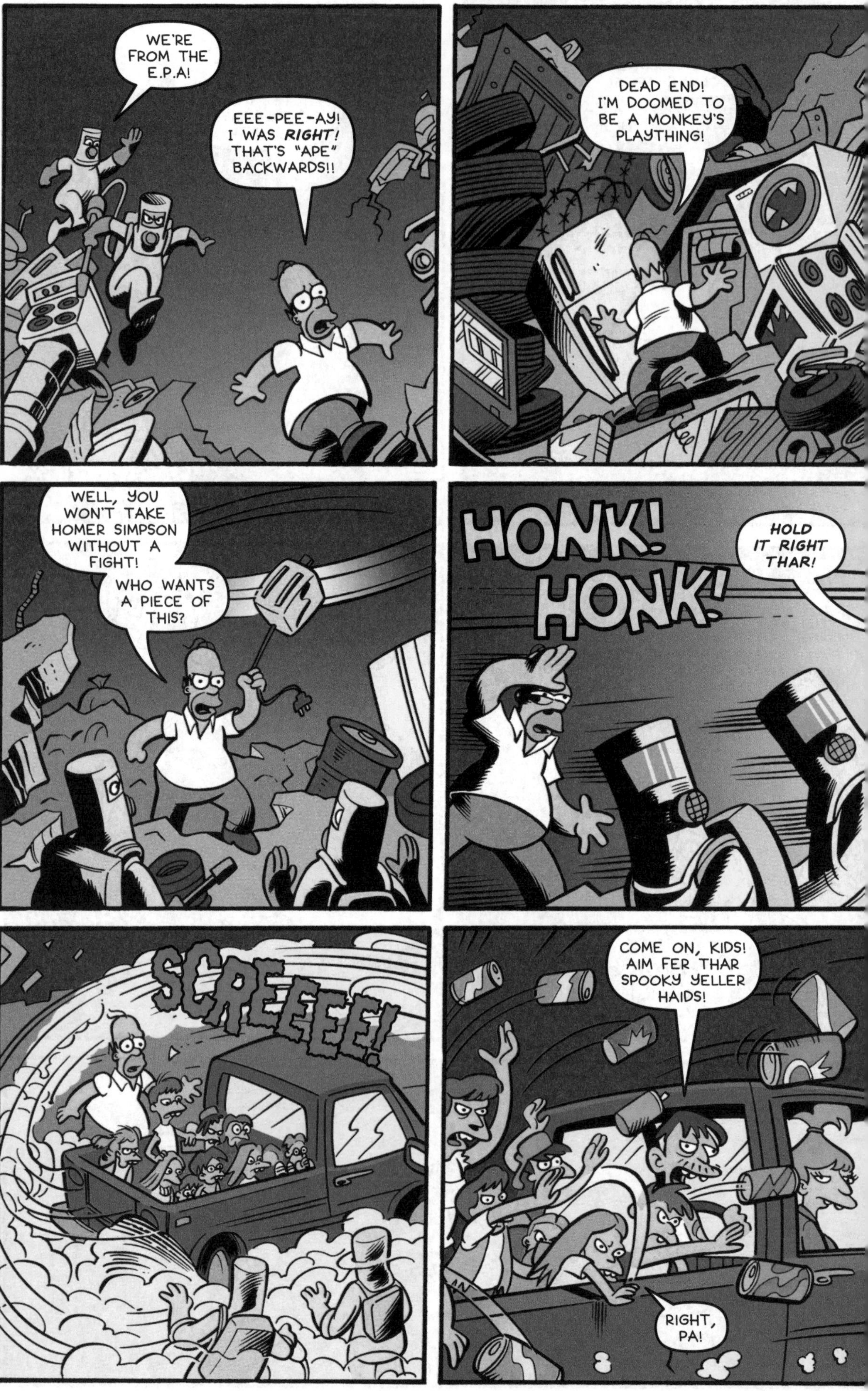
WE'RE FROM THE E.P.A!
EEE-PEE-AY! I WAS RIGHT! THAT'S "APE" BACKWARDS!!
DEAD END! I'M DOOMED TO BE A MONKEY'S PLAYTHING!
WELL, YOU WON'T TAKE HOMER SIMPSON WITHOUT A FIGHT!
WHO WANTS A PIECE OF THIS?
HONK! HONK!
HOLD IT RIGHT THAR!
SCREEEEE!
COME ON, KIDS! AIM FER THAR SPOOKY YELLER HAIDS!
RIGHT, PA!

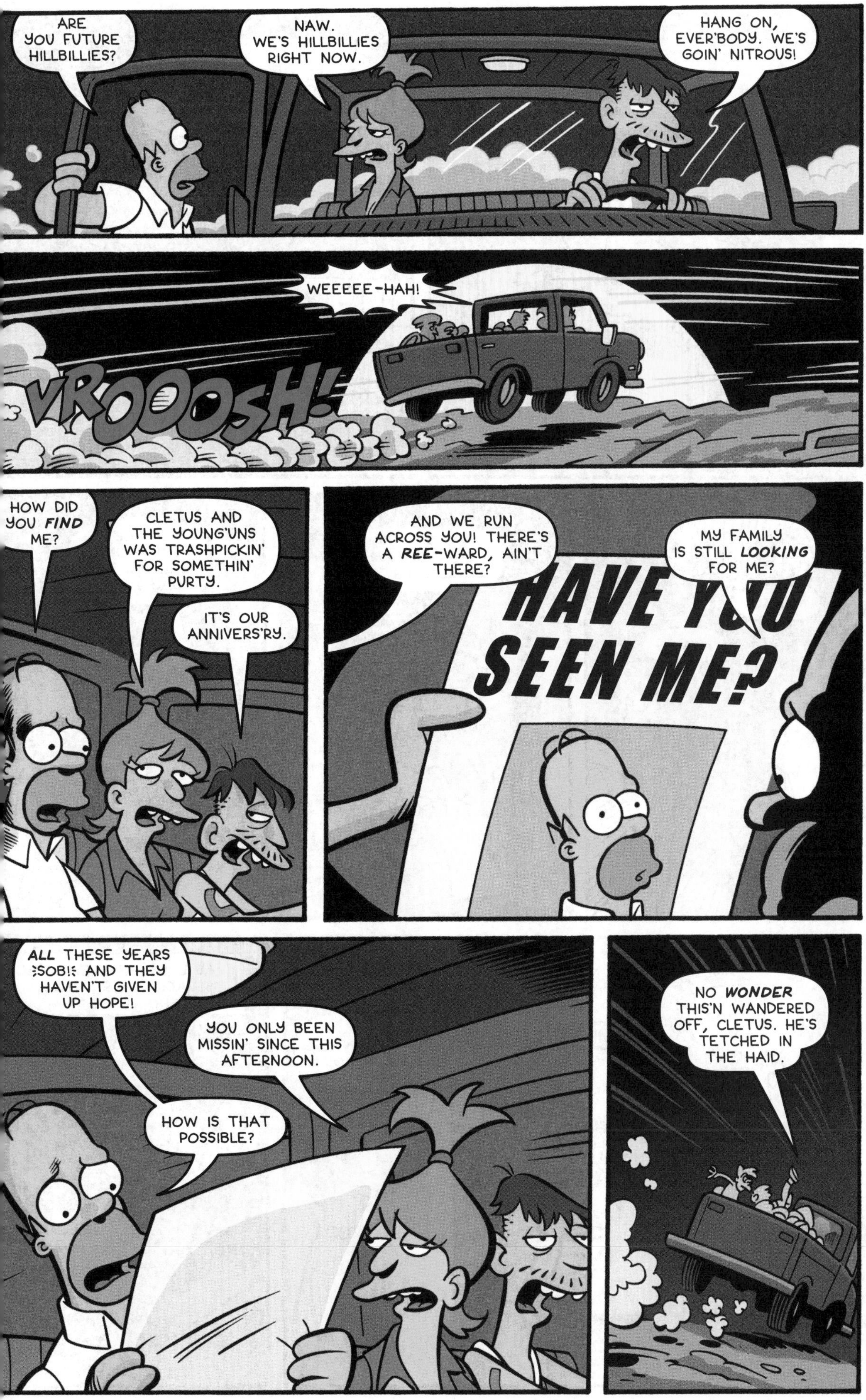

ARE YOU FUTURE HILLBILLIES?
NAW. WE'S HILLBILLIES RIGHT NOW.
HANG ON, EVER'BODY. WE'S GOIN' NITROUS!
WEEEEE-HAH!
VROOOOSH!
HOW DID YOU FIND ME?
CLETUS AND THE YOUNG'UNS WAS TRASHPICKIN' FOR SOMETHIN' PURTY.
IT'S OUR ANNIVERS'RY.
AND WE RUN ACROSS YOU! THERE'S A REE-WARD, AIN'T THERE?
MY FAMILY IS STILL LOOKING FOR ME?
HAVE YOU SEEN ME?
ALL THESE YEARS ;SOB!; AND THEY HAVEN'T GIVEN UP HOPE!
YOU ONLY BEEN MISSIN' SINCE THIS AFTERNOON.
HOW IS THAT POSSIBLE?
NO WONDER THIS'N WANDERED OFF, CLETUS. HE'S TETCHED IN THE HAID.

I WOULDN'T WORRY, MARGE. HOMER ALWAYS MANAGES TO COME BACK.

WILD HORSES COULDN'T KEEP HIM FROM YOUR SIDE FOR LONG.

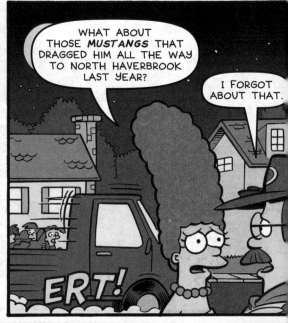

WHAT ABOUT THOSE *MUSTANGS* THAT DRAGGED HIM ALL THE WAY TO NORTH HAVERBROOK LAST YEAR?

I FORGOT ABOUT THAT.

ERT!

MARGE!

HOMIE!

HEY, KIDS! IT'S A GOL-DURNED YANKEE! *GET 'IM!*

MARGE, YOU WON'T *BELIEVE* THE DAY I HAD!

EEEK!

WHERE WERE YOU, DAD?

NOT "WHERE," LISA. THE QUESTION IS, *WHEN* WAS I?

WELL, I DON'T CARE WHERE *OR* WHEN YOU WERE...

"...AS LONG AS *EVERYONE* IS BACK WHERE THEY SHOULD BE."

HELLO?

THE END

THE MARTIN CHRONICLES!

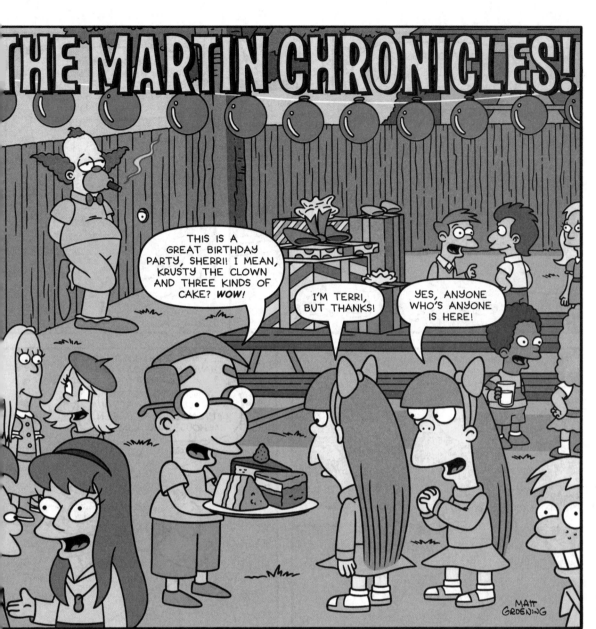

THIS IS A GREAT BIRTHDAY PARTY, SHERRI! I MEAN, KRUSTY THE CLOWN AND THREE KINDS OF CAKE? *WOW!*

I'M TERRI, BUT THANKS!

YES, ANYONE WHO'S ANYONE IS HERE!

CURSE MY UNPOPULARITY!

THAT DOES IT, MARTIN! IT'S TIME FOR YOU TO CLIMB THE SOCIAL LADDER!

I'LL USE *MATH* TO HELP ME! IT'S THE ONE FRIEND THAT'S ALWAYS CONSTANT!

ACCORDING TO MY CALCULATIONS, I'M THE *LEAST POPULAR* STUDENT AT SCHOOL. SO I CAN ADVANCE BY SIMPLY TAKING THE PLACE OF THE *SECOND LEAST* POPULAR!

AND THERE HE IS! *MILHOUSE VAN HOUTEN!*

N BOOTHBY
SCRIPT

PHIL ORTIZ
PENCILS

MIKE ROTE
INKS

NATHAN HAMILL
COLORS

KAREN BATES
LETTERS

NATHAN KANE
EDITOR

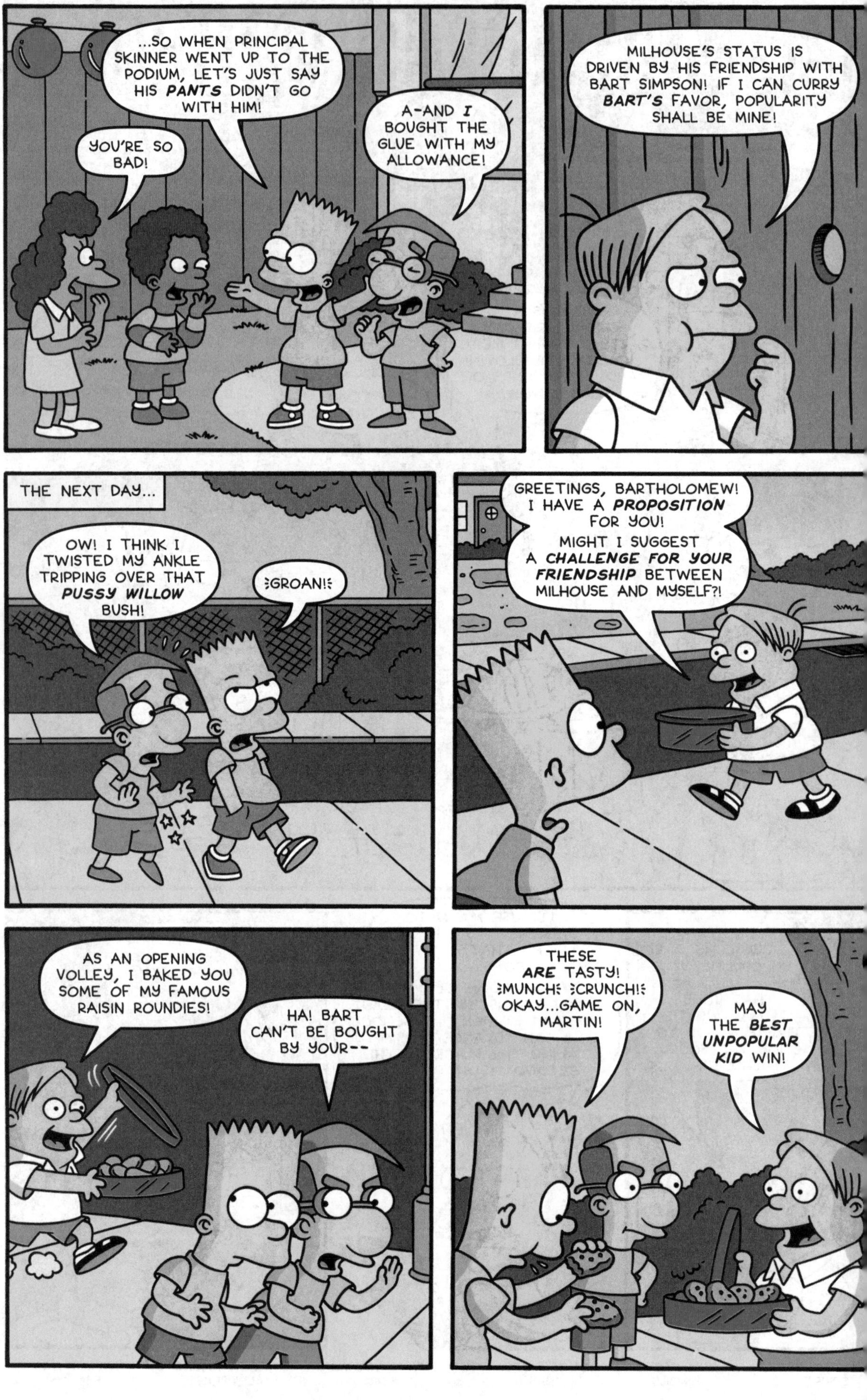
...SO WHEN PRINCIPAL SKINNER WENT UP TO THE PODIUM, LET'S JUST SAY HIS PANTS DIDN'T GO WITH HIM!
YOU'RE SO BAD!
A-AND I BOUGHT THE GLUE WITH MY ALLOWANCE!
MILHOUSE'S STATUS IS DRIVEN BY HIS FRIENDSHIP WITH BART SIMPSON! IF I CAN CURRY BART'S FAVOR, POPULARITY SHALL BE MINE!
THE NEXT DAY...
OW! I THINK I TWISTED MY ANKLE TRIPPING OVER THAT PUSSY WILLOW BUSH!
GROAN!
GREETINGS, BARTHOLOMEW! I HAVE A PROPOSITION FOR YOU!
MIGHT I SUGGEST A CHALLENGE FOR YOUR FRIENDSHIP BETWEEN MILHOUSE AND MYSELF?!
AS AN OPENING VOLLEY, I BAKED YOU SOME OF MY FAMOUS RAISIN ROUNDIES!
HA! BART CAN'T BE BOUGHT BY YOUR--
THESE ARE TASTY! MUNCH! CRUNCH! OKAY...GAME ON, MARTIN!
MAY THE BEST UNPOPULAR KID WIN!

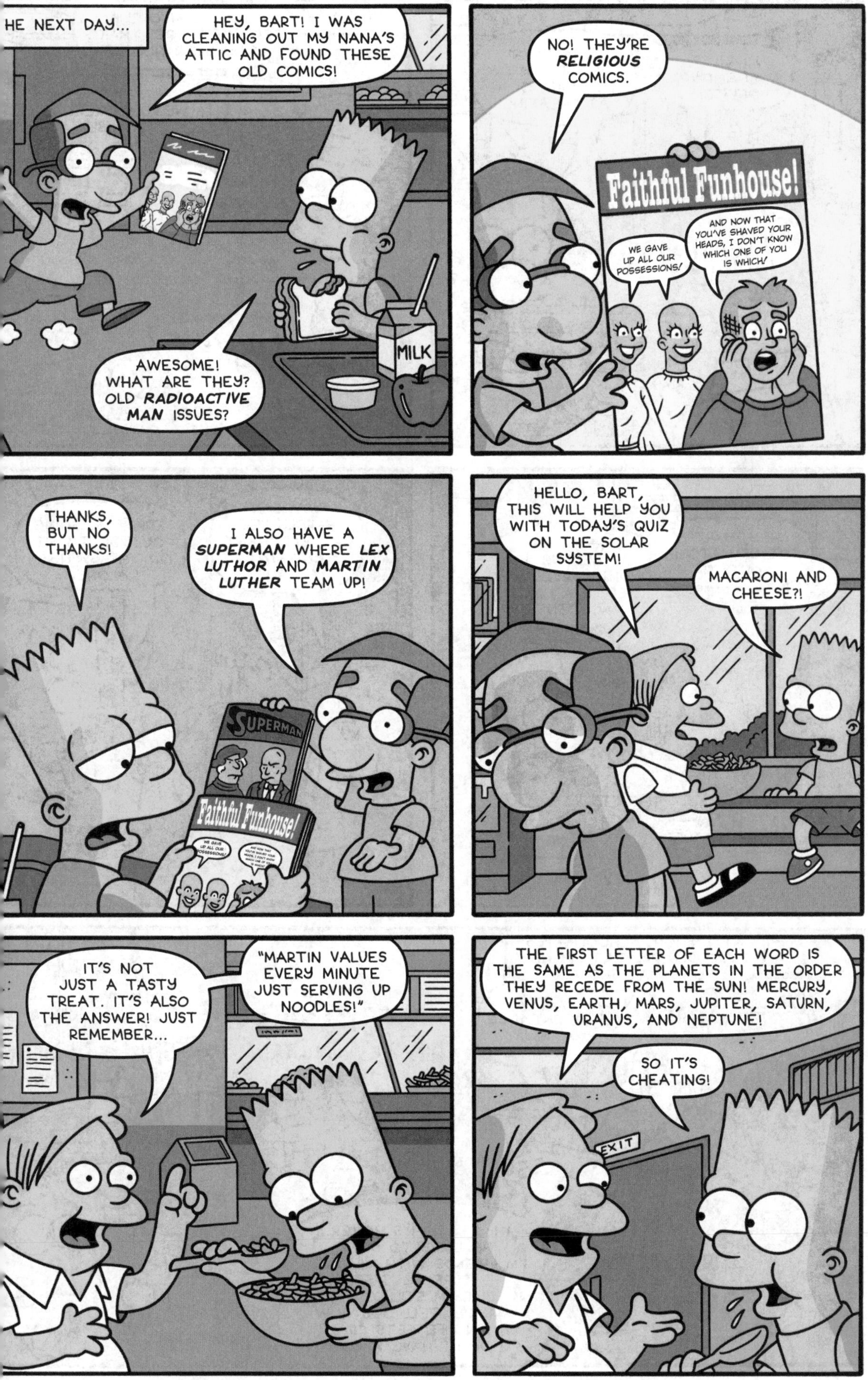

HE NEXT DAY...
HEY, BART! I WAS CLEANING OUT MY NANA'S ATTIC AND FOUND THESE OLD COMICS!
AWESOME! WHAT ARE THEY? OLD RADIOACTIVE MAN ISSUES?
MILK
NO! THEY'RE RELIGIOUS COMICS.
Faithful Funhouse!
WE GAVE UP ALL OUR POSSESSIONS!
AND NOW THAT YOU'VE SHAVED YOUR HEADS, I DON'T KNOW WHICH ONE OF YOU IS WHICH!
THANKS, BUT NO THANKS!
I ALSO HAVE A SUPERMAN WHERE LEX LUTHOR AND MARTIN LUTHER TEAM UP!
SUPERMAN
Faithful Funhouse!
HELLO, BART, THIS WILL HELP YOU WITH TODAY'S QUIZ ON THE SOLAR SYSTEM!
MACARONI AND CHEESE?!
IT'S NOT JUST A TASTY TREAT. IT'S ALSO THE ANSWER! JUST REMEMBER...
"MARTIN VALUES EVERY MINUTE JUST SERVING UP NOODLES!"
THE FIRST LETTER OF EACH WORD IS THE SAME AS THE PLANETS IN THE ORDER THEY RECEDE FROM THE SUN! MERCURY, VENUS, EARTH, MARS, JUPITER, SATURN, URANUS, AND NEPTUNE!
SO IT'S CHEATING!
EXIT

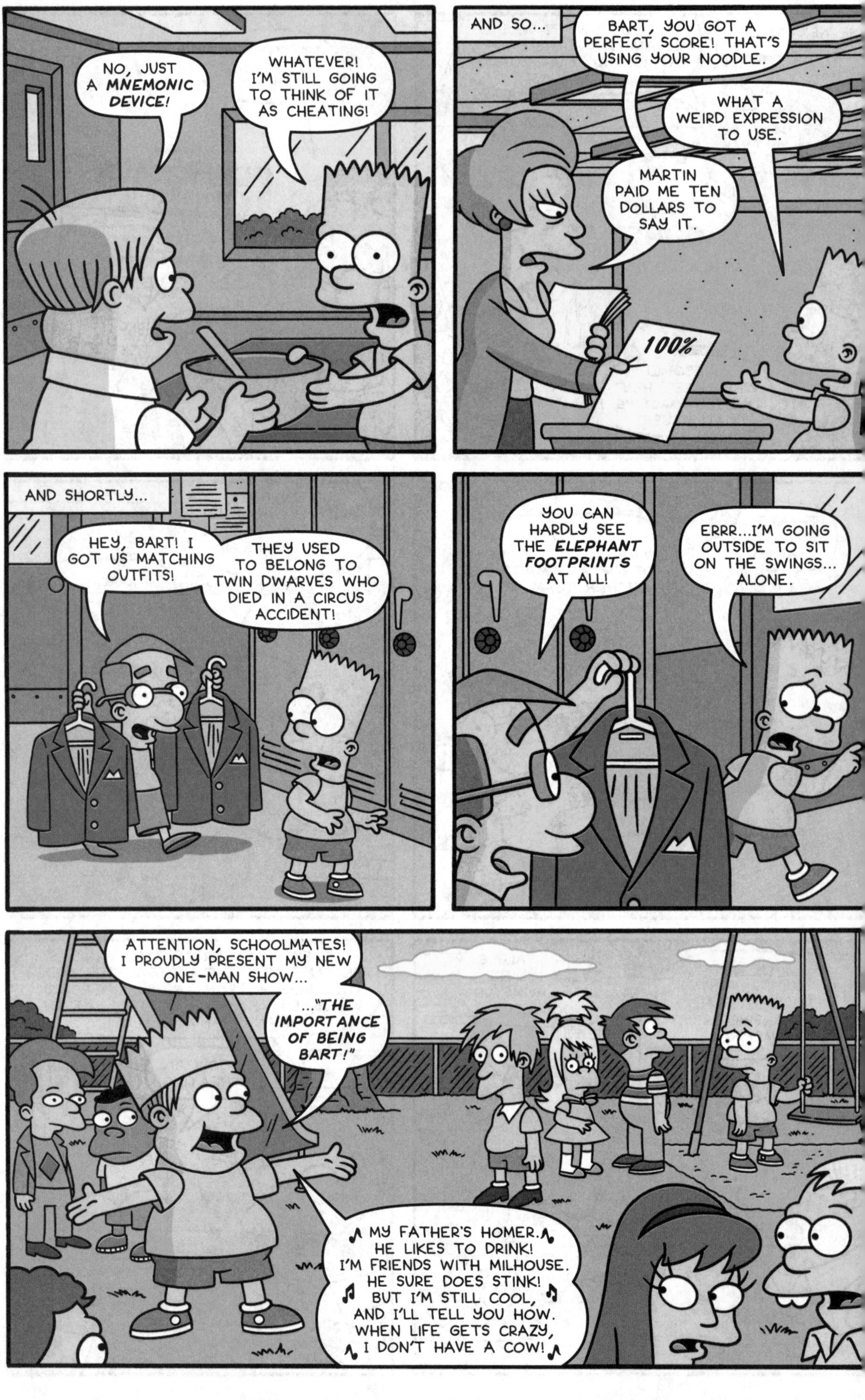
NO, JUST A MNEMONIC DEVICE!
WHATEVER! I'M STILL GOING TO THINK OF IT AS CHEATING!
AND SO...
BART, YOU GOT A PERFECT SCORE! THAT'S USING YOUR NOODLE.
WHAT A WEIRD EXPRESSION TO USE.
MARTIN PAID ME TEN DOLLARS TO SAY IT.
100%
AND SHORTLY...
HEY, BART! I GOT US MATCHING OUTFITS!
THEY USED TO BELONG TO TWIN DWARVES WHO DIED IN A CIRCUS ACCIDENT!
YOU CAN HARDLY SEE THE ELEPHANT FOOTPRINTS AT ALL!
ERRR...I'M GOING OUTSIDE TO SIT ON THE SWINGS... ALONE.
ATTENTION, SCHOOLMATES! I PROUDLY PRESENT MY NEW ONE-MAN SHOW...
..."THE IMPORTANCE OF BEING BART!"
MY FATHER'S HOMER. HE LIKES TO DRINK! I'M FRIENDS WITH MILHOUSE. HE SURE DOES STINK! BUT I'M STILL COOL, AND I'LL TELL YOU HOW. WHEN LIFE GETS CRAZY, I DON'T HAVE A COW!

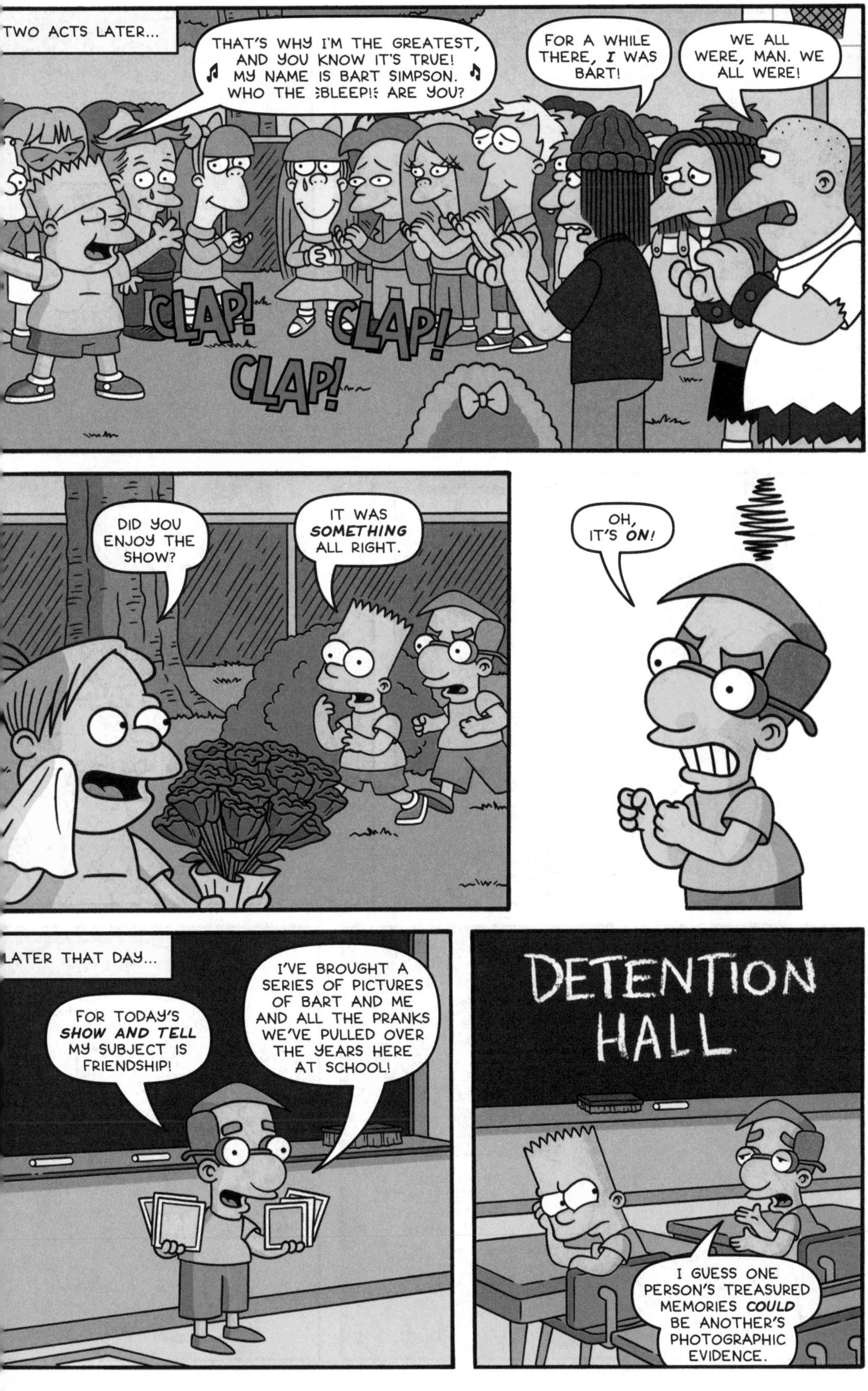

TWO ACTS LATER...
THAT'S WHY I'M THE GREATEST, AND YOU KNOW IT'S TRUE! MY NAME IS BART SIMPSON. WHO THE BLEEP! ARE YOU?
FOR A WHILE THERE, I WAS BART!
WE ALL WERE, MAN. WE ALL WERE!
CLAP! CLAP! CLAP!
DID YOU ENJOY THE SHOW?
IT WAS SOMETHING ALL RIGHT.
OH, IT'S ON!
LATER THAT DAY...
FOR TODAY'S SHOW AND TELL MY SUBJECT IS FRIENDSHIP!
I'VE BROUGHT A SERIES OF PICTURES OF BART AND ME AND ALL THE PRANKS WE'VE PULLED OVER THE YEARS HERE AT SCHOOL!
DETENTION HALL
I GUESS ONE PERSON'S TREASURED MEMORIES COULD BE ANOTHER'S PHOTOGRAPHIC EVIDENCE.

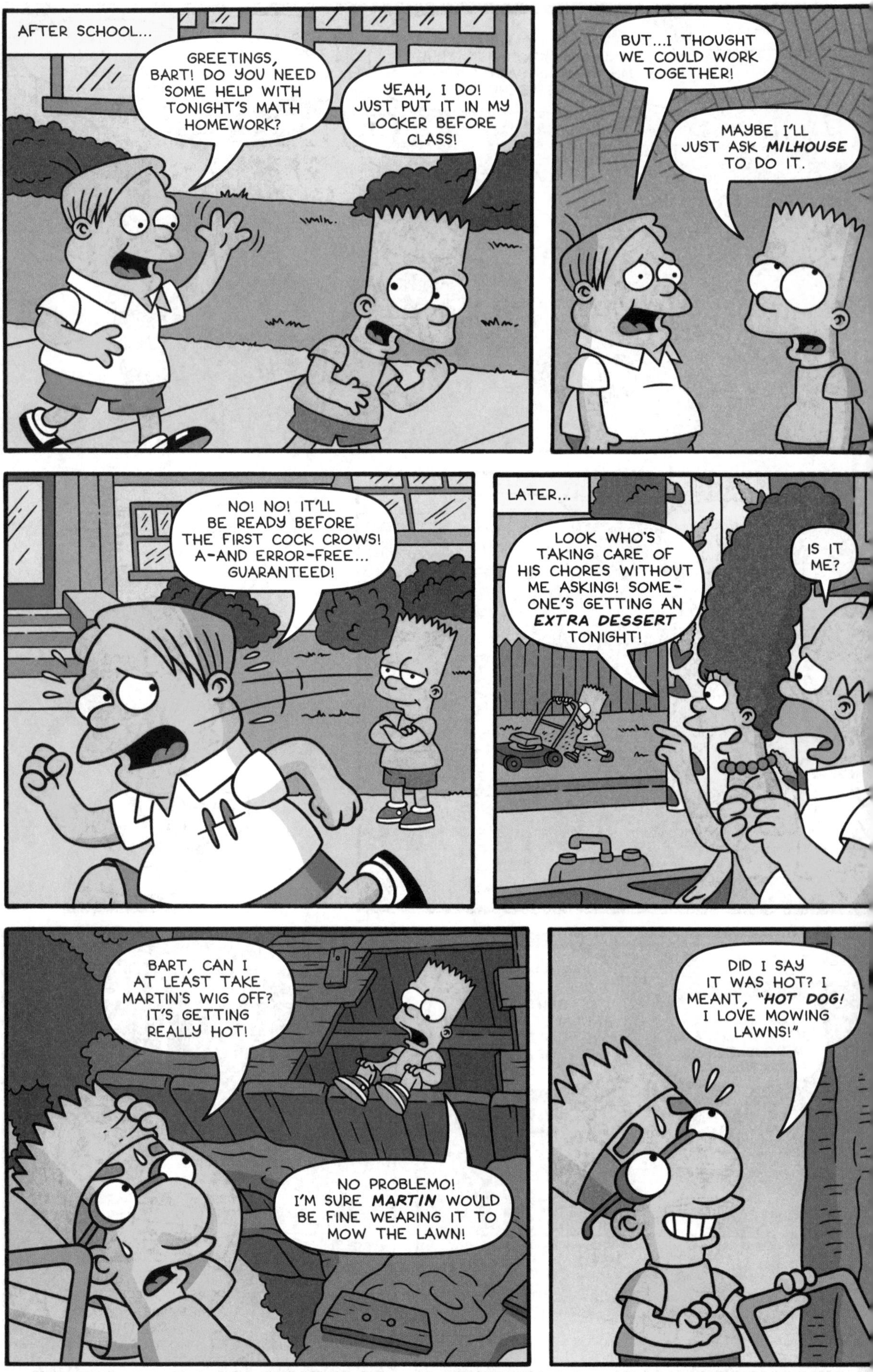
AFTER SCHOOL...
GREETINGS, BART! DO YOU NEED SOME HELP WITH TONIGHT'S MATH HOMEWORK?
YEAH, I DO! JUST PUT IT IN MY LOCKER BEFORE CLASS!
BUT...I THOUGHT WE COULD WORK TOGETHER!
MAYBE I'LL JUST ASK ***MILHOUSE*** TO DO IT.
NO! NO! IT'LL BE READY BEFORE THE FIRST COCK CROWS! A-AND ERROR-FREE... GUARANTEED!
LATER...
LOOK WHO'S TAKING CARE OF HIS CHORES WITHOUT ME ASKING! SOMEONE'S GETTING AN ***EXTRA DESSERT*** TONIGHT!
IS IT ME?
BART, CAN I AT LEAST TAKE MARTIN'S WIG OFF? IT'S GETTING REALLY HOT!
NO PROBLEMO! I'M SURE ***MARTIN*** WOULD BE FINE WEARING IT TO MOW THE LAWN!
DID I SAY IT WAS HOT? I MEANT, "***HOT DOG!*** I LOVE MOWING LAWNS!"

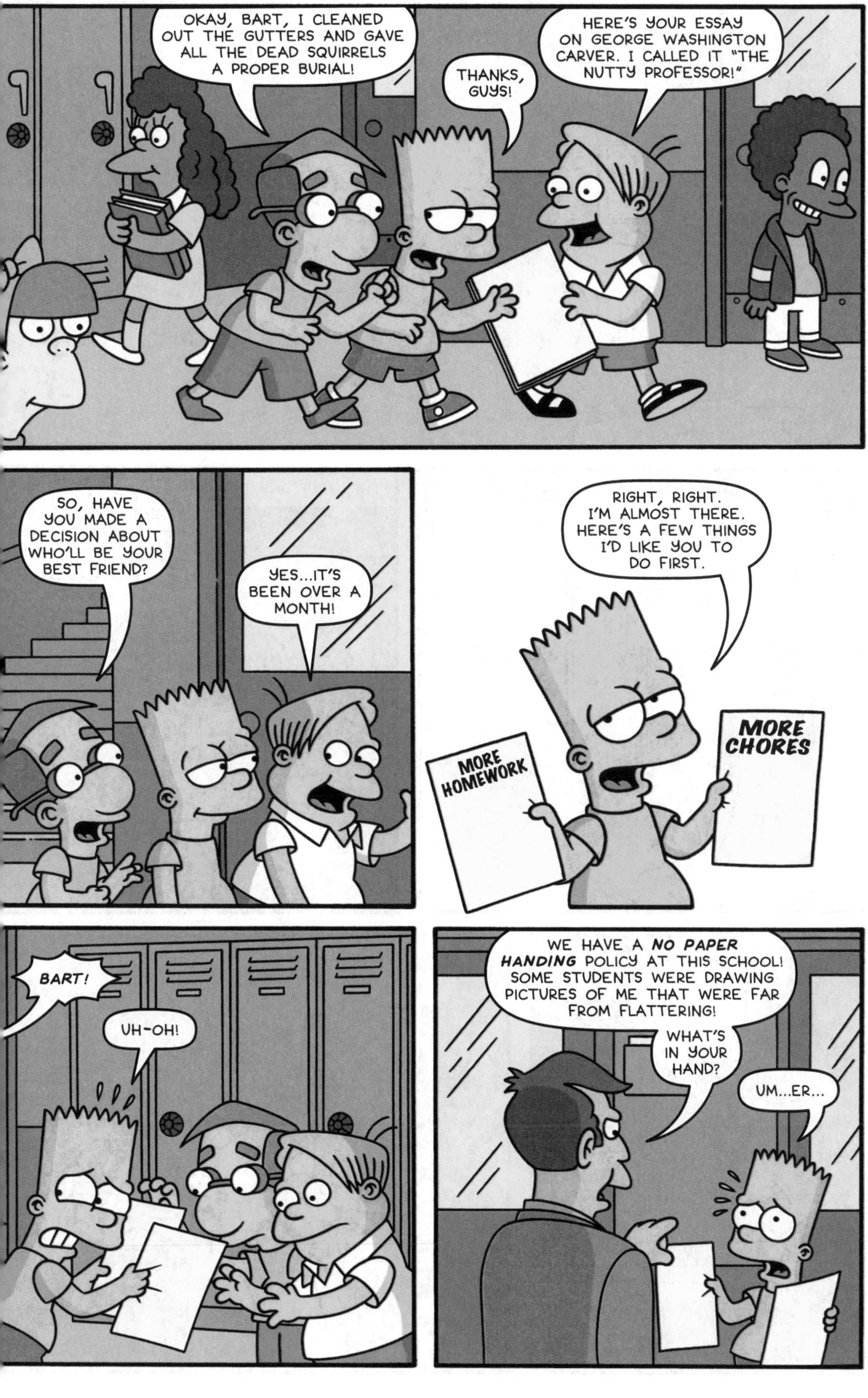

OKAY, BART, I CLEANED OUT THE GUTTERS AND GAVE ALL THE DEAD SQUIRRELS A PROPER BURIAL!
THANKS, GUYS!
HERE'S YOUR ESSAY ON GEORGE WASHINGTON CARVER. I CALLED IT "THE NUTTY PROFESSOR!"
SO, HAVE YOU MADE A DECISION ABOUT WHO'LL BE YOUR BEST FRIEND?
YES...IT'S BEEN OVER A MONTH!
RIGHT, RIGHT. I'M ALMOST THERE. HERE'S A FEW THINGS I'D LIKE YOU TO DO FIRST.
MORE HOMEWORK
MORE CHORES
BART!
UH-OH!
WE HAVE A ***NO PAPER HANDING*** POLICY AT THIS SCHOOL! SOME STUDENTS WERE DRAWING PICTURES OF ME THAT WERE FAR FROM FLATTERING!
WHAT'S IN YOUR HAND?
UM...ER...

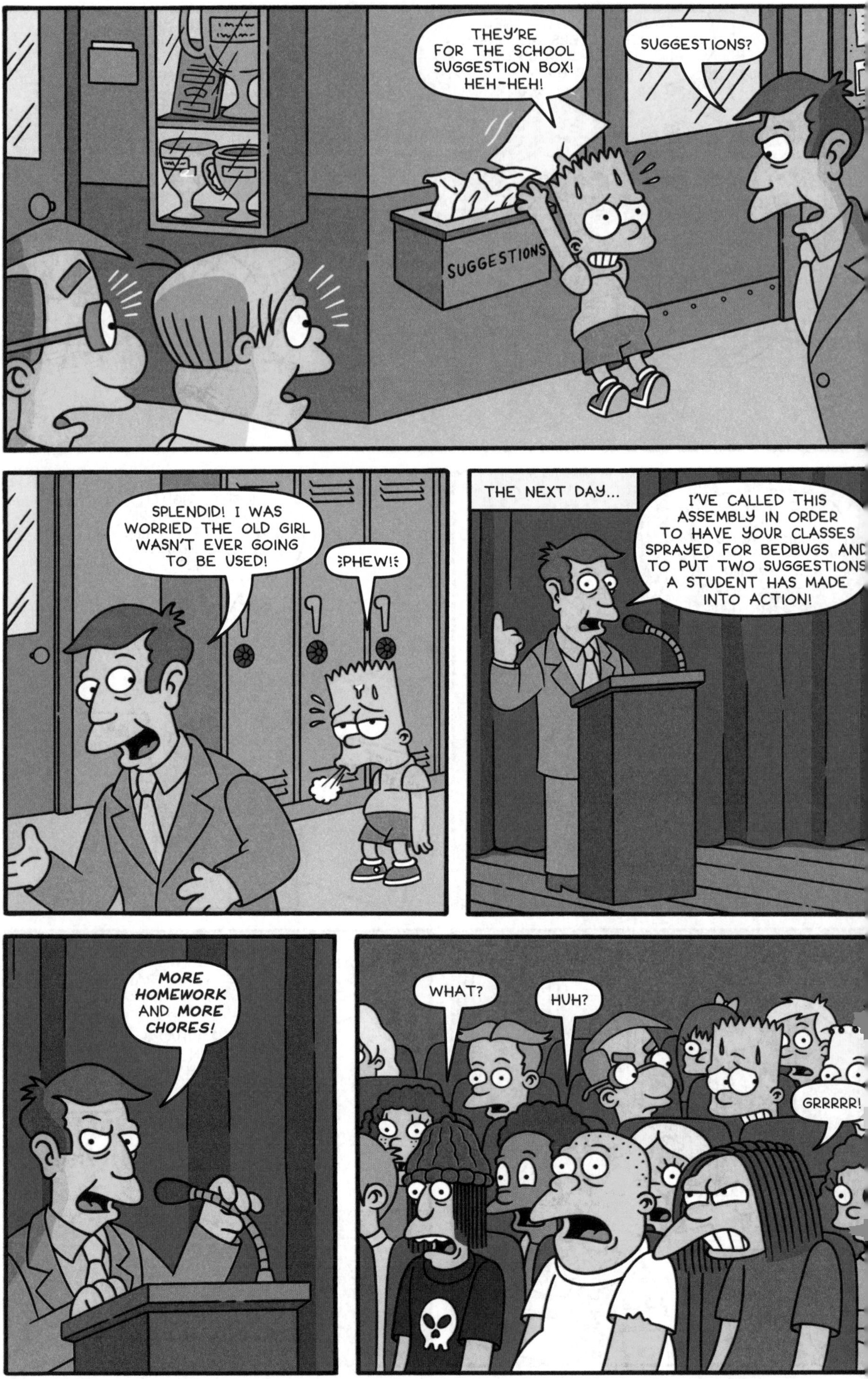
THEY'RE FOR THE SCHOOL SUGGESTION BOX! HEH-HEH!
SUGGESTIONS?
SUGGESTIONS
SPLENDID! I WAS WORRIED THE OLD GIRL WASN'T EVER GOING TO BE USED!
PHEW!
THE NEXT DAY...
I'VE CALLED THIS ASSEMBLY IN ORDER TO HAVE YOUR CLASSES SPRAYED FOR BEDBUGS AND TO PUT TWO SUGGESTIONS A STUDENT HAS MADE INTO ACTION!
MORE HOMEWORK AND MORE CHORES!
WHAT?
HUH?
GRRRRR!

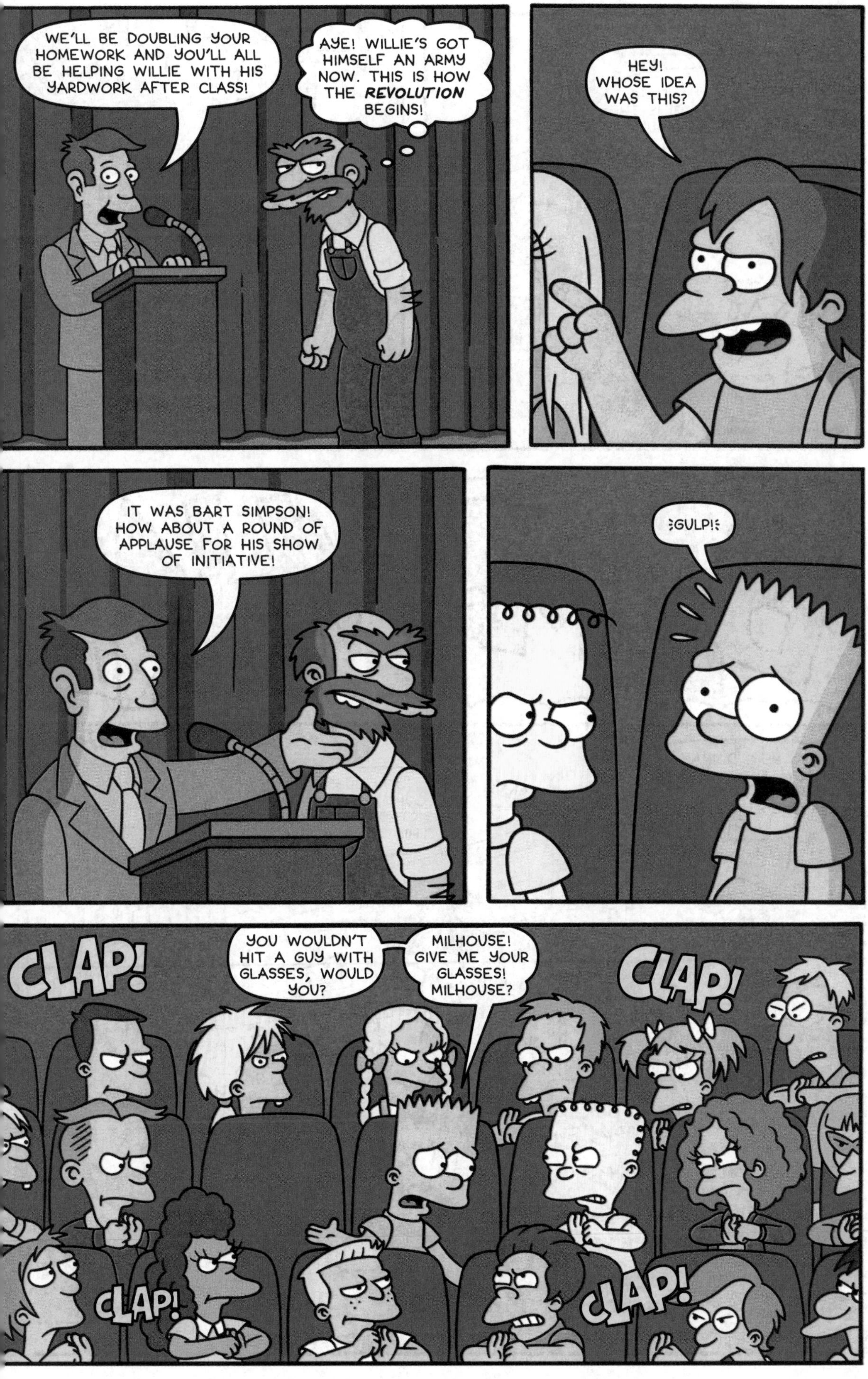
WE'LL BE DOUBLING YOUR HOMEWORK AND YOU'LL ALL BE HELPING WILLIE WITH HIS YARDWORK AFTER CLASS!
AYE! WILLIE'S GOT HIMSELF AN ARMY NOW. THIS IS HOW THE REVOLUTION BEGINS!
HEY! WHOSE IDEA WAS THIS?
IT WAS BART SIMPSON! HOW ABOUT A ROUND OF APPLAUSE FOR HIS SHOW OF INITIATIVE!
GULP!
CLAP!
YOU WOULDN'T HIT A GUY WITH GLASSES, WOULD YOU?
MILHOUSE! GIVE ME YOUR GLASSES! MILHOUSE?
CLAP!
CLAP!
CLAP!

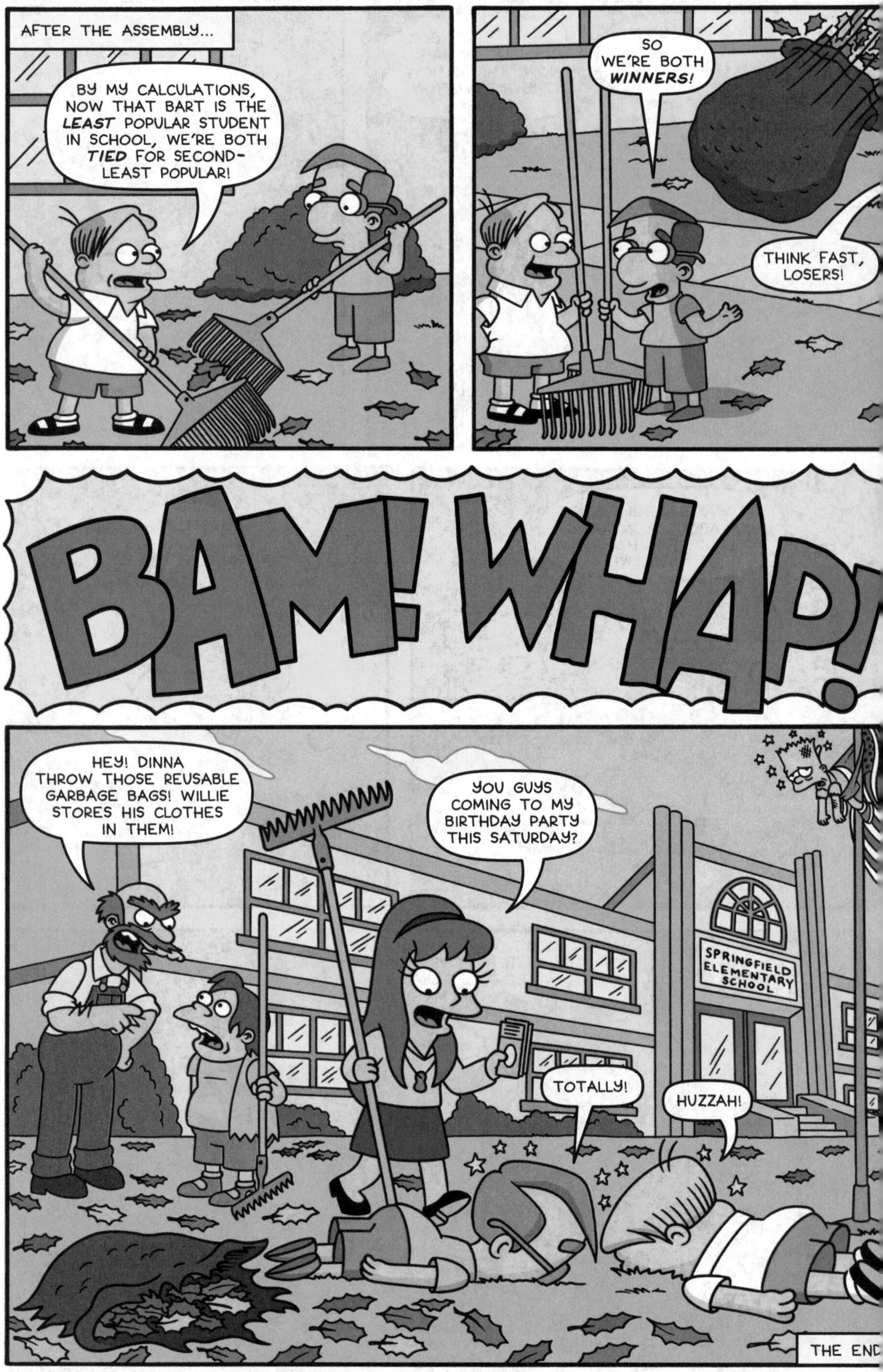

AFTER THE ASSEMBLY...
BY MY CALCULATIONS, NOW THAT BART IS THE LEAST POPULAR STUDENT IN SCHOOL, WE'RE BOTH TIED FOR SECOND-LEAST POPULAR!
SO WE'RE BOTH WINNERS!
THINK FAST, LOSERS!
BAM! WHAP!
HEY! DINNA THROW THOSE REUSABLE GARBAGE BAGS! WILLIE STORES HIS CLOTHES IN THEM!
YOU GUYS COMING TO MY BIRTHDAY PARTY THIS SATURDAY?
SPRINGFIELD ELEMENTARY SCHOOL
TOTALLY!
HUZZAH!
THE END

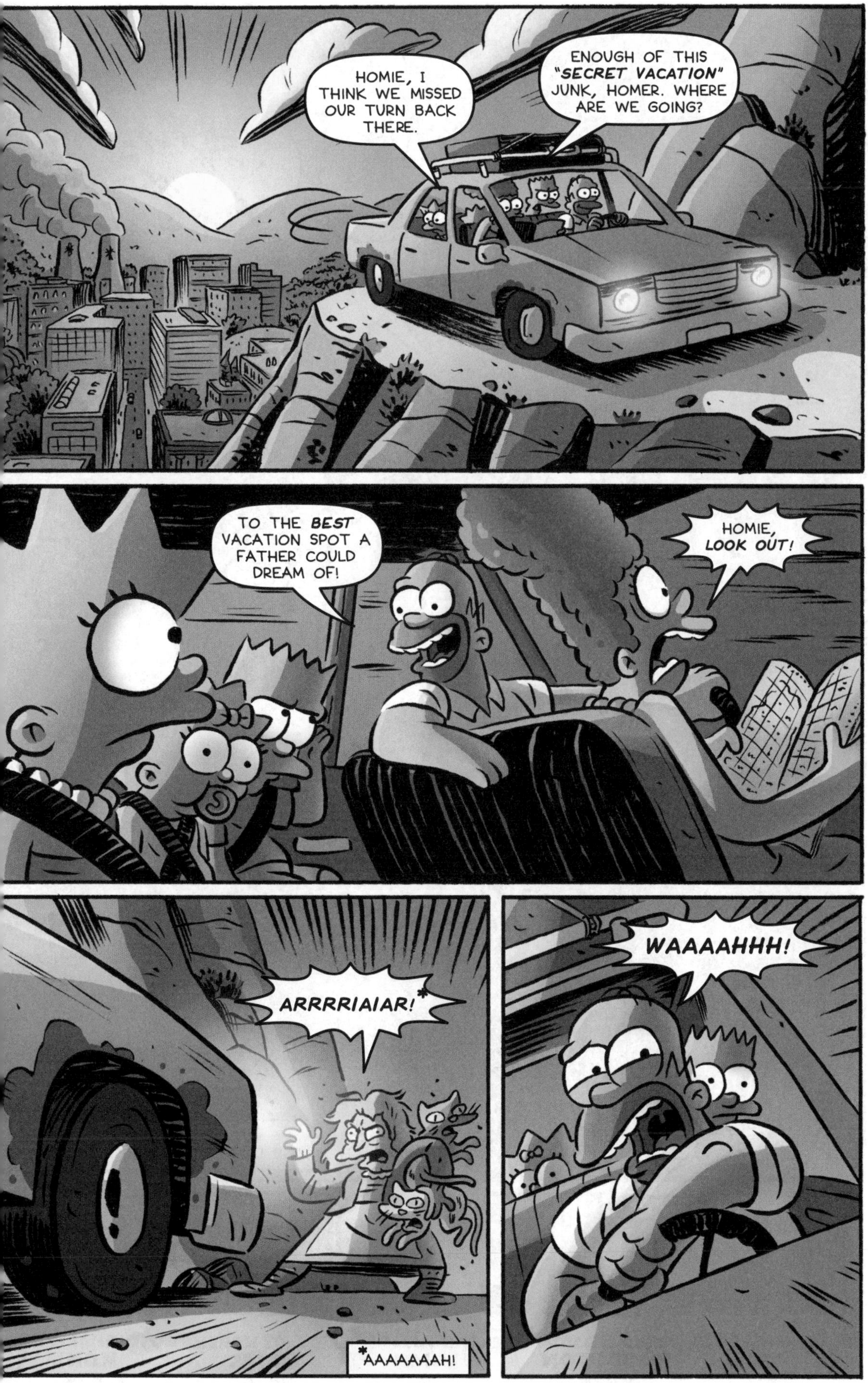
HOMIE, I THINK WE MISSED OUR TURN BACK THERE.
ENOUGH OF THIS "SECRET VACATION" JUNK, HOMER. WHERE ARE WE GOING?
TO THE BEST VACATION SPOT A FATHER COULD DREAM OF!
HOMIE, LOOK OUT!
ARRRRIAIAR!*
*AAAAAAAH!
WAAAAHHH!

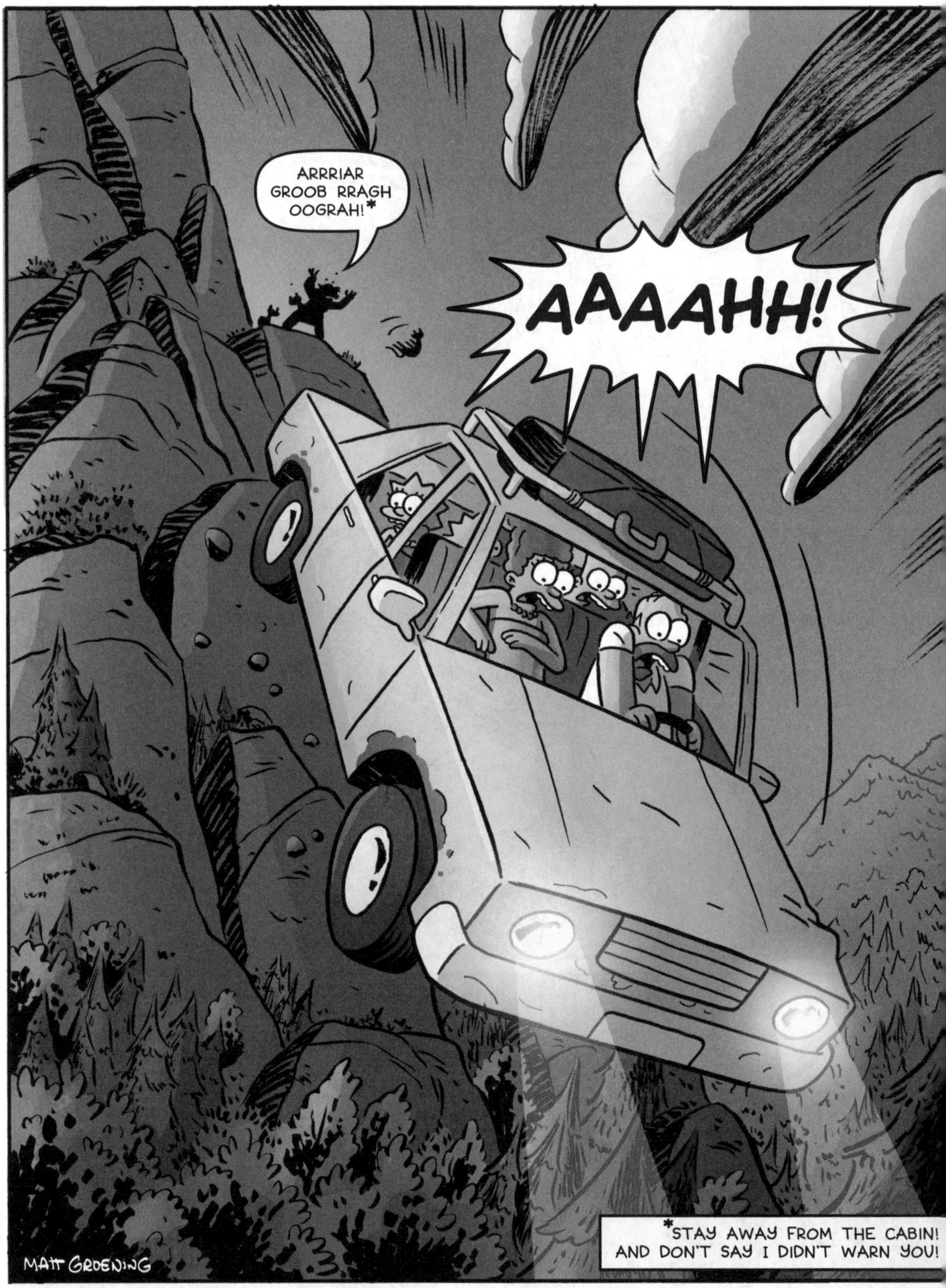
ARRRIAR GROOB RRAGH OOGRAH!*
AAAAHH!
*STAY AWAY FROM THE CABIN! AND DON'T SAY I DIDN'T WARN YOU!
MATT GROENING

EERIE BEERY

SHANE of the DEAD HOUGHTON STORY
CHRIS of DEATH HOUGHTON PENCILS & INKS
GELATINOUS JOSH ULRICH COLORS
KREEPY KAREN BATES LETTERS
NOCTURNAL NATHA KANE EDITOR

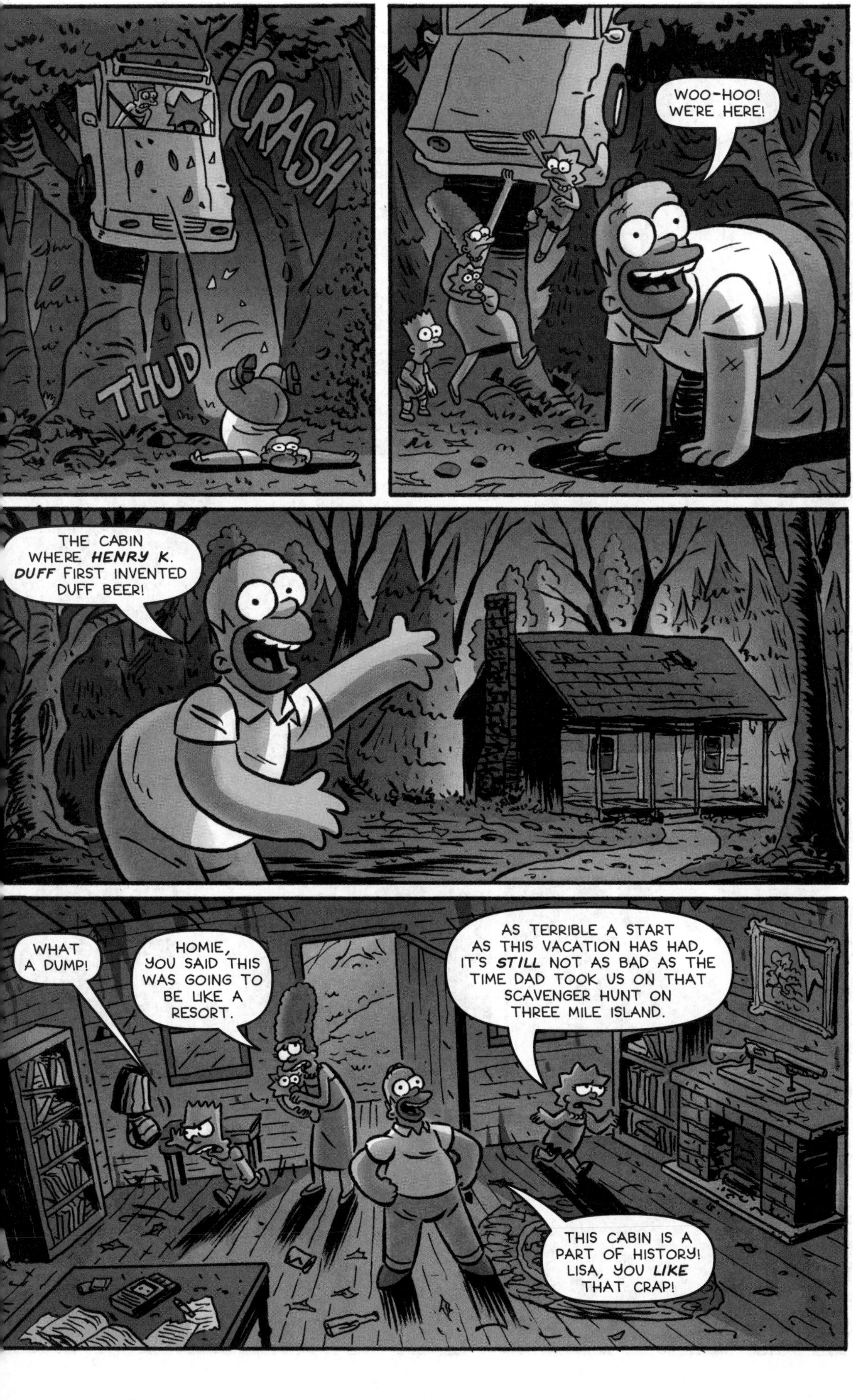
CRASH
THUD
WOO-HOO! WE'RE HERE!
THE CABIN WHERE **HENRY K. DUFF** FIRST INVENTED DUFF BEER!
WHAT A DUMP!
HOMIE, YOU SAID THIS WAS GOING TO BE LIKE A RESORT.
AS TERRIBLE A START AS THIS VACATION HAS HAD, IT'S ***STILL*** NOT AS BAD AS THE TIME DAD TOOK US ON THAT SCAVENGER HUNT ON THREE MILE ISLAND.
THIS CABIN IS A PART OF HISTORY! LISA, YOU ***LIKE*** THAT CRAP!

IF IT WASN'T FOR HENRY K. DUFF'S BEER RECIPE RESEARCH HERE AT THIS CABIN, DADDY NEVER WOULD HAVE HAD ENOUGH CONFIDENCE TO MAKE MOST OF THE MAJOR LIFE DECISIONS HE'S MADE!

KZZKKZZ

HENRY K. DUFF HERE, RECORDING MY FINDINGS ONE LAST TIME BEFORE WHAT WILL MOST LIKELY BE MY UNTIMELY DEMISE.

BOOORRRRING

IN MY SEARCH FOR THE MOST DELICIOUS, YET WATERED-DOWN FLAVOR OF BEER, I DISCOVERED SOMETHING TRULY FRIGHTENING.

WHEN READ ALOUD, THE RECIPE AWAKENS ANCIENT EVIL SPIRITS THAT SEEM TO HAVE POSSESSED MY WIFE AND CHILDREN.

AS TEMPTING AS IT MAY BE, DO NOT...I REPEAT, DO NOT READ THE RECIPE FOR DUFF BEER OUT LOUD!

FOR THE LOVE OF ALL THINGS HOLY, DO NOT--

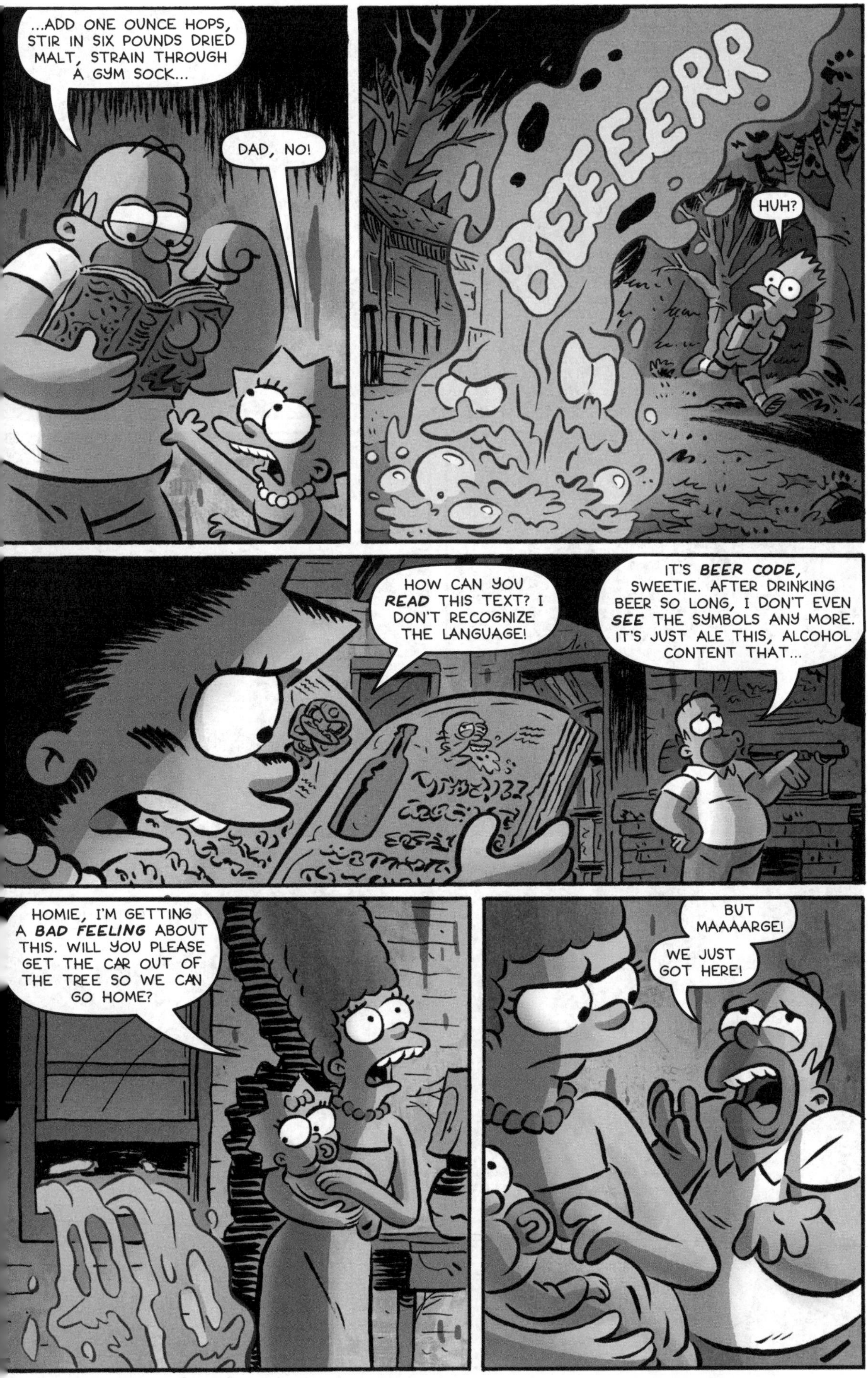
...ADD ONE OUNCE HOPS, STIR IN SIX POUNDS DRIED MALT, STRAIN THROUGH A GYM SOCK...
DAD, NO!
BEEEERR
HUH?
HOW CAN YOU READ THIS TEXT? I DON'T RECOGNIZE THE LANGUAGE!
IT'S BEER CODE, SWEETIE. AFTER DRINKING BEER SO LONG, I DON'T EVEN SEE THE SYMBOLS ANY MORE. IT'S JUST ALE THIS, ALCOHOL CONTENT THAT...
HOMIE, I'M GETTING A BAD FEELING ABOUT THIS. WILL YOU PLEASE GET THE CAR OUT OF THE TREE SO WE CAN GO HOME?
BUT MAAAARGE!
WE JUST GOT HERE!

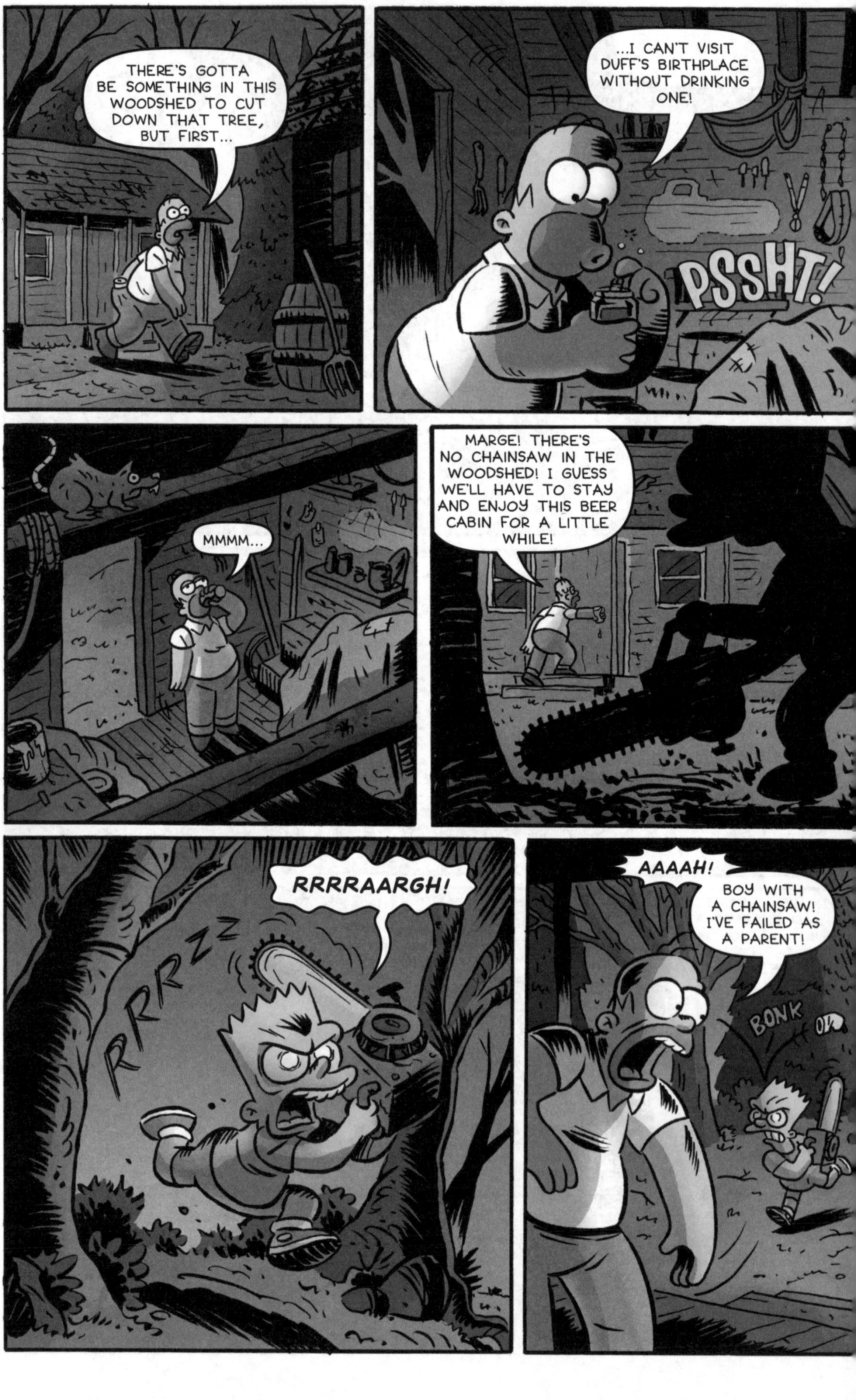
THERE'S GOTTA BE SOMETHING IN THIS WOODSHED TO CUT DOWN THAT TREE, BUT FIRST...
...I CAN'T VISIT DUFF'S BIRTHPLACE WITHOUT DRINKING ONE!
PSSHT!
MMMM...
MARGE! THERE'S NO CHAINSAW IN THE WOODSHED! I GUESS WE'LL HAVE TO STAY AND ENJOY THIS BEER CABIN FOR A LITTLE WHILE!
RRRRAARGH!
AAAAH!
BOY WITH A CHAINSAW! I'VE FAILED AS A PARENT!
BONK

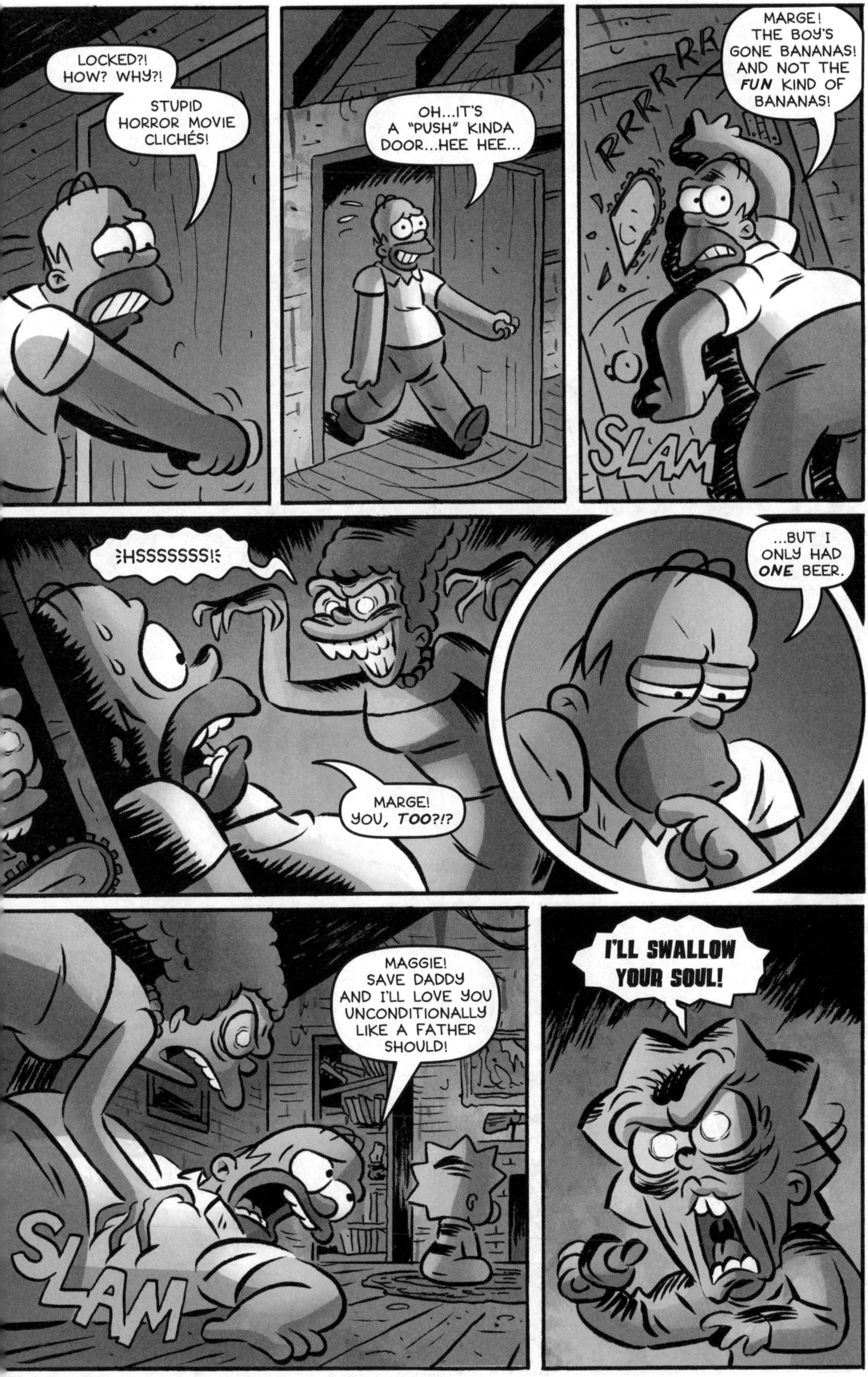
LOCKED?! HOW? WHY?!
STUPID HORROR MOVIE CLICHÉS!
OH...IT'S A "PUSH" KINDA DOOR...HEE HEE...
MARGE! THE BOY'S GONE BANANAS! AND NOT THE FUN KIND OF BANANAS!
RRRRRRR
SLAM
HSSSSSSS!
MARGE! YOU, TOO?!?
...BUT I ONLY HAD ONE BEER.
MAGGIE! SAVE DADDY AND I'LL LOVE YOU UNCONDITIONALLY LIKE A FATHER SHOULD!
SLAM
I'LL SWALLOW YOUR SOUL!

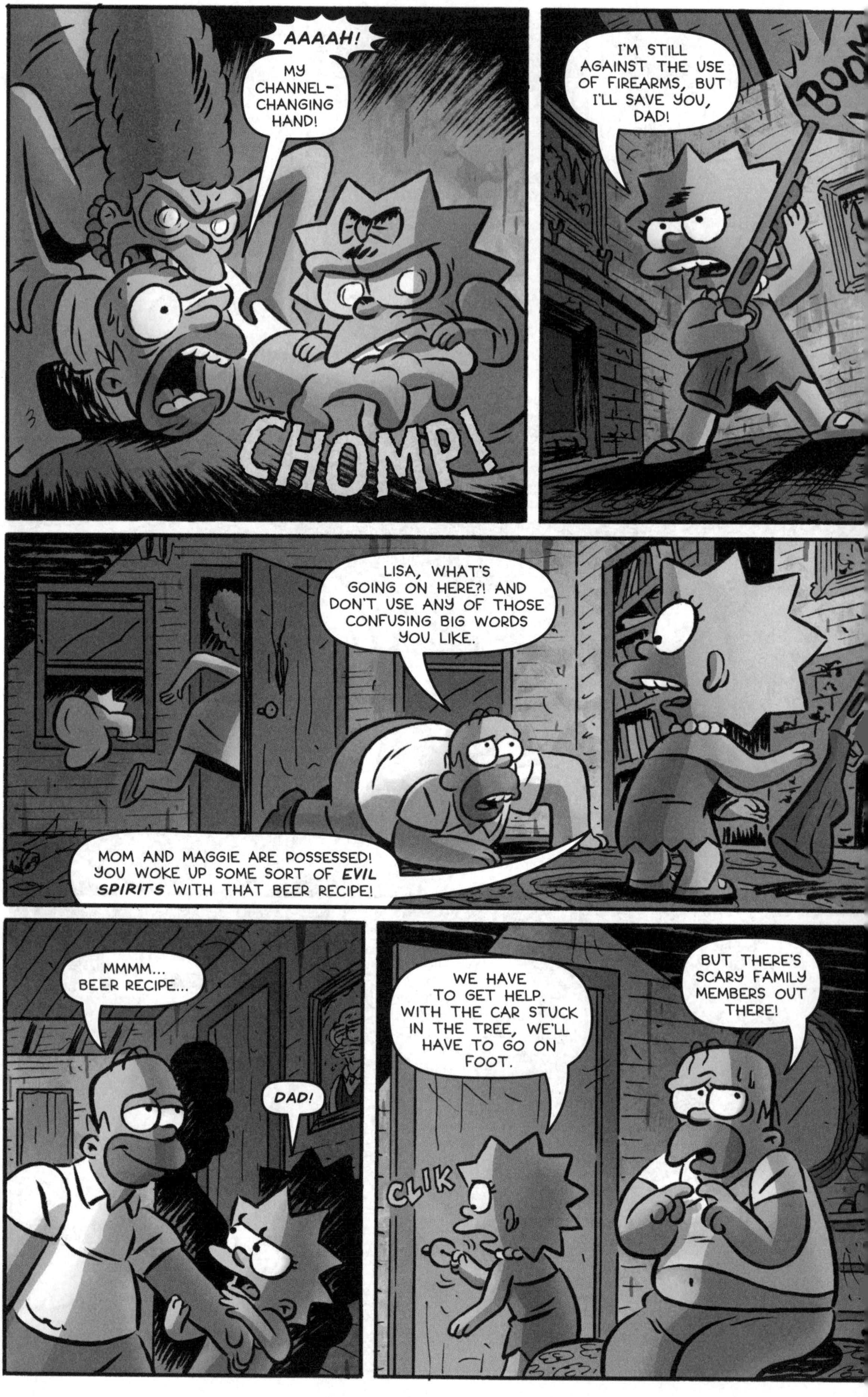
AAAAH!
MY CHANNEL-CHANGING HAND!
CHOMP!
I'M STILL AGAINST THE USE OF FIREARMS, BUT I'LL SAVE YOU, DAD!
LISA, WHAT'S GOING ON HERE?! AND DON'T USE ANY OF THOSE CONFUSING BIG WORDS YOU LIKE.
MOM AND MAGGIE ARE POSSESSED! YOU WOKE UP SOME SORT OF *EVIL SPIRITS* WITH THAT BEER RECIPE!
MMMM... BEER RECIPE...
DAD!
WE HAVE TO GET HELP. WITH THE CAR STUCK IN THE TREE, WE'LL HAVE TO GO ON FOOT.
CLIK
BUT THERE'S SCARY FAMILY MEMBERS OUT THERE!

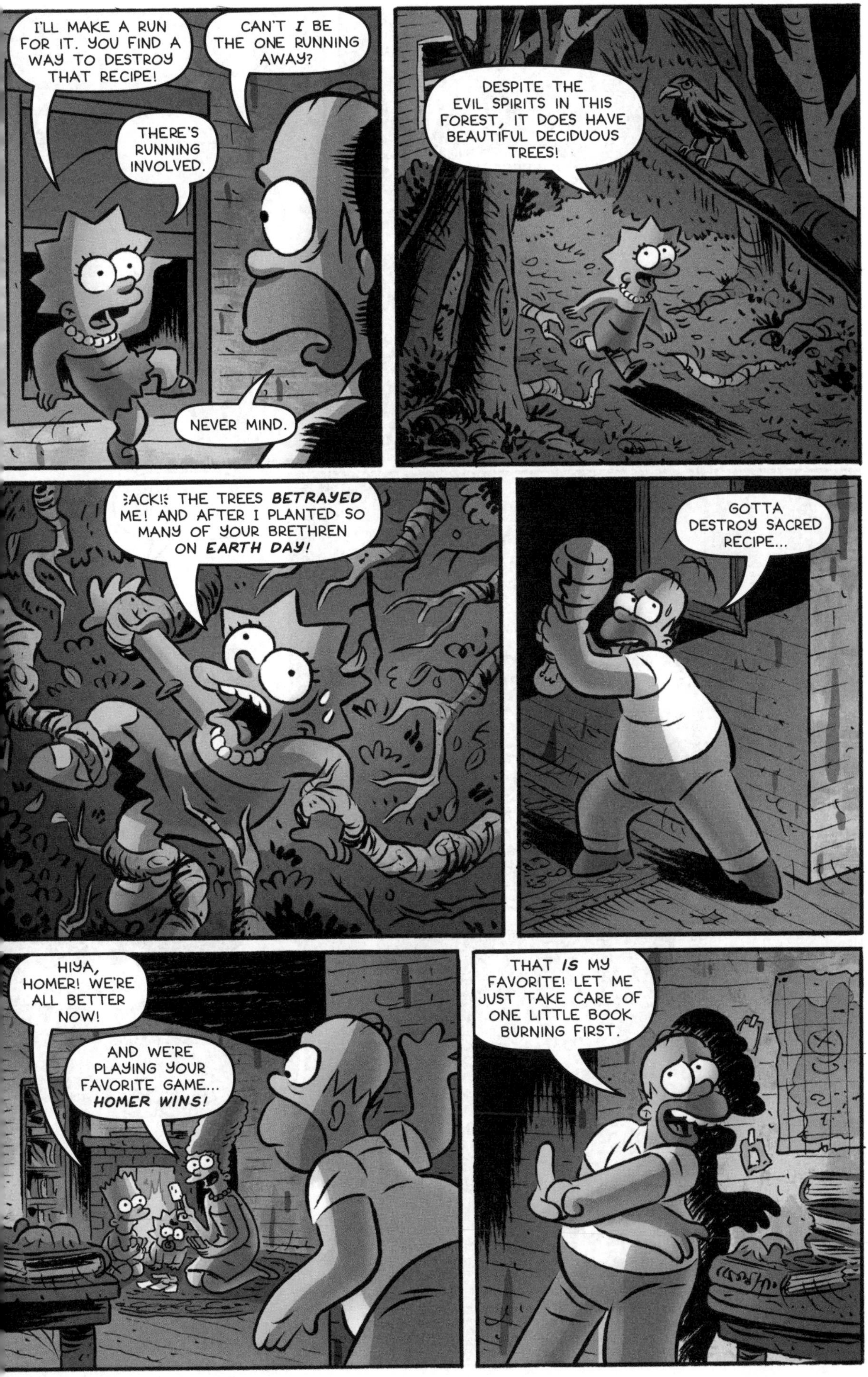
I'LL MAKE A RUN FOR IT. YOU FIND A WAY TO DESTROY THAT RECIPE!
CAN'T *I* BE THE ONE RUNNING AWAY?
THERE'S RUNNING INVOLVED.
NEVER MIND.
DESPITE THE EVIL SPIRITS IN THIS FOREST, IT DOES HAVE BEAUTIFUL DECIDUOUS TREES!
ACK! THE TREES **BETRAYED** ME! AND AFTER I PLANTED SO MANY OF YOUR BRETHREN ON **EARTH DAY!**
GOTTA DESTROY SACRED RECIPE...
HIYA, HOMER! WE'RE ALL BETTER NOW!
AND WE'RE PLAYING YOUR FAVORITE GAME... **HOMER WINS!**
THAT **IS** MY FAVORITE! LET ME JUST TAKE CARE OF ONE LITTLE BOOK BURNING FIRST.

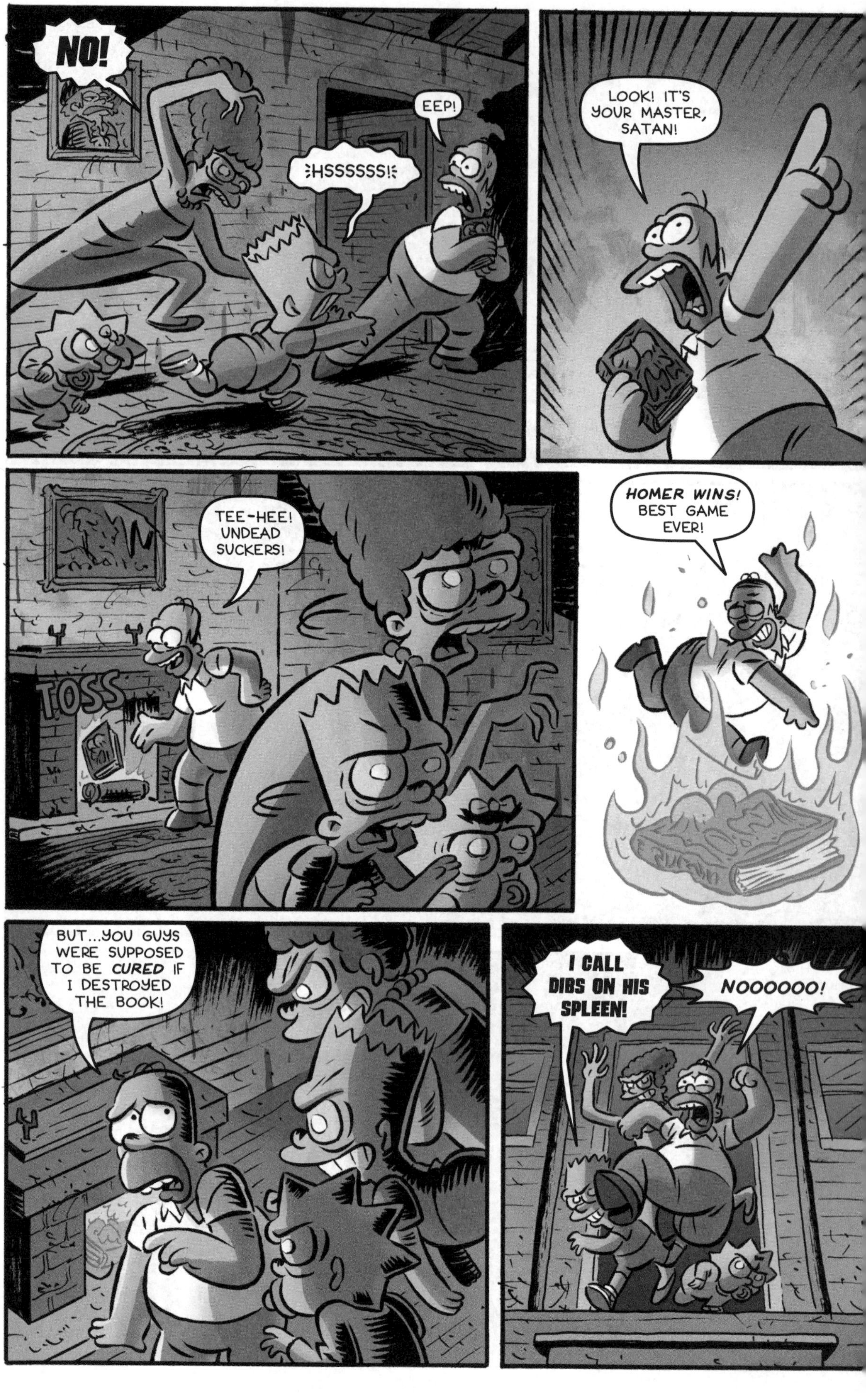
NO!
EEP!
HSSSSSS!
LOOK! IT'S YOUR MASTER, SATAN!
TEE-HEE! UNDEAD SUCKERS!
TOSS
HOMER WINS! BEST GAME EVER!
BUT...YOU GUYS WERE SUPPOSED TO BE CURED IF I DESTROYED THE BOOK!
I CALL DIBS ON HIS SPLEEN!
NOOOOOO!

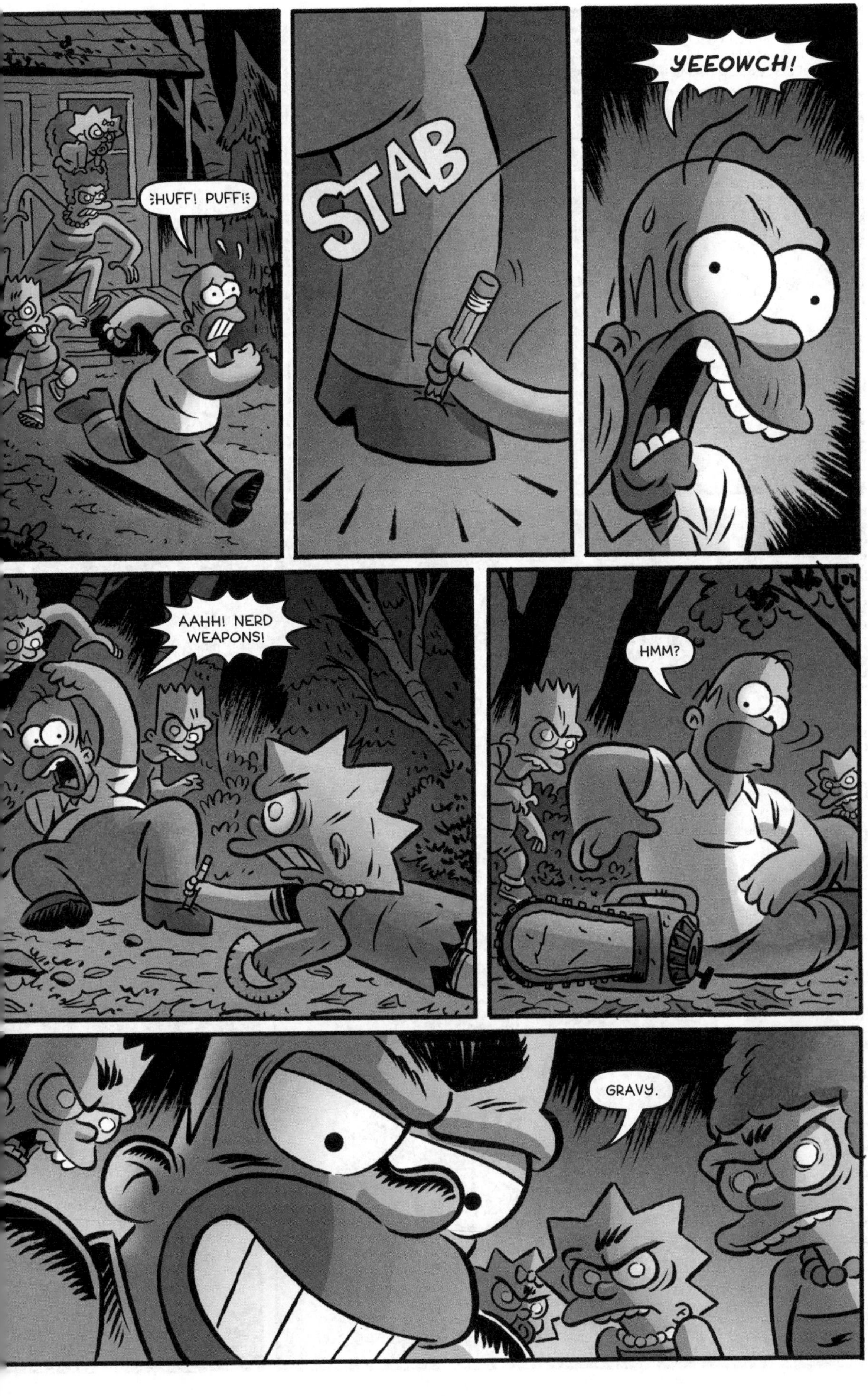
HUFF! PUFF!
STAB
YEEOWCH!
AAHH! NERD WEAPONS!
HMM?
GRAVY.

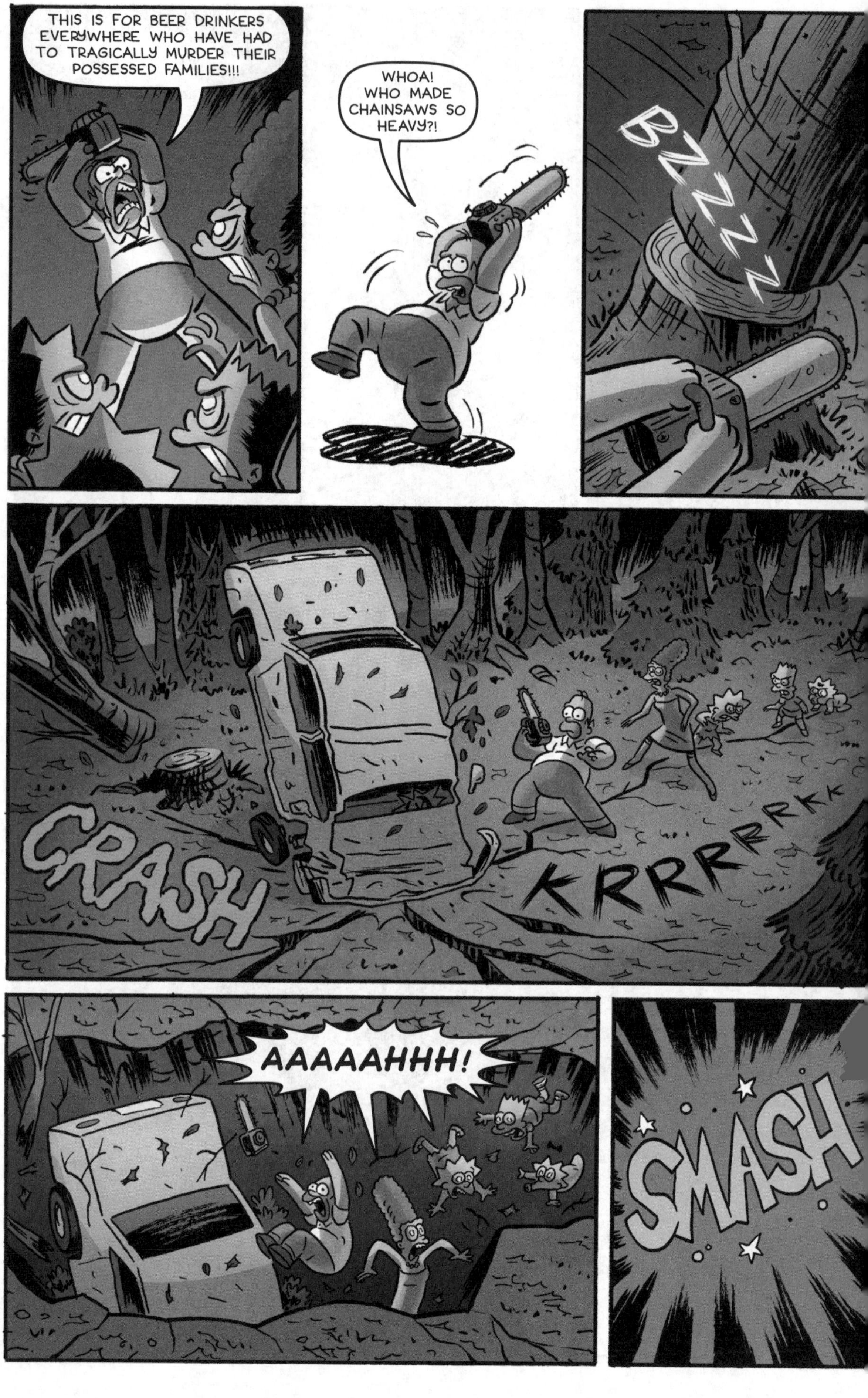
THIS IS FOR BEER DRINKERS EVERYWHERE WHO HAVE HAD TO TRAGICALLY MURDER THEIR POSSESSED FAMILIES!!!
WHOA! WHO MADE CHAINSAWS SO HEAVY?!
BZZZZ
CRASH
KRRRRRRKK
AAAAAHHH!
SMASH

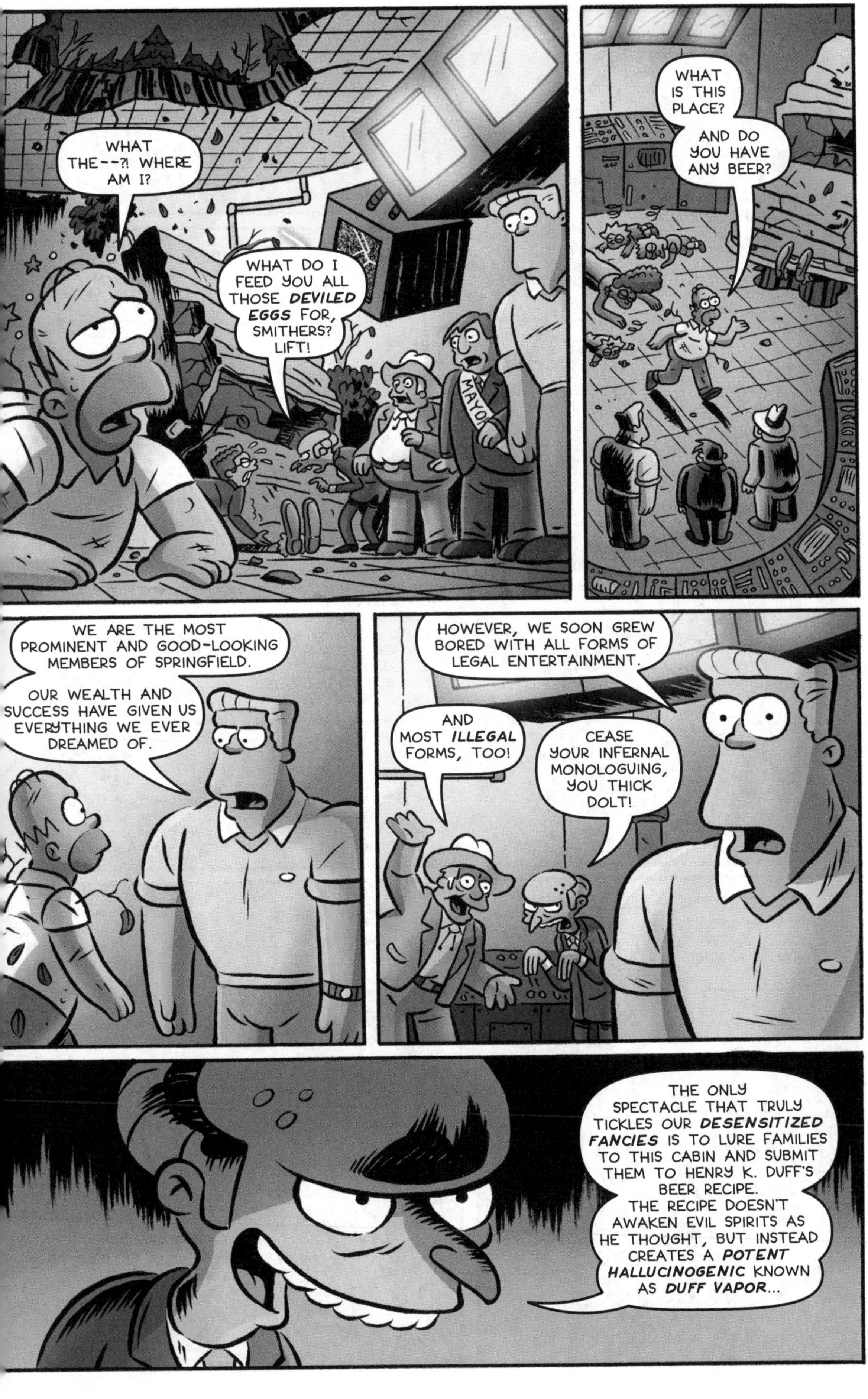
WHAT THE--?! WHERE AM I?
WHAT DO I FEED YOU ALL THOSE DEVILED EGGS FOR, SMITHERS? LIFT!
MAYO
WHAT IS THIS PLACE?
AND DO YOU HAVE ANY BEER?
WE ARE THE MOST PROMINENT AND GOOD-LOOKING MEMBERS OF SPRINGFIELD.
OUR WEALTH AND SUCCESS HAVE GIVEN US EVERYTHING WE EVER DREAMED OF.
HOWEVER, WE SOON GREW BORED WITH ALL FORMS OF LEGAL ENTERTAINMENT.
AND MOST ILLEGAL FORMS, TOO!
CEASE YOUR INFERNAL MONOLOGUING, YOU THICK DOLT!
THE ONLY SPECTACLE THAT TRULY TICKLES OUR DESENSITIZED FANCIES IS TO LURE FAMILIES TO THIS CABIN AND SUBMIT THEM TO HENRY K. DUFF'S BEER RECIPE.
THE RECIPE DOESN'T AWAKEN EVIL SPIRITS AS HE THOUGHT, BUT INSTEAD CREATES A POTENT HALLUCINOGENIC KNOWN AS DUFF VAPOR...

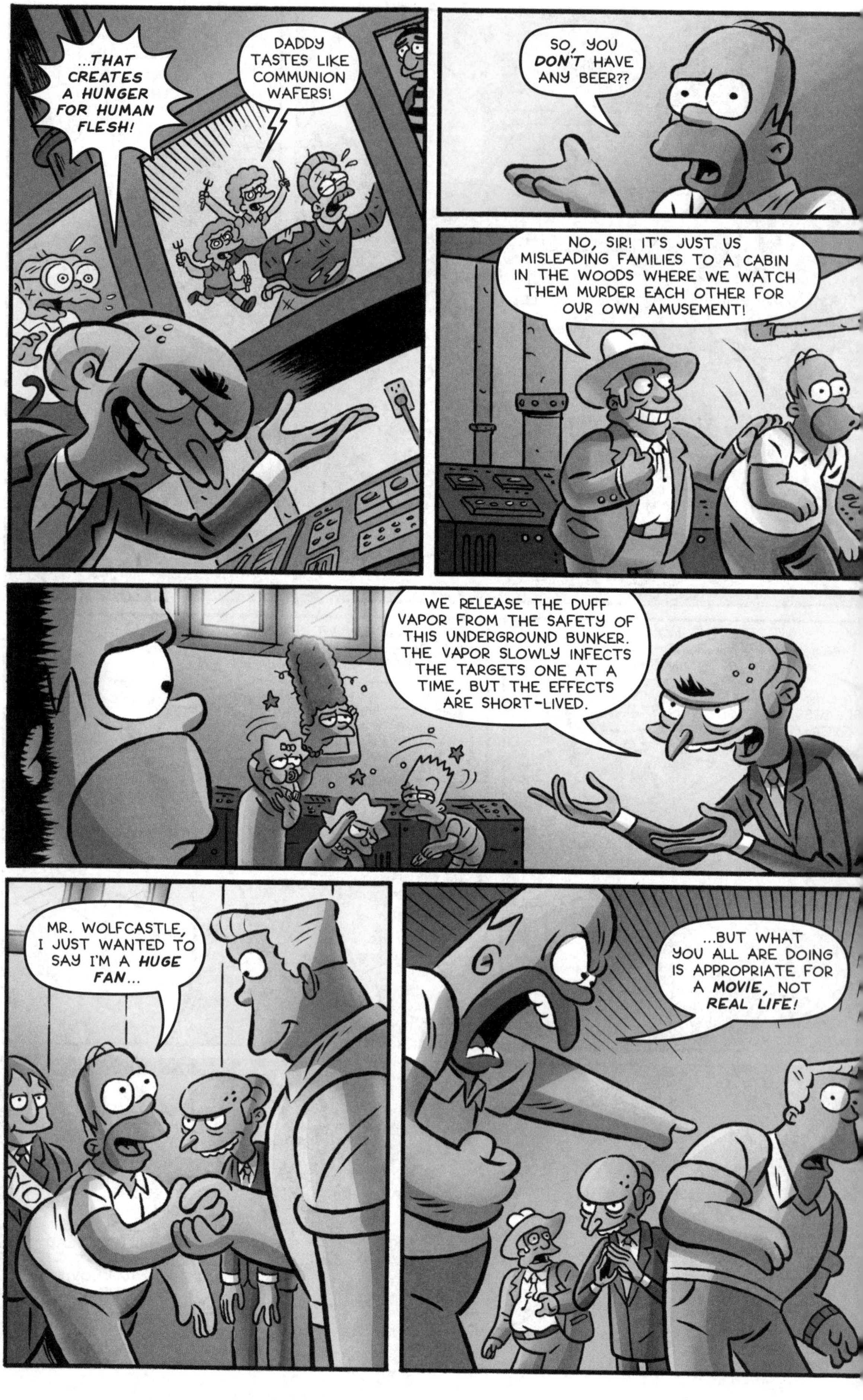
...THAT CREATES A HUNGER FOR HUMAN FLESH!
DADDY TASTES LIKE COMMUNION WAFERS!
SO, YOU DON'T HAVE ANY BEER??
NO, SIR! IT'S JUST US MISLEADING FAMILIES TO A CABIN IN THE WOODS WHERE WE WATCH THEM MURDER EACH OTHER FOR OUR OWN AMUSEMENT!
WE RELEASE THE DUFF VAPOR FROM THE SAFETY OF THIS UNDERGROUND BUNKER. THE VAPOR SLOWLY INFECTS THE TARGETS ONE AT A TIME, BUT THE EFFECTS ARE SHORT-LIVED.
MR. WOLFCASTLE, I JUST WANTED TO SAY I'M A HUGE FAN...
...BUT WHAT YOU ALL ARE DOING IS APPROPRIATE FOR A MOVIE, NOT REAL LIFE!

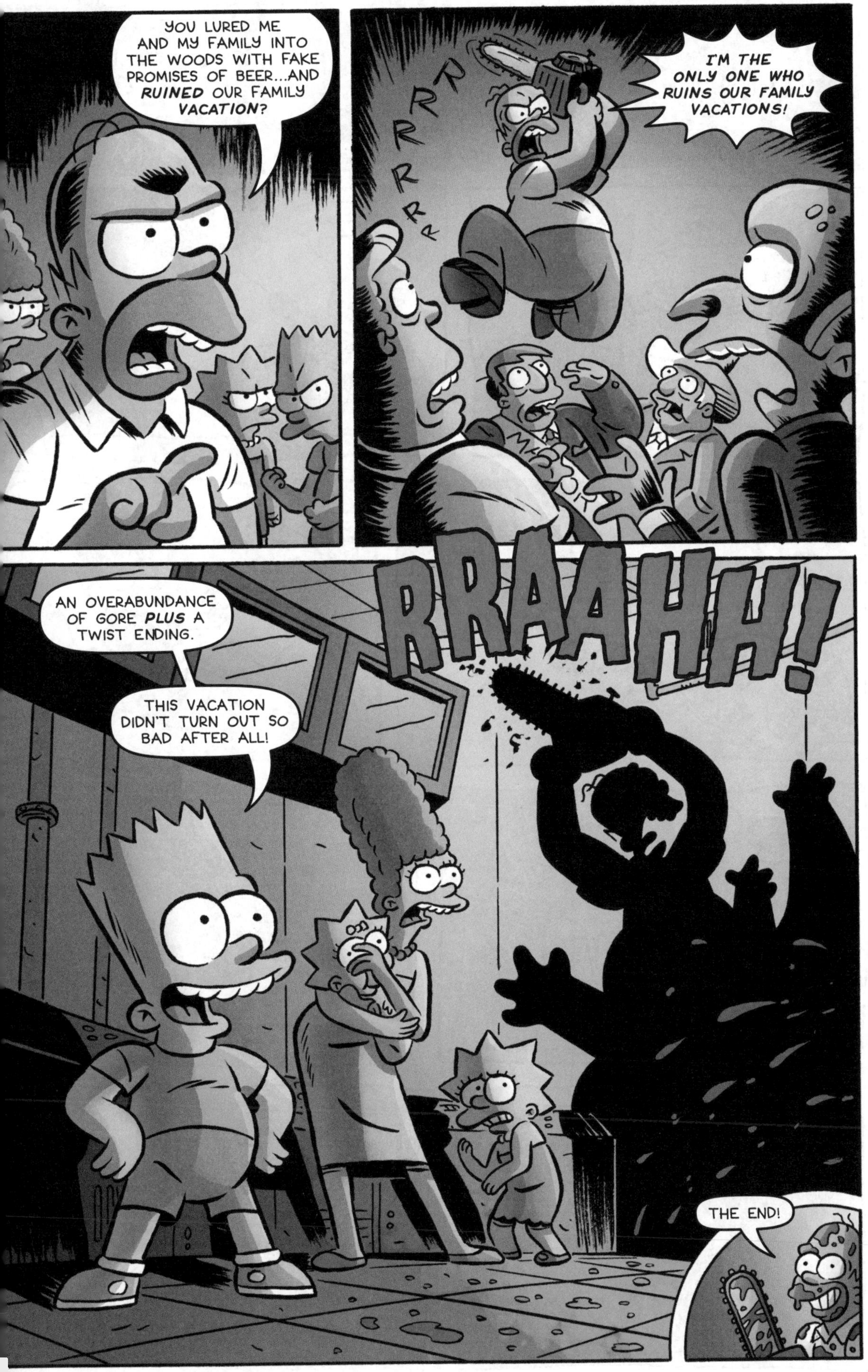

YOU LURED ME AND MY FAMILY INTO THE WOODS WITH FAKE PROMISES OF BEER...AND RUINED OUR FAMILY VACATION?
RRRRRRR
I'M THE ONLY ONE WHO RUINS OUR FAMILY VACATIONS!
RRAAHH!
AN OVERABUNDANCE OF GORE PLUS A TWIST ENDING.
THIS VACATION DIDN'T TURN OUT SO BAD AFTER ALL!
THE END!

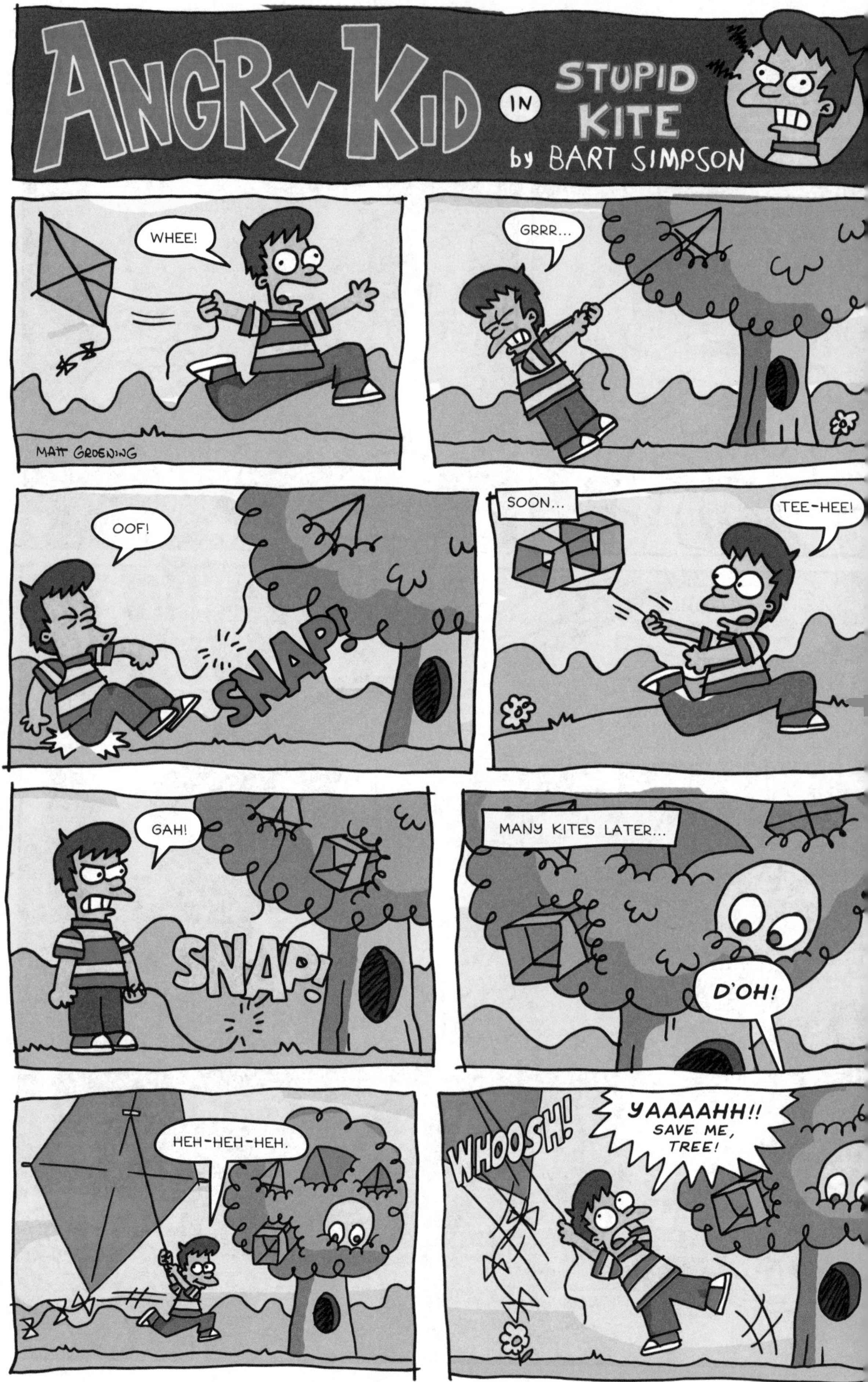
ANGRY KID
IN
STUPID KITE
by BART SIMPSON
WHEE!
MATT GROENING
GRRR...
OOF!
SNAP!
SOON...
TEE-HEE!
GAH!
SNAP!
MANY KITES LATER...
D'OH!
HEH-HEH-HEH.
WHOOSH!
YAAAAHH!! SAVE ME, TREE!

TONY DIGEROLAMO SCRIPT · MIKE ROTE PENCILS · JASON HO INKS · NATHAN HAMILL COLORS · KAREN BATES LETTERS · BILL MORRISON EDITOR

LISA'S LAUGHATORY

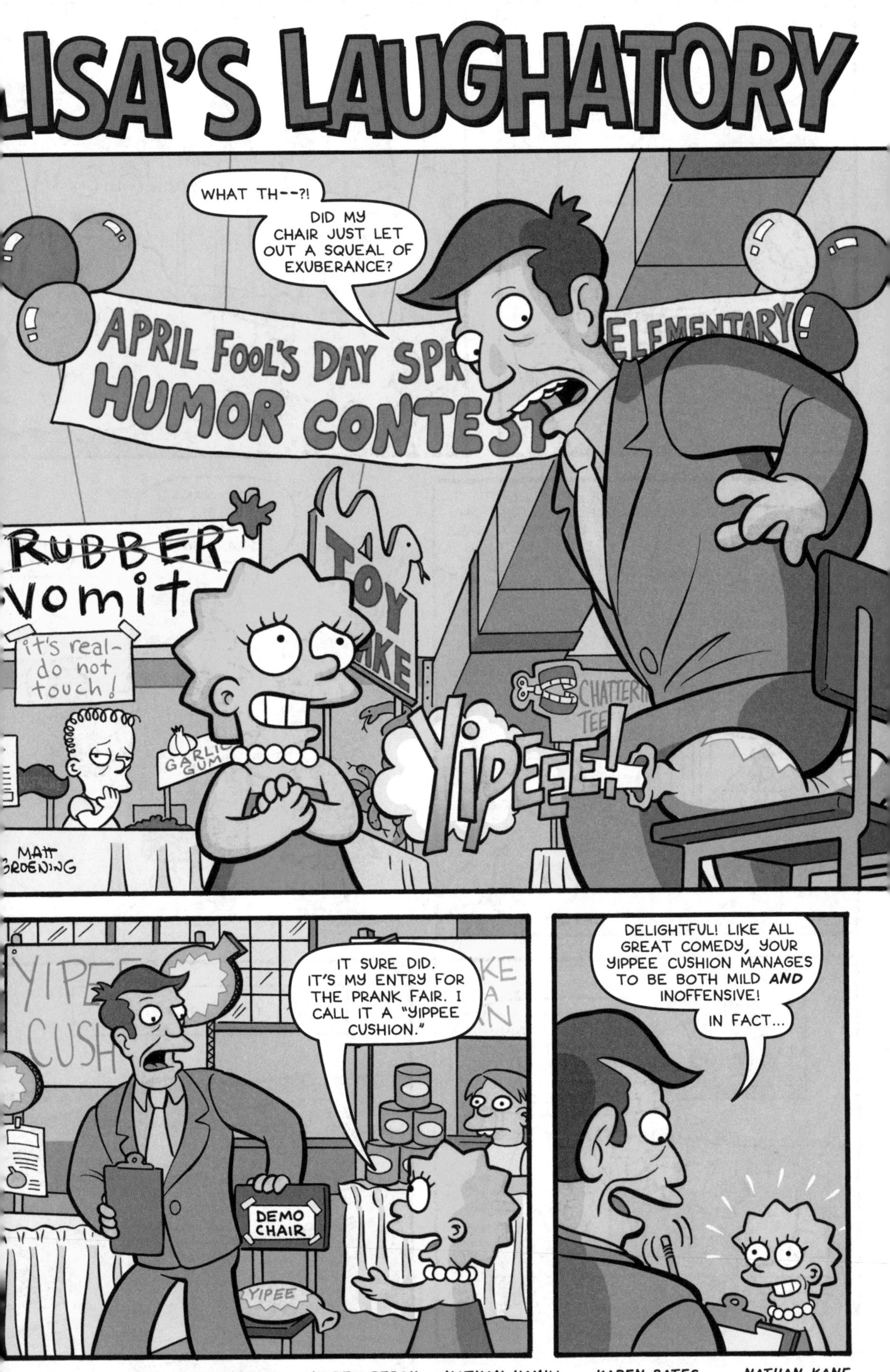
WHAT TH--?!
DID MY CHAIR JUST LET OUT A SQUEAL OF EXUBERANCE?
APRIL FOOL'S DAY SPR HUMOR CONTEST
ELEMENTARY
RUBBER vomit
it's real- do not touch!
TOY
GARLIC GUM
CHATTERI TEE
YIPEEE!
MATT GROENING
YIPEE CUSH
DEMO CHAIR
YIPEE
IT SURE DID. IT'S MY ENTRY FOR THE PRANK FAIR. I CALL IT A "YIPPEE CUSHION."
DELIGHTFUL! LIKE ALL GREAT COMEDY, YOUR YIPPEE CUSHION MANAGES TO BE BOTH MILD ***AND*** INOFFENSIVE!
IN FACT...

ARIE KAPLAN SCRIPT
NINA MATSUMOTO PENCILS
ANDREW PEPOY INKS
NATHAN HAMILL COLORS
KAREN BATES LETTERS
NATHAN KANE EDITOR

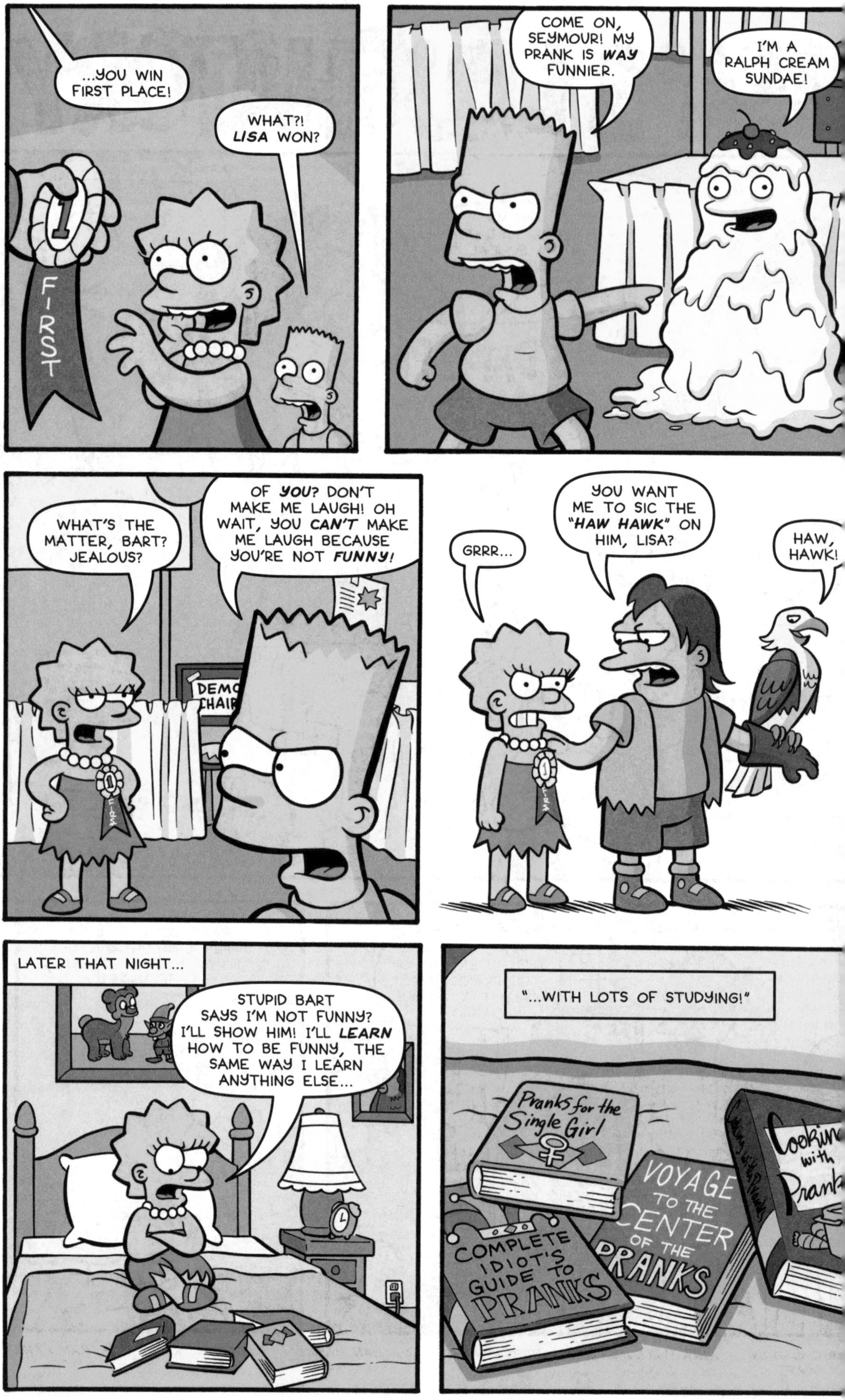

...YOU WIN FIRST PLACE!
WHAT?! LISA WON?
1
FIRST
COME ON, SEYMOUR! MY PRANK IS WAY FUNNIER.
I'M A RALPH CREAM SUNDAE!
WHAT'S THE MATTER, BART? JEALOUS?
OF YOU? DON'T MAKE ME LAUGH! OH WAIT, YOU CAN'T MAKE ME LAUGH BECAUSE YOU'RE NOT FUNNY!
GRRR...
YOU WANT ME TO SIC THE "HAW HAWK" ON HIM, LISA?
HAW, HAWK!
LATER THAT NIGHT...
STUPID BART SAYS I'M NOT FUNNY? I'LL SHOW HIM! I'LL LEARN HOW TO BE FUNNY, THE SAME WAY I LEARN ANYTHING ELSE...
"...WITH LOTS OF STUDYING!"
Pranks for the Single Girl
VOYAGE TO THE CENTER OF THE PRANKS
COMPLETE IDIOT'S GUIDE TO PRANKS

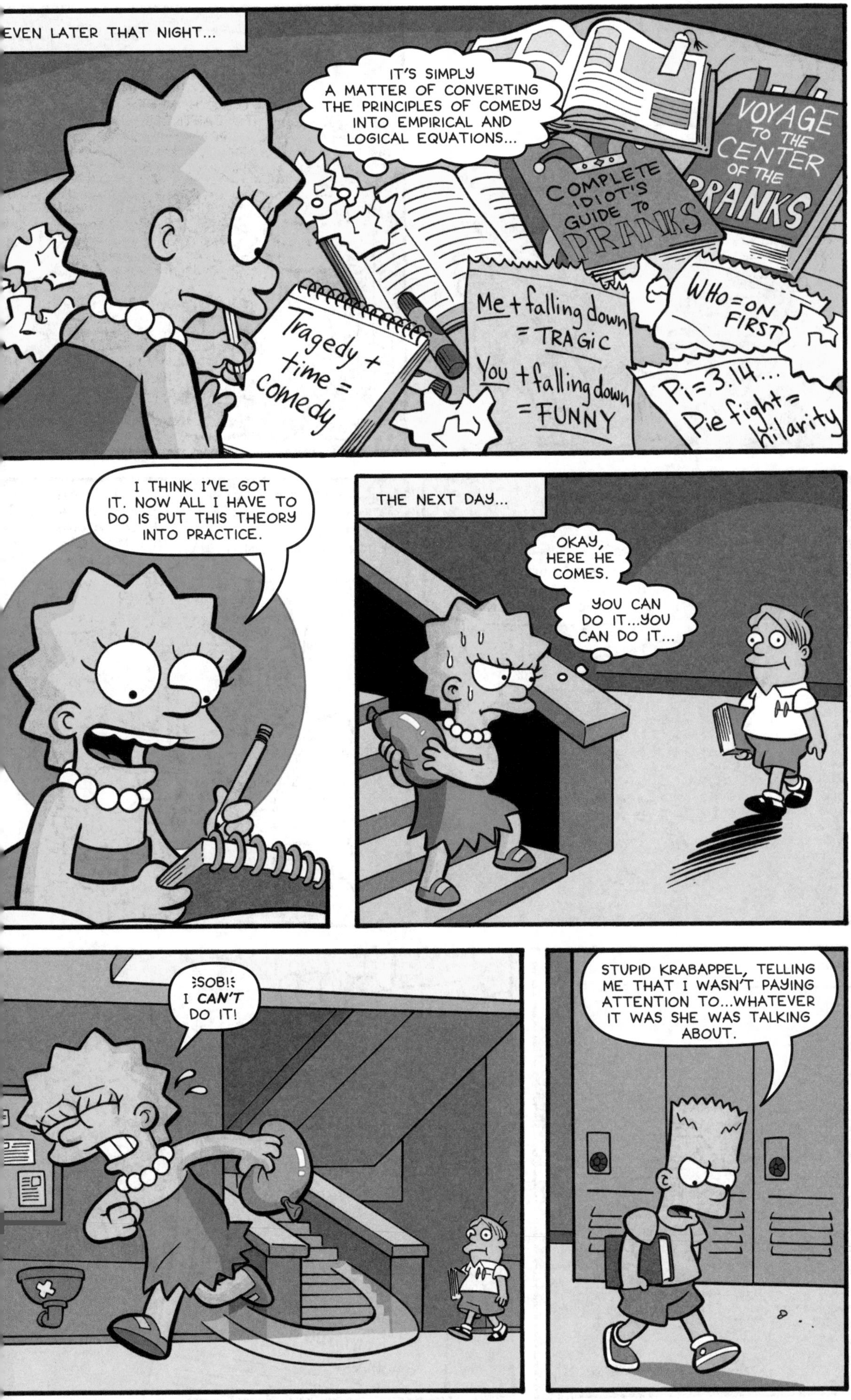
EVEN LATER THAT NIGHT...
IT'S SIMPLY A MATTER OF CONVERTING THE PRINCIPLES OF COMEDY INTO EMPIRICAL AND LOGICAL EQUATIONS...
COMPLETE IDIOT'S GUIDE TO PRANKS
VOYAGE TO THE CENTER OF THE PRANKS
Tragedy + time = comedy
Me + falling down = TRAGIC
You + falling down = FUNNY
WHO = ON FIRST
Pi = 3.14... Pie fight = hilarity
I THINK I'VE GOT IT. NOW ALL I HAVE TO DO IS PUT THIS THEORY INTO PRACTICE.
THE NEXT DAY...
OKAY, HERE HE COMES.
YOU CAN DO IT...YOU CAN DO IT...
SOB! I CAN'T DO IT!
STUPID KRABAPPEL, TELLING ME THAT I WASN'T PAYING ATTENTION TO...WHATEVER IT WAS SHE WAS TALKING ABOUT.

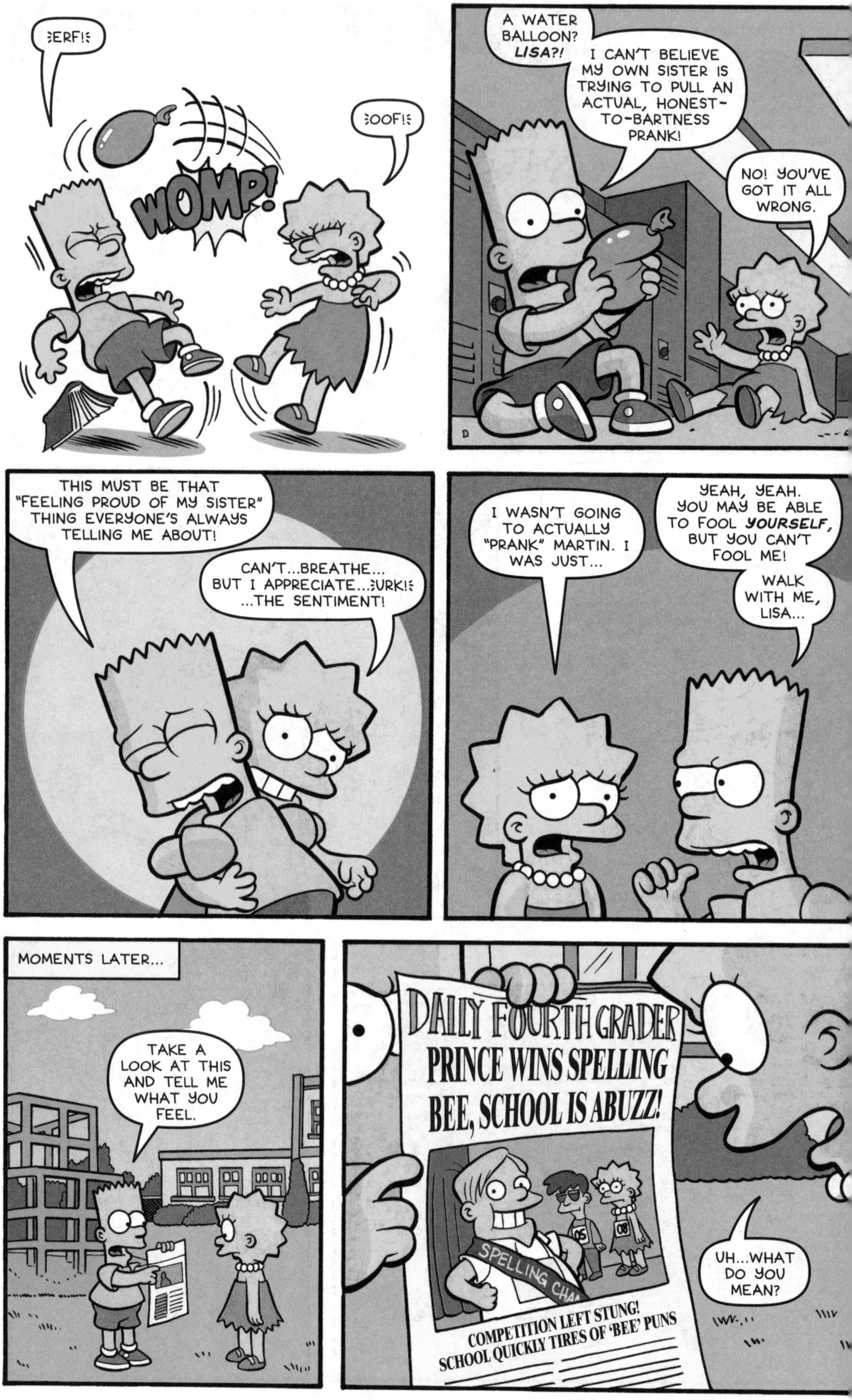
ERF!
WOMP!
OOF!
A WATER BALLOON? LISA?!
I CAN'T BELIEVE MY OWN SISTER IS TRYING TO PULL AN ACTUAL, HONEST-TO-BARTNESS PRANK!
NO! YOU'VE GOT IT ALL WRONG.
THIS MUST BE THAT "FEELING PROUD OF MY SISTER" THING EVERYONE'S ALWAYS TELLING ME ABOUT!
CAN'T...BREATHE... BUT I APPRECIATE...URK! ...THE SENTIMENT!
I WASN'T GOING TO ACTUALLY "PRANK" MARTIN. I WAS JUST...
YEAH, YEAH. YOU MAY BE ABLE TO FOOL YOURSELF, BUT YOU CAN'T FOOL ME!
WALK WITH ME, LISA...
MOMENTS LATER...
TAKE A LOOK AT THIS AND TELL ME WHAT YOU FEEL.
DAILY FOURTH GRADER
PRINCE WINS SPELLING BEE, SCHOOL IS ABUZZ!
SPELLING CHA
05
08
COMPETITION LEFT STUNG!
SCHOOL QUICKLY TIRES OF 'BEE' PUNS
UH...WHAT DO YOU MEAN?

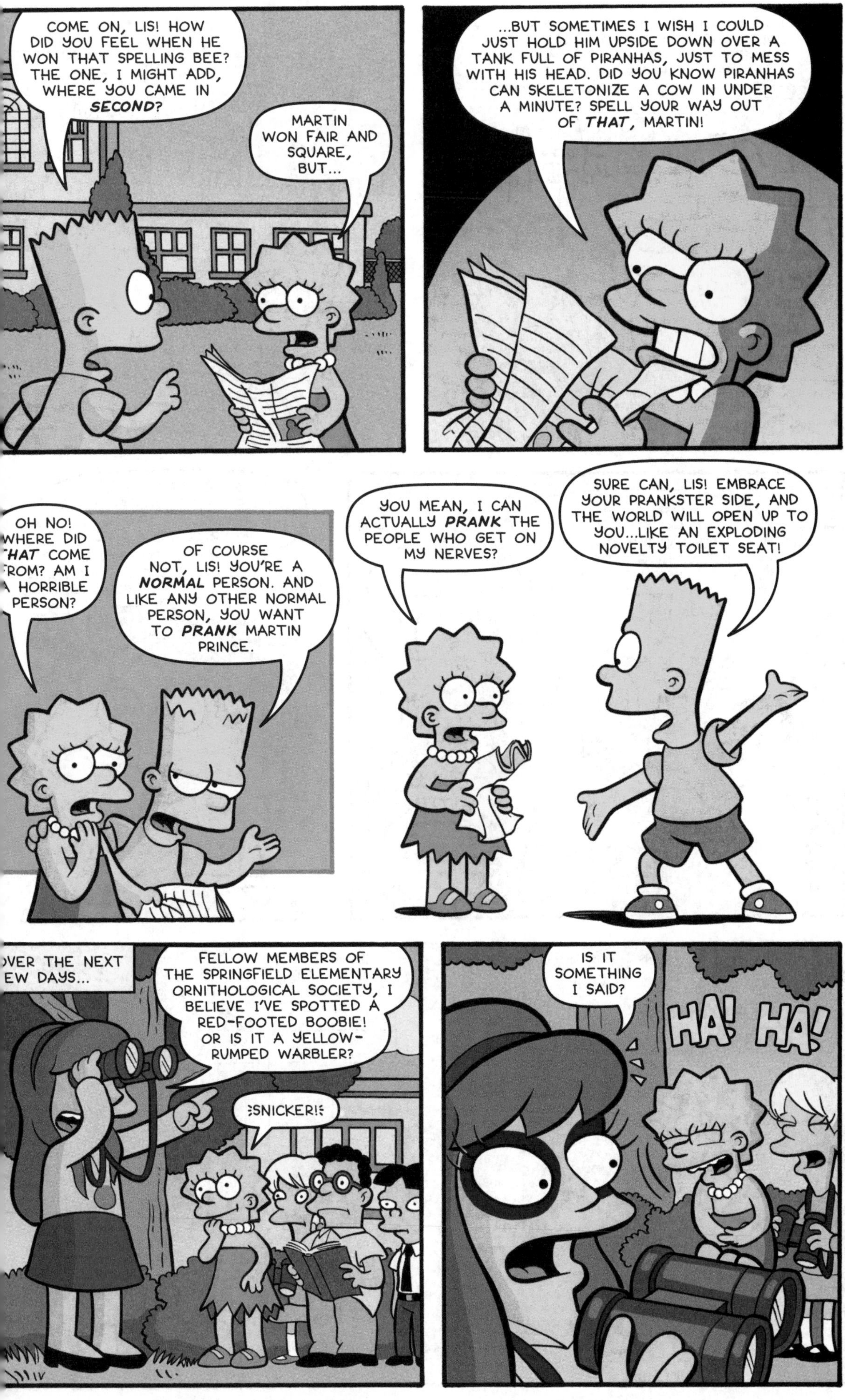
COME ON, LIS! HOW DID YOU FEEL WHEN HE WON THAT SPELLING BEE? THE ONE, I MIGHT ADD, WHERE YOU CAME IN ***SECOND***?
MARTIN WON FAIR AND SQUARE, BUT...
...BUT SOMETIMES I WISH I COULD JUST HOLD HIM UPSIDE DOWN OVER A TANK FULL OF PIRANHAS, JUST TO MESS WITH HIS HEAD. DID YOU KNOW PIRANHAS CAN SKELETONIZE A COW IN UNDER A MINUTE? SPELL YOUR WAY OUT OF ***THAT***, MARTIN!
OH NO! HERE DID HAT COME ROM? AM I HORRIBLE PERSON?
OF COURSE NOT, LIS! YOU'RE A ***NORMAL*** PERSON. AND LIKE ANY OTHER NORMAL PERSON, YOU WANT TO ***PRANK*** MARTIN PRINCE.
YOU MEAN, I CAN ACTUALLY ***PRANK*** THE PEOPLE WHO GET ON MY NERVES?
SURE CAN, LIS! EMBRACE YOUR PRANKSTER SIDE, AND THE WORLD WILL OPEN UP TO YOU...LIKE AN EXPLODING NOVELTY TOILET SEAT!
VER THE NEXT EW DAYS...
FELLOW MEMBERS OF THE SPRINGFIELD ELEMENTARY ORNITHOLOGICAL SOCIETY, I BELIEVE I'VE SPOTTED A RED-FOOTED BOOBIE! OR IS IT A YELLOW-RUMPED WARBLER?
SNICKER!
IS IT SOMETHING I SAID?
HA! HA!

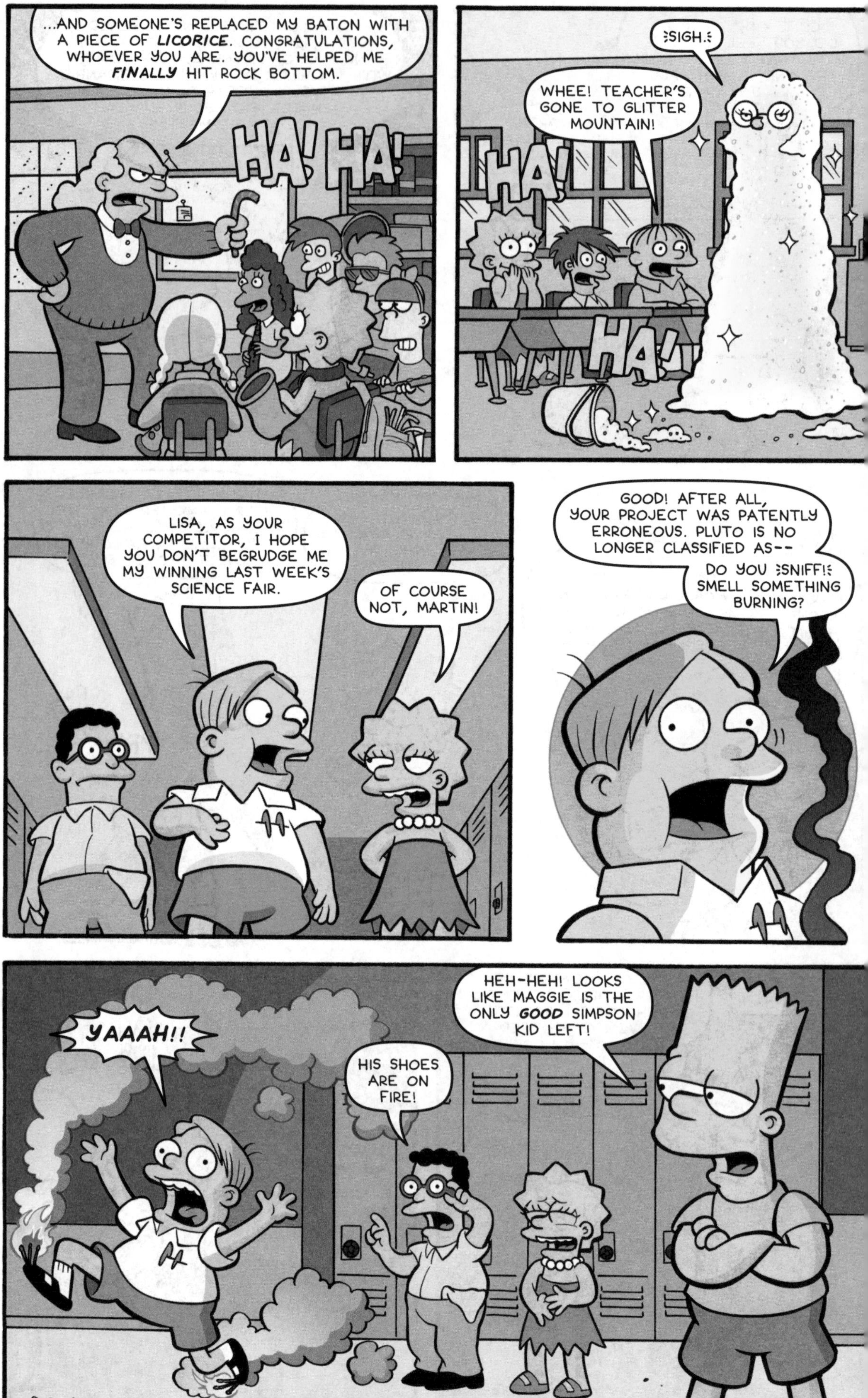
...AND SOMEONE'S REPLACED MY BATON WITH A PIECE OF LICORICE. CONGRATULATIONS, WHOEVER YOU ARE. YOU'VE HELPED ME FINALLY HIT ROCK BOTTOM.
HA! HA!
:SIGH.:
WHEE! TEACHER'S GONE TO GLITTER MOUNTAIN!
HA!
HA!
LISA, AS YOUR COMPETITOR, I HOPE YOU DON'T BEGRUDGE ME MY WINNING LAST WEEK'S SCIENCE FAIR.
OF COURSE NOT, MARTIN!
GOOD! AFTER ALL, YOUR PROJECT WAS PATENTLY ERRONEOUS. PLUTO IS NO LONGER CLASSIFIED AS--
DO YOU :SNIFF!: SMELL SOMETHING BURNING?
YAAAH!!
HIS SHOES ARE ON FIRE!
HEH-HEH! LOOKS LIKE MAGGIE IS THE ONLY GOOD SIMPSON KID LEFT!

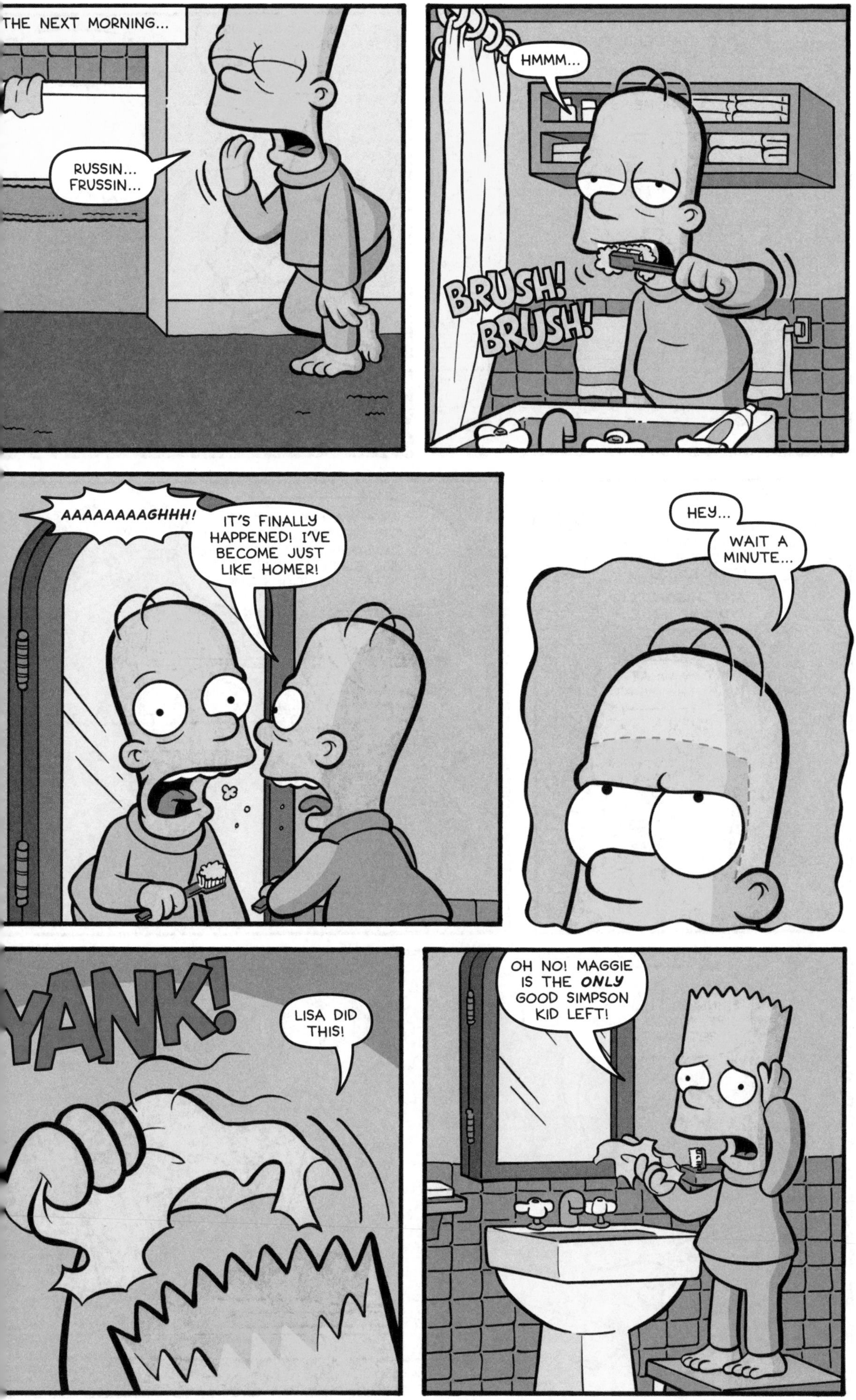
THE NEXT MORNING...
RUSSIN... FRUSSIN...
HMMM...
BRUSH! BRUSH!
AAAAAAAAGHHH!
IT'S FINALLY HAPPENED! I'VE BECOME JUST LIKE HOMER!
HEY...
WAIT A MINUTE...
YANK!
LISA DID THIS!
OH NO! MAGGIE IS THE ONLY GOOD SIMPSON KID LEFT!

SOON...

IT'S TIME TO PUT AN END TO THIS, LISA. KEEP ACTING LIKE ME AND YOUR GRADES ARE GONNA PLUNGE LOWER THAN HOMER'S RETIREMENT FUND!

I THINK YOU'RE JUST JEALOUS BECAUSE *I'M* THE SCHOOL'S NEW CLASS CLOWN.

WHAT?!? ARE YOU KIDDING--

ATTENTION STUDENTS...

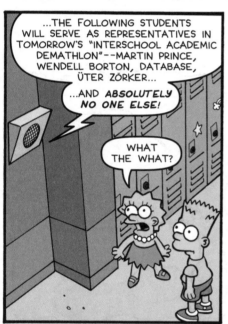

...THE FOLLOWING STUDENTS WILL SERVE AS REPRESENTATIVES IN TOMORROW'S "INTERSCHOOL ACADEMIC DEMATHLON"--MARTIN PRINCE, WENDELL BORTON, DATABASE, ÜTER ZÖRKER...

...AND *ABSOLUTELY NO ONE ELSE!*

WHAT THE WHAT?

WHY WASN'T I PICKED FOR THE DEMATHLON TEAM? I'M LISA SIMPSON! I GET PICKED FOR STUFF! ESPECIALLY IF THAT "STUFF" CONTAINS THE WORD "MATH."

COME ON, PRINCIPAL SKINNER! THERE'S GOT TO BE A WAY FOR ME TO GET ON THAT TEAM!

SORRY, LISA. YOUR RECENT INCORRIGIBILITY LEAVES ME NO OTHER CHOICE.

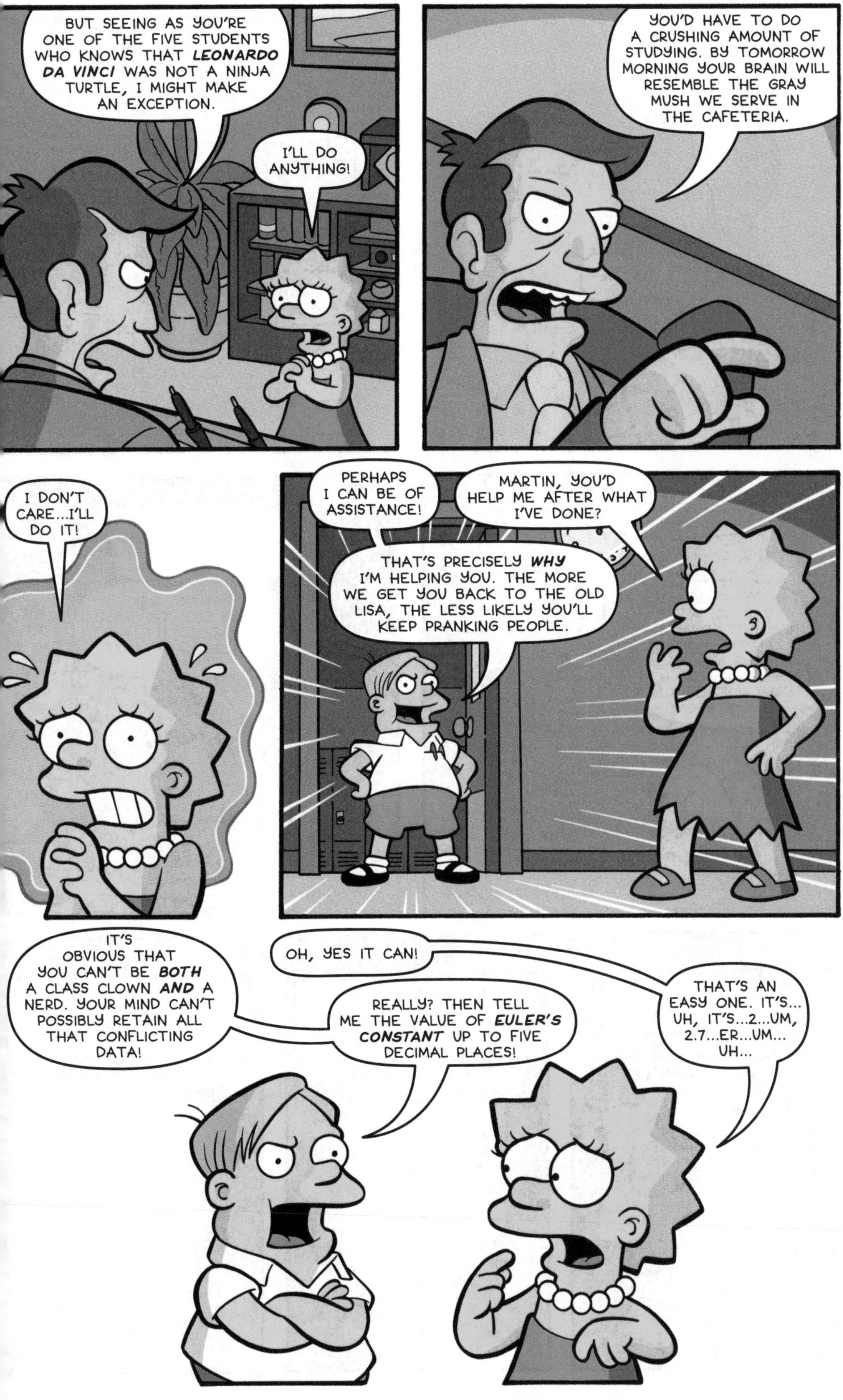
BUT SEEING AS YOU'RE ONE OF THE FIVE STUDENTS WHO KNOWS THAT ***LEONARDO DA VINCI*** WAS NOT A NINJA TURTLE, I MIGHT MAKE AN EXCEPTION.
I'LL DO ANYTHING!
YOU'D HAVE TO DO A CRUSHING AMOUNT OF STUDYING. BY TOMORROW MORNING YOUR BRAIN WILL RESEMBLE THE GRAY MUSH WE SERVE IN THE CAFETERIA.
I DON'T CARE...I'LL DO IT!
PERHAPS I CAN BE OF ASSISTANCE!
MARTIN, YOU'D HELP ME AFTER WHAT I'VE DONE?
THAT'S PRECISELY ***WHY*** I'M HELPING YOU. THE MORE WE GET YOU BACK TO THE OLD LISA, THE LESS LIKELY YOU'LL KEEP PRANKING PEOPLE.
IT'S OBVIOUS THAT YOU CAN'T BE ***BOTH*** A CLASS CLOWN ***AND*** A NERD. YOUR MIND CAN'T POSSIBLY RETAIN ALL THAT CONFLICTING DATA!
OH, YES IT CAN!
REALLY? THEN TELL ME THE VALUE OF ***EULER'S CONSTANT*** UP TO FIVE DECIMAL PLACES!
THAT'S AN EASY ONE. IT'S... UH, IT'S...2...UM, 2.7...ER...UM... UH...

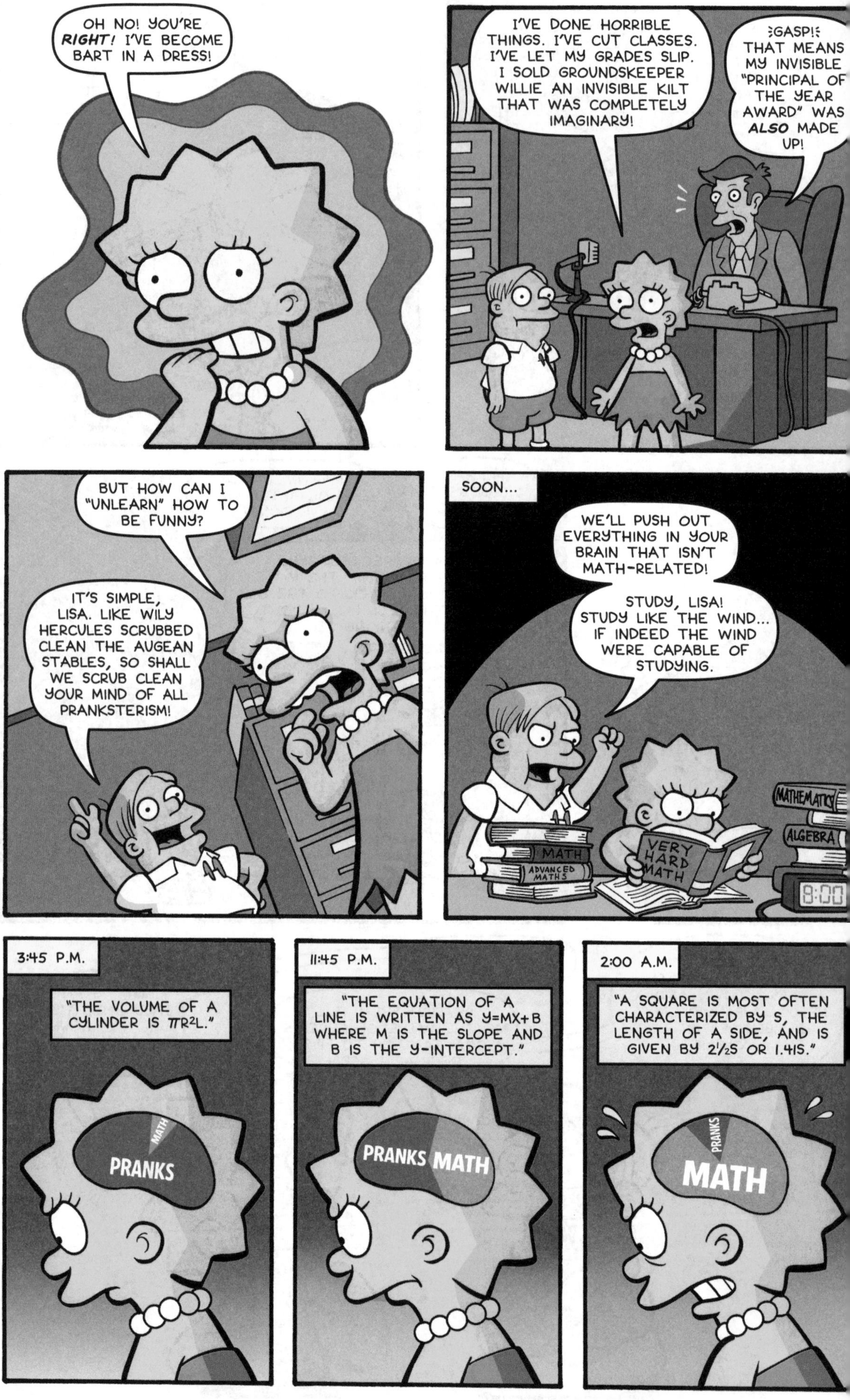
OH NO! YOU'RE *RIGHT!* I'VE BECOME BART IN A DRESS!
I'VE DONE HORRIBLE THINGS. I'VE CUT CLASSES. I'VE LET MY GRADES SLIP. I SOLD GROUNDSKEEPER WILLIE AN INVISIBLE KILT THAT WAS COMPLETELY IMAGINARY!
GASP! THAT MEANS MY INVISIBLE "PRINCIPAL OF THE YEAR AWARD" WAS *ALSO* MADE UP!
BUT HOW CAN I "UNLEARN" HOW TO BE FUNNY?
IT'S SIMPLE, LISA. LIKE WILY HERCULES SCRUBBED CLEAN THE AUGEAN STABLES, SO SHALL WE SCRUB CLEAN YOUR MIND OF ALL PRANKSTERISM!
SOON...
WE'LL PUSH OUT EVERYTHING IN YOUR BRAIN THAT ISN'T MATH-RELATED!
STUDY, LISA! STUDY LIKE THE WIND... IF INDEED THE WIND WERE CAPABLE OF STUDYING.
MATH
ADVANCED MATHS
VERY HARD MATH
MATHEMATICS
ALGEBRA
8:00
3:45 P.M.
"THE VOLUME OF A CYLINDER IS πR²L."
MATH
PRANKS
11:45 P.M.
"THE EQUATION OF A LINE IS WRITTEN AS Y=MX+B WHERE M IS THE SLOPE AND B IS THE Y-INTERCEPT."
PRANKS MATH
2:00 A.M.
"A SQUARE IS MOST OFTEN CHARACTERIZED BY S, THE LENGTH OF A SIDE, AND IS GIVEN BY 2½S OR 1.41S."
PRANKS
MATH

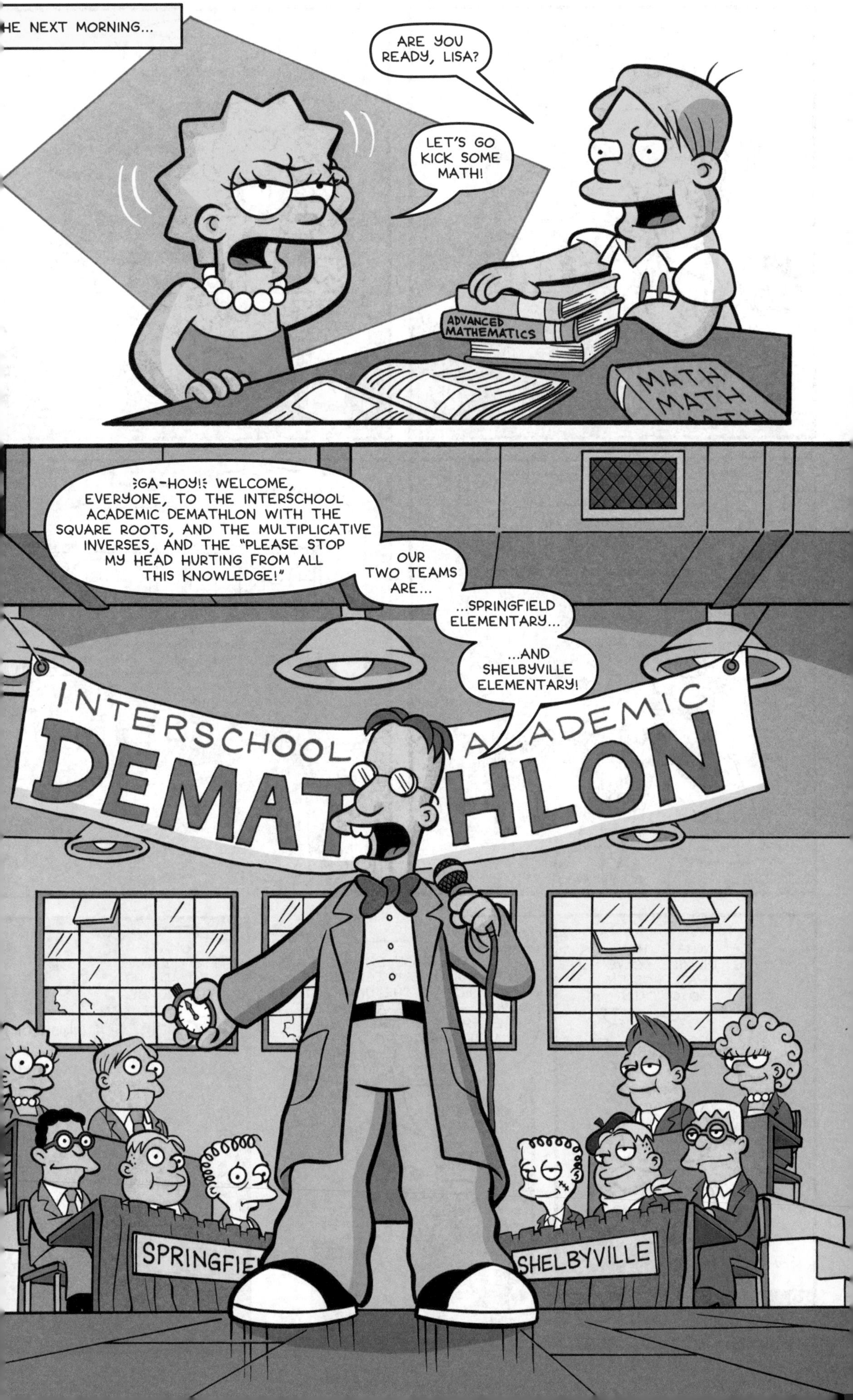
HE NEXT MORNING...
ARE YOU READY, LISA?
LET'S GO KICK SOME MATH!
ADVANCED MATHEMATICS
MATH MATH
¡GA-HOY!¡ WELCOME, EVERYONE, TO THE INTERSCHOOL ACADEMIC DEMATHLON WITH THE SQUARE ROOTS, AND THE MULTIPLICATIVE INVERSES, AND THE "PLEASE STOP MY HEAD HURTING FROM ALL THIS KNOWLEDGE!"
OUR TWO TEAMS ARE...
...SPRINGFIELD ELEMENTARY...
...AND SHELBYVILLE ELEMENTARY!
INTERSCHOOL ACADEMIC DEMATHLON
SPRINGFIE
SHELBYVILLE

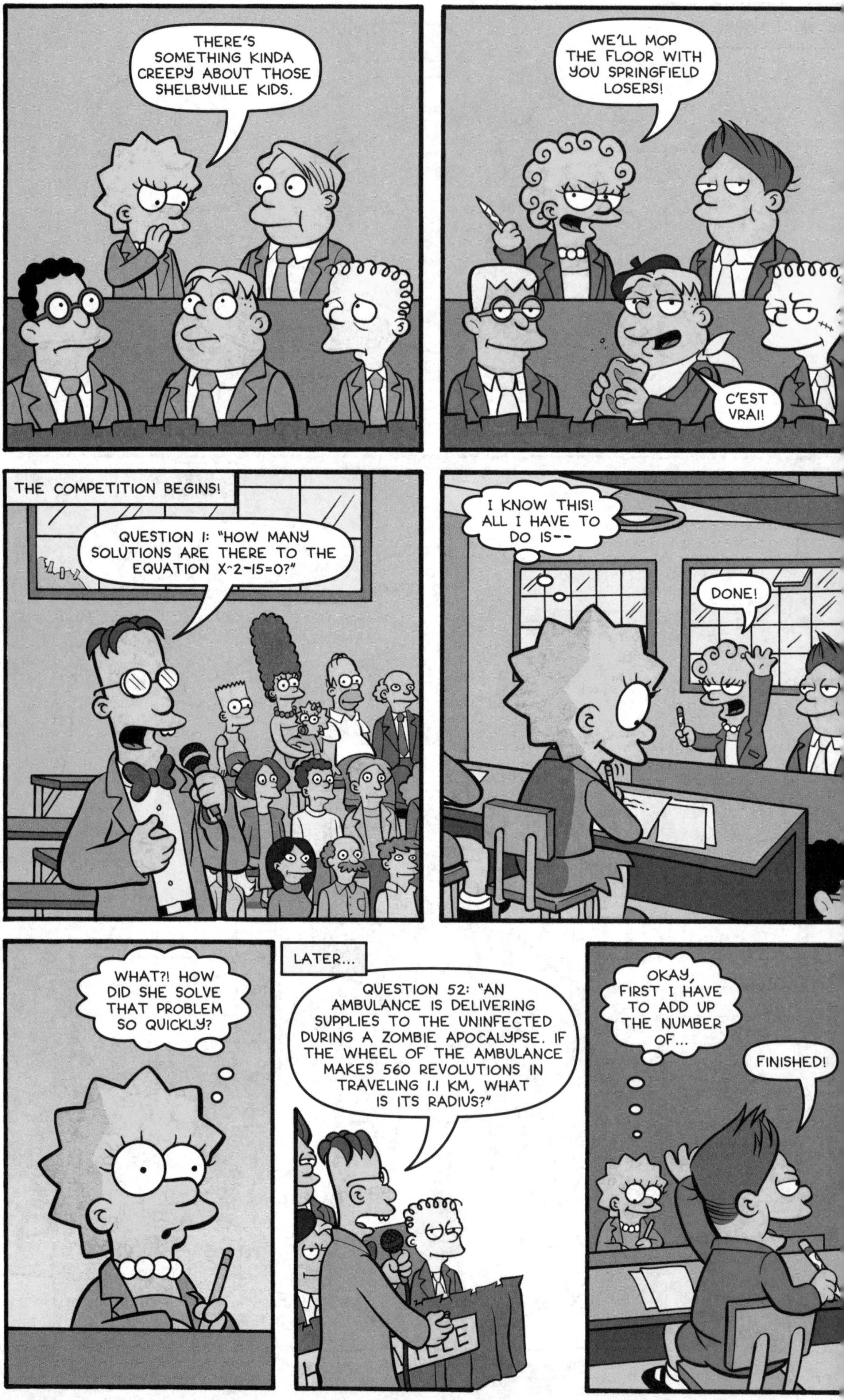
THERE'S SOMETHING KINDA CREEPY ABOUT THOSE SHELBYVILLE KIDS.
WE'LL MOP THE FLOOR WITH YOU SPRINGFIELD LOSERS!
C'EST VRAI!
THE COMPETITION BEGINS!
QUESTION 1: "HOW MANY SOLUTIONS ARE THERE TO THE EQUATION X^2-15=0?"
I KNOW THIS! ALL I HAVE TO DO IS--
DONE!
WHAT?! HOW DID SHE SOLVE THAT PROBLEM SO QUICKLY?
LATER...
QUESTION 52: "AN AMBULANCE IS DELIVERING SUPPLIES TO THE UNINFECTED DURING A ZOMBIE APOCALYPSE. IF THE WHEEL OF THE AMBULANCE MAKES 560 REVOLUTIONS IN TRAVELING 1.1 KM, WHAT IS ITS RADIUS?"
OKAY, FIRST I HAVE TO ADD UP THE NUMBER OF...
FINISHED!

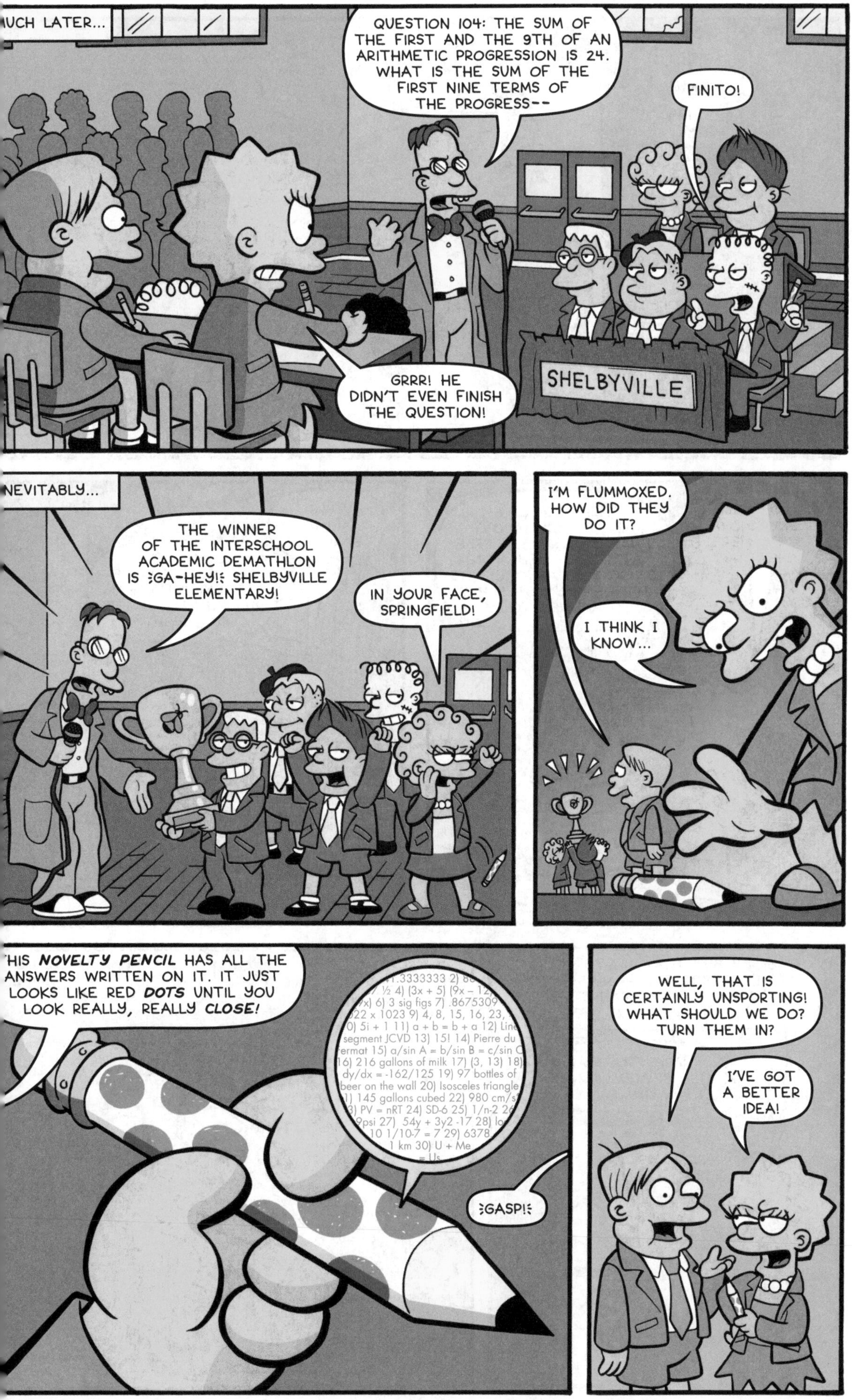

MUCH LATER...
QUESTION 104: THE SUM OF THE FIRST AND THE 9TH OF AN ARITHMETIC PROGRESSION IS 24. WHAT IS THE SUM OF THE FIRST NINE TERMS OF THE PROGRESS--
FINITO!
GRRR! HE DIDN'T EVEN FINISH THE QUESTION!
SHELBYVILLE
INEVITABLY...
THE WINNER OF THE INTERSCHOOL ACADEMIC DEMATHLON IS GA-HEY! SHELBYVILLE ELEMENTARY!
IN YOUR FACE, SPRINGFIELD!
I'M FLUMMOXED. HOW DID THEY DO IT?
I THINK I KNOW...
THIS NOVELTY PENCIL HAS ALL THE ANSWERS WRITTEN ON IT. IT JUST LOOKS LIKE RED DOTS UNTIL YOU LOOK REALLY, REALLY CLOSE!
1.3333333 2)
½ 4) (3x + 5) (9x – 12
x) 6) 3 sig figs 7) .8675309
22 x 1023 9) 4, 8, 15, 16, 23,
0) 5i + 1 11) a + b = b + a 12) Line
segment JCVD 13) 15! 14) Pierre du
ermat 15) a/sin A = b/sin B = c/sin C
16) 216 gallons of milk 17) (3, 13) 18)
dy/dx = -162/125 19) 97 bottles of
beer on the wall 20) Isosceles triangle
1) 145 gallons cubed 22) 980 cm/s
3) PV = nRT 24) SD-6 25) 1/n-2 2
9psi 27) 54y + 3y2 -17 28) lo
10 1/10-7 = 7 29) 6378
1 km 30) U + Me
GASP!
WELL, THAT IS CERTAINLY UNSPORTING! WHAT SHOULD WE DO? TURN THEM IN?
I'VE GOT A BETTER IDEA!

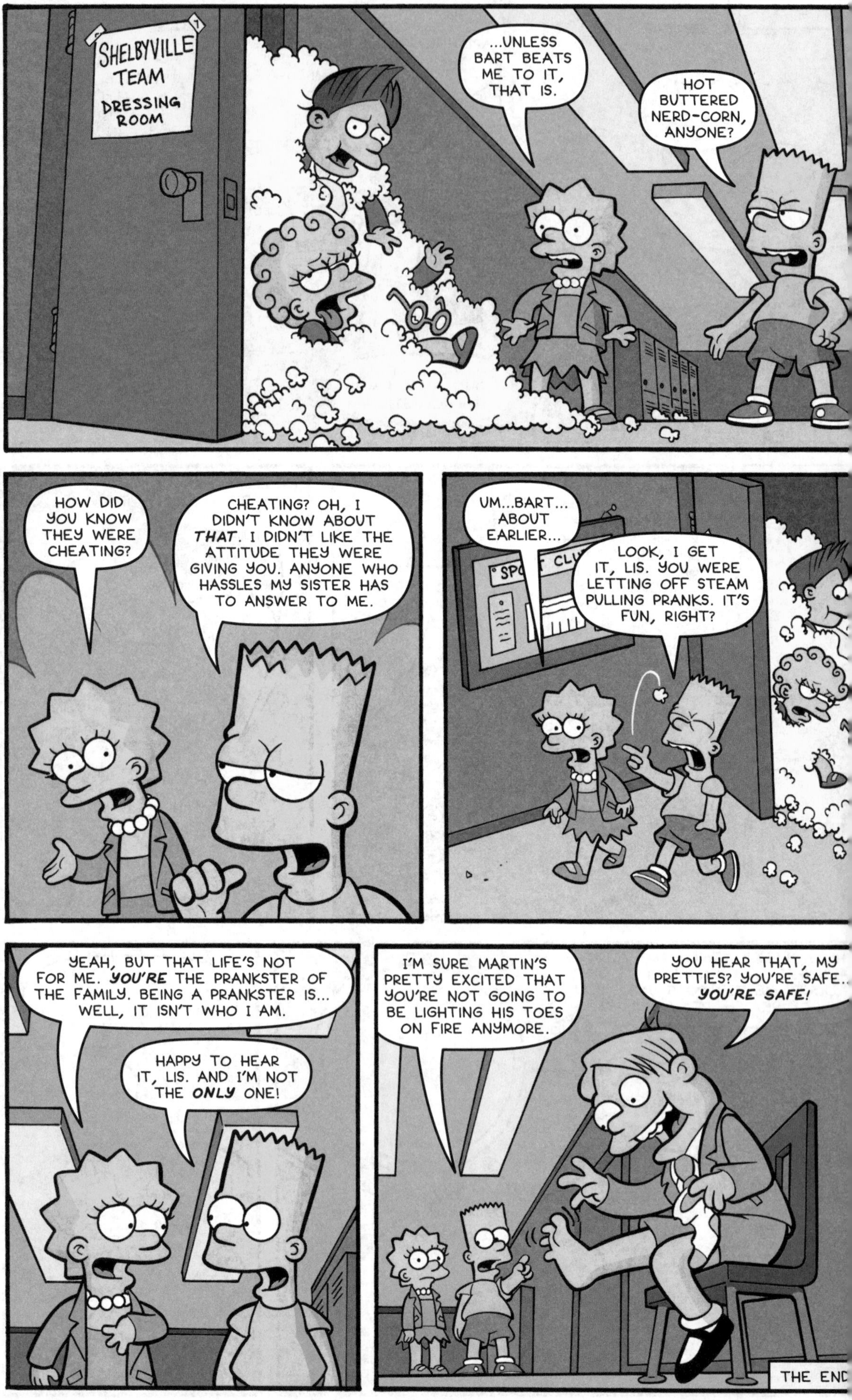
SHELBYVILLE TEAM DRESSING ROOM
...UNLESS BART BEATS ME TO IT, THAT IS.
HOT BUTTERED NERD-CORN, ANYONE?
HOW DID YOU KNOW THEY WERE CHEATING?
CHEATING? OH, I DIDN'T KNOW ABOUT *THAT*. I DIDN'T LIKE THE ATTITUDE THEY WERE GIVING YOU. ANYONE WHO HASSLES MY SISTER HAS TO ANSWER TO ME.
UM...BART... ABOUT EARLIER...
LOOK, I GET IT, LIS. YOU WERE LETTING OFF STEAM PULLING PRANKS. IT'S FUN, RIGHT?
YEAH, BUT THAT LIFE'S NOT FOR ME. ***YOU'RE*** THE PRANKSTER OF THE FAMILY. BEING A PRANKSTER IS... WELL, IT ISN'T WHO I AM.
HAPPY TO HEAR IT, LIS. AND I'M NOT THE ***ONLY*** ONE!
I'M SURE MARTIN'S PRETTY EXCITED THAT YOU'RE NOT GOING TO BE LIGHTING HIS TOES ON FIRE ANYMORE.
YOU HEAR THAT, MY PRETTIES? YOU'RE SAFE... ***YOU'RE SAFE!***
THE END

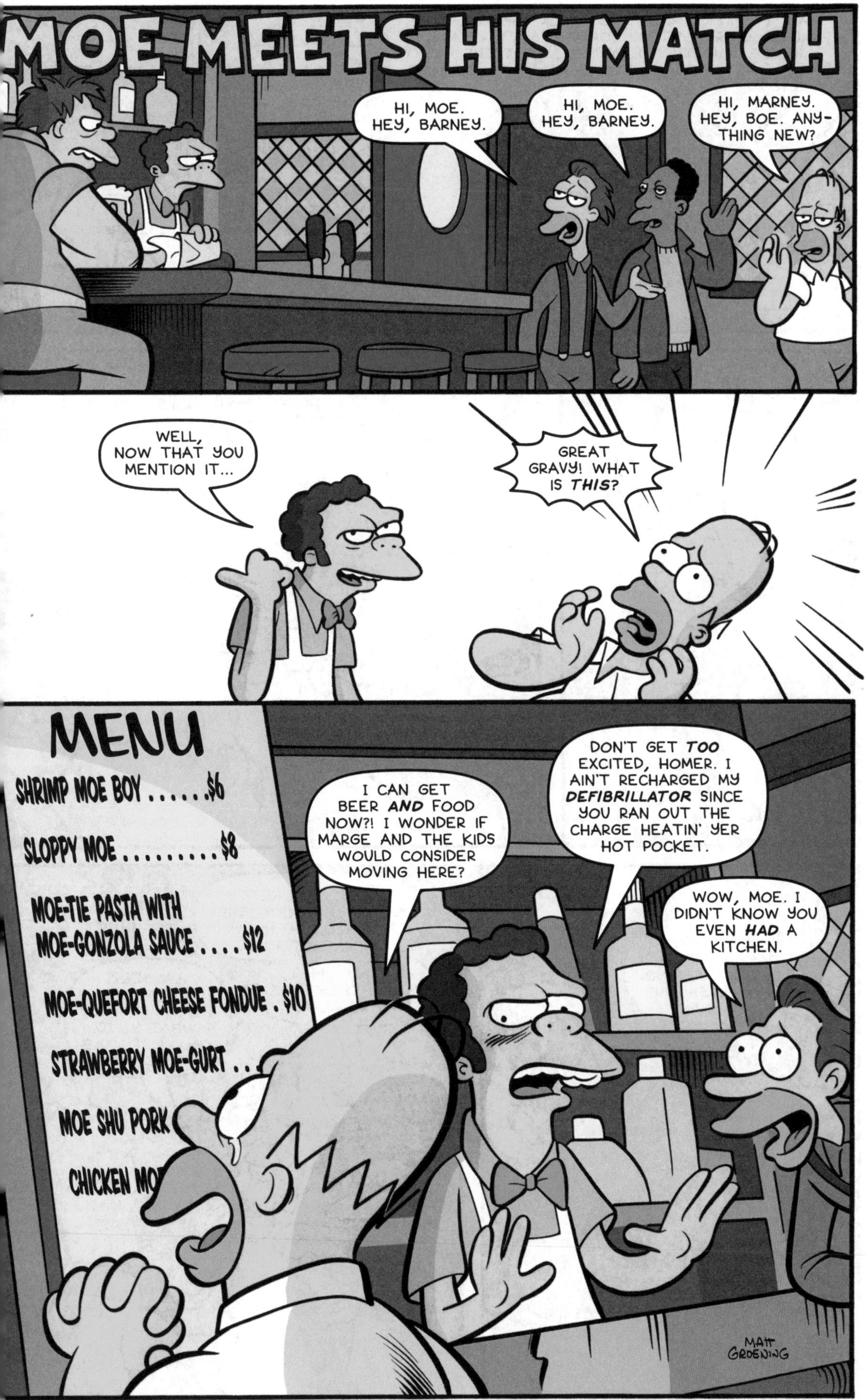
MOE MEETS HIS MATCH
HI, MOE. HEY, BARNEY.
HI, MOE. HEY, BARNEY.
HI, MARNEY. HEY, BOE. ANY-THING NEW?
WELL, NOW THAT YOU MENTION IT...
GREAT GRAVY! WHAT IS *THIS*?
MENU
SHRIMP MOE BOY $6
SLOPPY MOE $8
MOE-TIE PASTA WITH MOE-GONZOLA SAUCE $12
MOE-QUEFORT CHEESE FONDUE . $10
STRAWBERRY MOE-GURT ..
MOE SHU PORK
I CAN GET BEER *AND* FOOD NOW?! I WONDER IF MARGE AND THE KIDS WOULD CONSIDER MOVING HERE?
DON'T GET *TOO* EXCITED, HOMER. I AIN'T RECHARGED MY *DEFIBRILLATOR* SINCE YOU RAN OUT THE CHARGE HEATIN' YER HOT POCKET.
WOW, MOE. I DIDN'T KNOW YOU EVEN *HAD* A KITCHEN.
MATT GROENING

ONY DIGEROLAMO & MAX DAVISON SCRIPT | JOHN DELANEY PENCILS | ANDREW PEPOY INKS | NATHAN HAMILL COLORS | KAREN BATES LETTERS | NATHAN KANE EDITOR

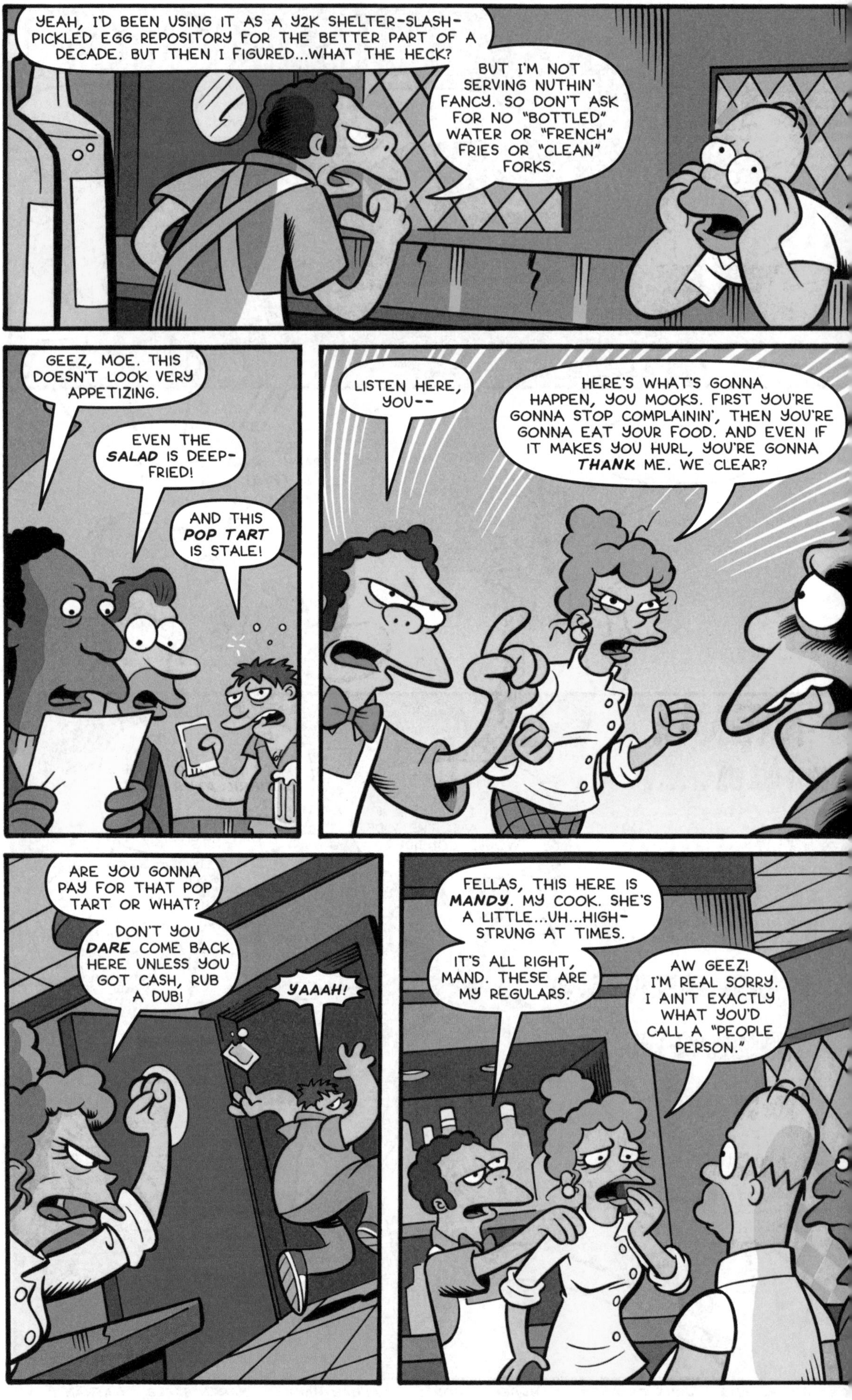
YEAH, I'D BEEN USING IT AS A Y2K SHELTER-SLASH-PICKLED EGG REPOSITORY FOR THE BETTER PART OF A DECADE. BUT THEN I FIGURED...WHAT THE HECK?
BUT I'M NOT SERVING NUTHIN' FANCY. SO DON'T ASK FOR NO "BOTTLED" WATER OR "FRENCH" FRIES OR "CLEAN" FORKS.
GEEZ, MOE. THIS DOESN'T LOOK VERY APPETIZING.
EVEN THE SALAD IS DEEP-FRIED!
AND THIS POP TART IS STALE!
LISTEN HERE, YOU--
HERE'S WHAT'S GONNA HAPPEN, YOU MOOKS. FIRST YOU'RE GONNA STOP COMPLAININ', THEN YOU'RE GONNA EAT YOUR FOOD. AND EVEN IF IT MAKES YOU HURL, YOU'RE GONNA THANK ME. WE CLEAR?
ARE YOU GONNA PAY FOR THAT POP TART OR WHAT?
DON'T YOU DARE COME BACK HERE UNLESS YOU GOT CASH, RUB A DUB!
YAAAH!
FELLAS, THIS HERE IS MANDY. MY COOK. SHE'S A LITTLE...UH...HIGH-STRUNG AT TIMES.
IT'S ALL RIGHT, MAND. THESE ARE MY REGULARS.
AW GEEZ! I'M REAL SORRY. I AIN'T EXACTLY WHAT YOU'D CALL A "PEOPLE PERSON."

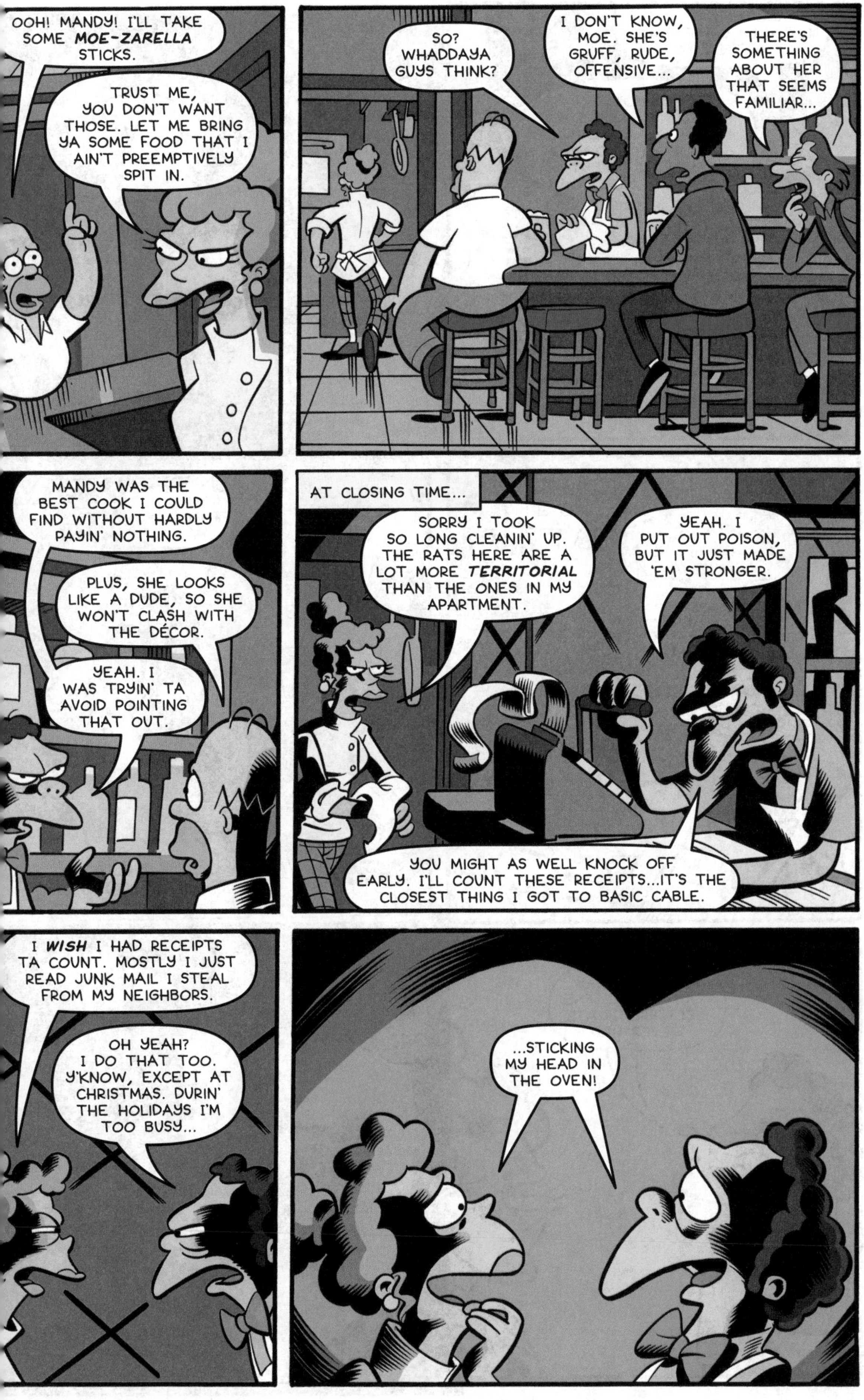
OOH! MANDY! I'LL TAKE SOME MOE-ZARELLA STICKS.
TRUST ME, YOU DON'T WANT THOSE. LET ME BRING YA SOME FOOD THAT I AIN'T PREEMPTIVELY SPIT IN.
SO? WHADDAYA GUYS THINK?
I DON'T KNOW, MOE. SHE'S GRUFF, RUDE, OFFENSIVE...
THERE'S SOMETHING ABOUT HER THAT SEEMS FAMILIAR...
MANDY WAS THE BEST COOK I COULD FIND WITHOUT HARDLY PAYIN' NOTHING.
PLUS, SHE LOOKS LIKE A DUDE, SO SHE WON'T CLASH WITH THE DÉCOR.
YEAH. I WAS TRYIN' TA AVOID POINTING THAT OUT.
AT CLOSING TIME...
SORRY I TOOK SO LONG CLEANIN' UP. THE RATS HERE ARE A LOT MORE TERRITORIAL THAN THE ONES IN MY APARTMENT.
YEAH. I PUT OUT POISON, BUT IT JUST MADE 'EM STRONGER.
YOU MIGHT AS WELL KNOCK OFF EARLY. I'LL COUNT THESE RECEIPTS...IT'S THE CLOSEST THING I GOT TO BASIC CABLE.
I WISH I HAD RECEIPTS TA COUNT. MOSTLY I JUST READ JUNK MAIL I STEAL FROM MY NEIGHBORS.
OH YEAH? I DO THAT TOO. Y'KNOW, EXCEPT AT CHRISTMAS. DURIN' THE HOLIDAYS I'M TOO BUSY...
...STICKING MY HEAD IN THE OVEN!

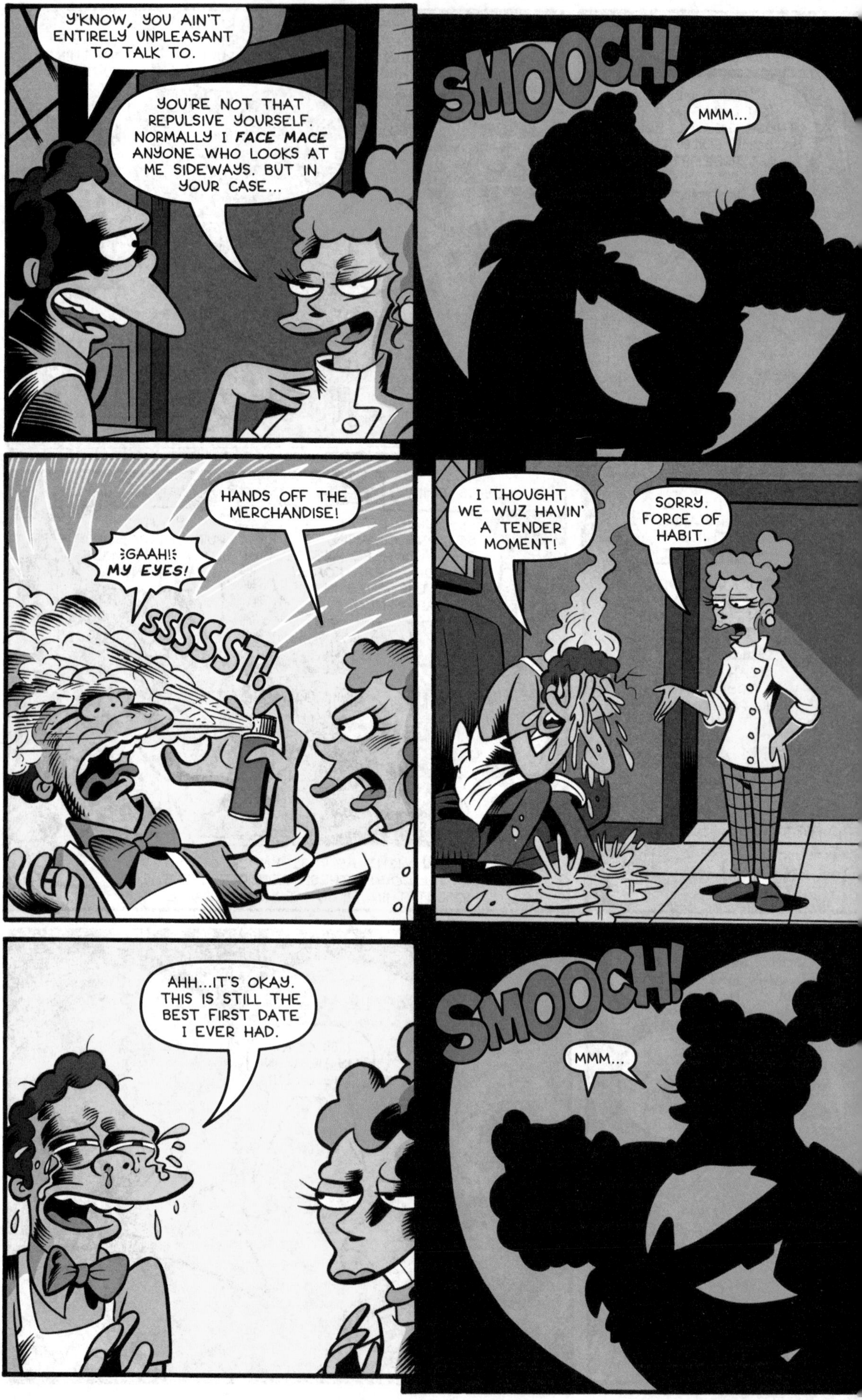
Y'KNOW, YOU AIN'T ENTIRELY UNPLEASANT TO TALK TO.
YOU'RE NOT THAT REPULSIVE YOURSELF. NORMALLY I FACE MACE ANYONE WHO LOOKS AT ME SIDEWAYS. BUT IN YOUR CASE...
SMOOCH!
MMM...
HANDS OFF THE MERCHANDISE!
GAAH! MY EYES!
SSSSST!
I THOUGHT WE WUZ HAVIN' A TENDER MOMENT!
SORRY. FORCE OF HABIT.
AHH...IT'S OKAY. THIS IS STILL THE BEST FIRST DATE I EVER HAD.
SMOOCH!
MMM...

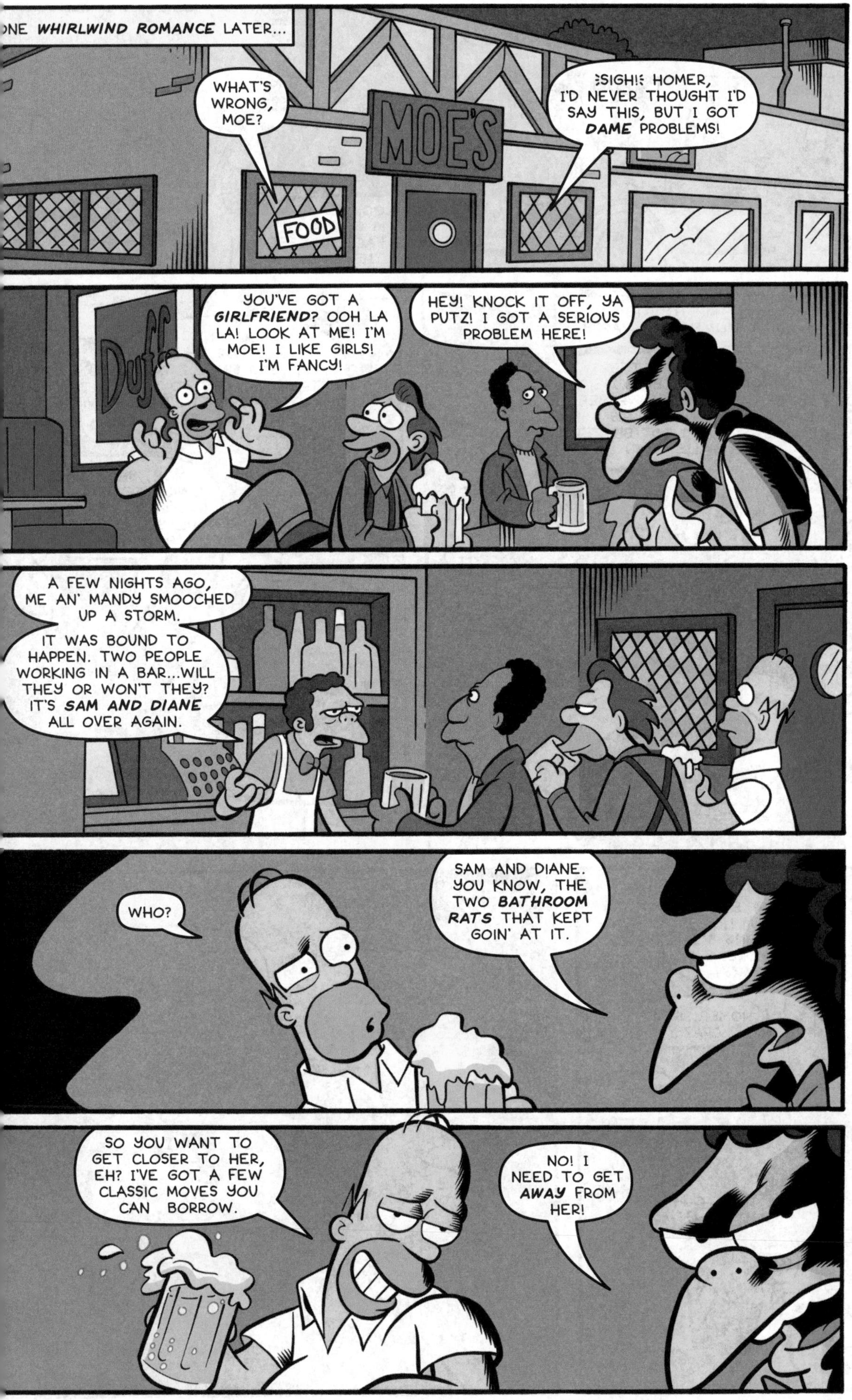
ONE WHIRLWIND ROMANCE LATER...
WHAT'S WRONG, MOE?
MOE'S
FOOD
SIGH! HOMER, I'D NEVER THOUGHT I'D SAY THIS, BUT I GOT DAME PROBLEMS!
Duff
YOU'VE GOT A GIRLFRIEND? OOH LA LA! LOOK AT ME! I'M MOE! I LIKE GIRLS! I'M FANCY!
HEY! KNOCK IT OFF, YA PUTZ! I GOT A SERIOUS PROBLEM HERE!
A FEW NIGHTS AGO, ME AN' MANDY SMOOCHED UP A STORM.
IT WAS BOUND TO HAPPEN. TWO PEOPLE WORKING IN A BAR...WILL THEY OR WON'T THEY? IT'S SAM AND DIANE ALL OVER AGAIN.
WHO?
SAM AND DIANE. YOU KNOW, THE TWO BATHROOM RATS THAT KEPT GOIN' AT IT.
SO YOU WANT TO GET CLOSER TO HER, EH? I'VE GOT A FEW CLASSIC MOVES YOU CAN BORROW.
NO! I NEED TO GET AWAY FROM HER!

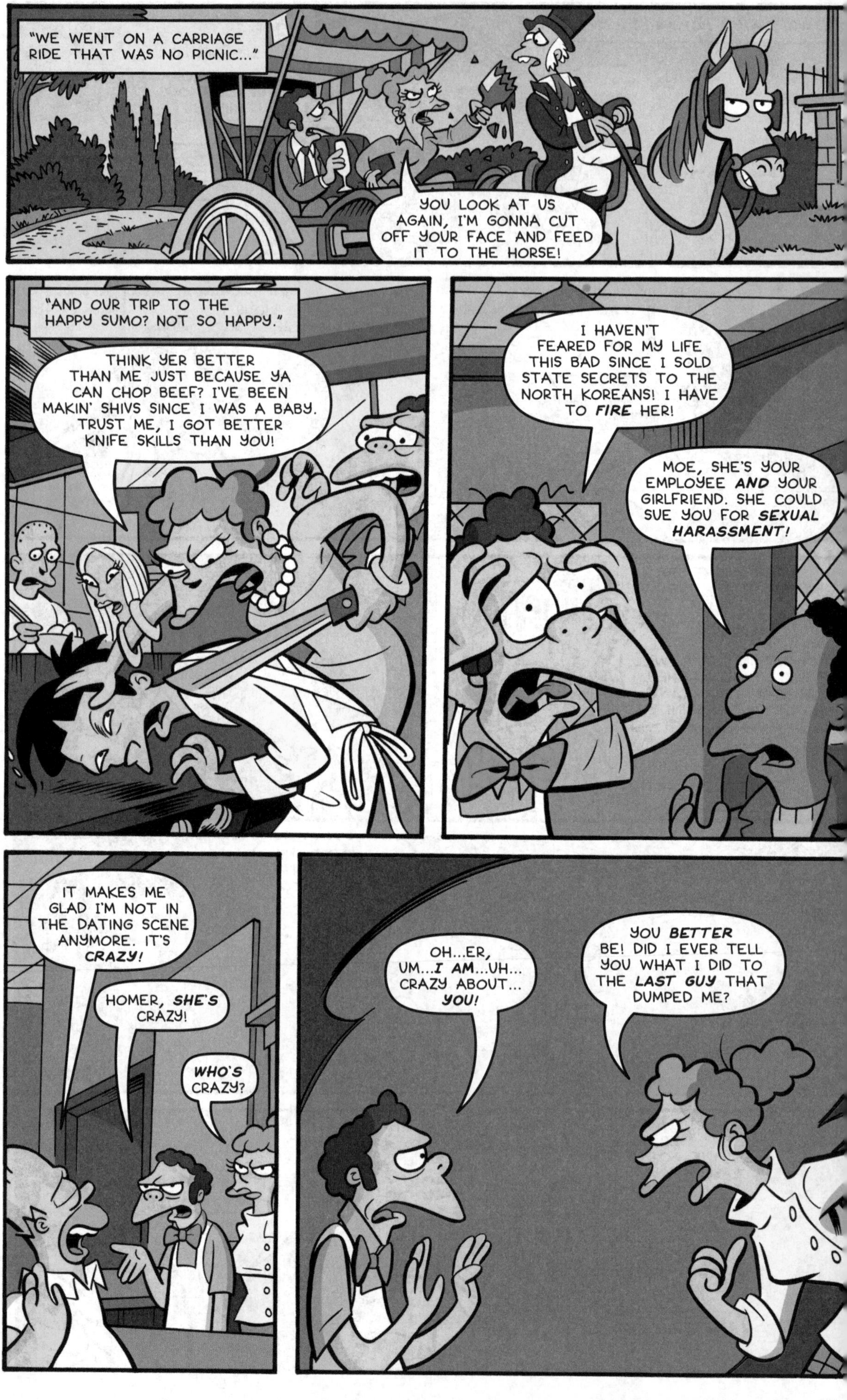
"WE WENT ON A CARRIAGE RIDE THAT WAS NO PICNIC..."
YOU LOOK AT US AGAIN, I'M GONNA CUT OFF YOUR FACE AND FEED IT TO THE HORSE!
"AND OUR TRIP TO THE HAPPY SUMO? NOT SO HAPPY."
THINK YER BETTER THAN ME JUST BECAUSE YA CAN CHOP BEEF? I'VE BEEN MAKIN' SHIVS SINCE I WAS A BABY. TRUST ME, I GOT BETTER KNIFE SKILLS THAN YOU!
I HAVEN'T FEARED FOR MY LIFE THIS BAD SINCE I SOLD STATE SECRETS TO THE NORTH KOREANS! I HAVE TO FIRE HER!
MOE, SHE'S YOUR EMPLOYEE AND YOUR GIRLFRIEND. SHE COULD SUE YOU FOR SEXUAL HARASSMENT!
IT MAKES ME GLAD I'M NOT IN THE DATING SCENE ANYMORE. IT'S CRAZY!
HOMER, SHE'S CRAZY!
WHO'S CRAZY?
OH...ER, UM...I AM...UH... CRAZY ABOUT... YOU!
YOU BETTER BE! DID I EVER TELL YOU WHAT I DID TO THE LAST GUY THAT DUMPED ME?

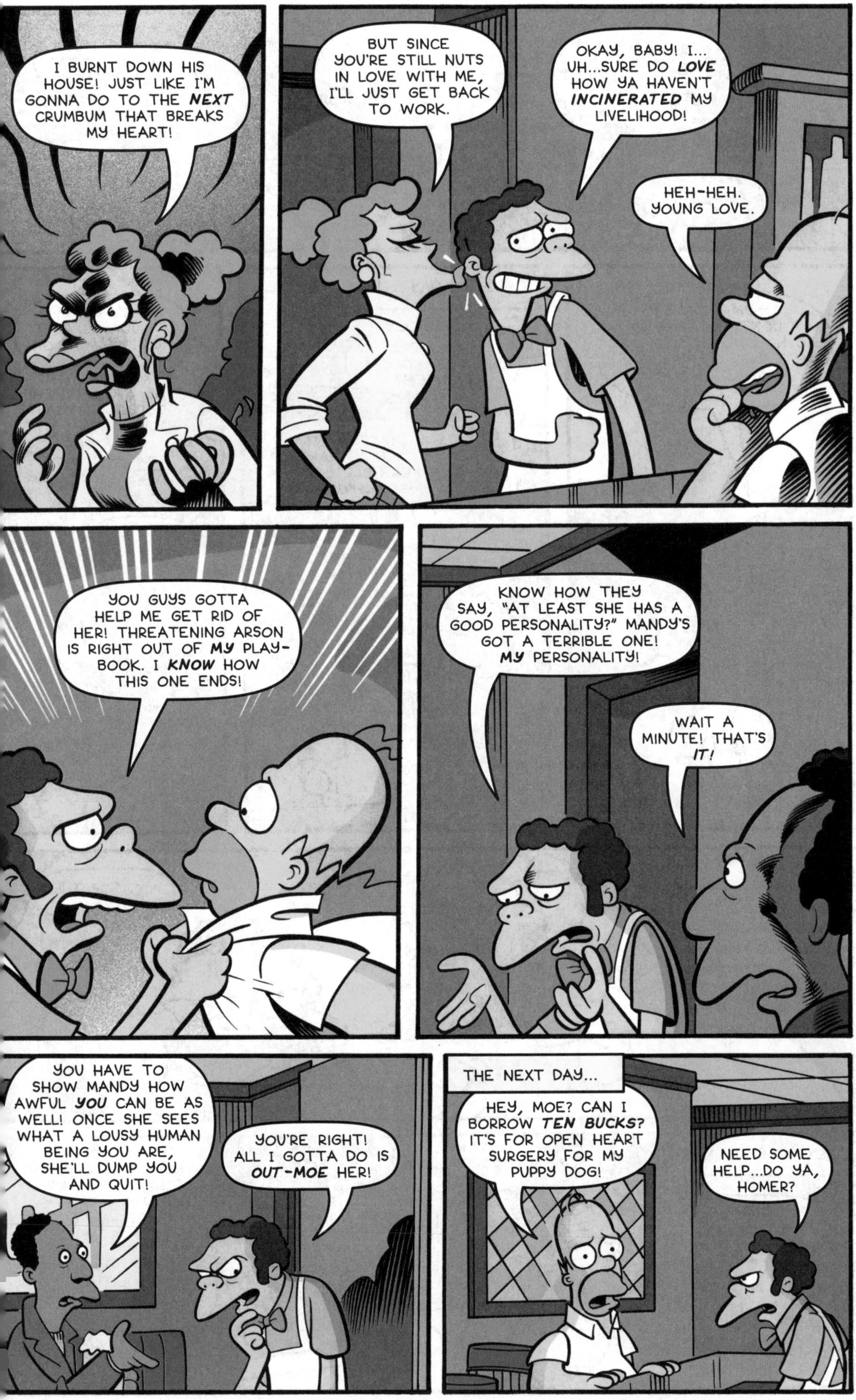
I BURNT DOWN HIS HOUSE! JUST LIKE I'M GONNA DO TO THE NEXT CRUMBUM THAT BREAKS MY HEART!
BUT SINCE YOU'RE STILL NUTS IN LOVE WITH ME, I'LL JUST GET BACK TO WORK.
OKAY, BABY! I... UH...SURE DO LOVE HOW YA HAVEN'T INCINERATED MY LIVELIHOOD!
HEH-HEH. YOUNG LOVE.
YOU GUYS GOTTA HELP ME GET RID OF HER! THREATENING ARSON IS RIGHT OUT OF MY PLAY-BOOK. I KNOW HOW THIS ONE ENDS!
KNOW HOW THEY SAY, "AT LEAST SHE HAS A GOOD PERSONALITY?" MANDY'S GOT A TERRIBLE ONE! MY PERSONALITY!
WAIT A MINUTE! THAT'S IT!
YOU HAVE TO SHOW MANDY HOW AWFUL YOU CAN BE AS WELL! ONCE SHE SEES WHAT A LOUSY HUMAN BEING YOU ARE, SHE'LL DUMP YOU AND QUIT!
YOU'RE RIGHT! ALL I GOTTA DO IS OUT-MOE HER!
THE NEXT DAY...
HEY, MOE? CAN I BORROW TEN BUCKS? IT'S FOR OPEN HEART SURGERY FOR MY PUPPY DOG!
NEED SOME HELP...DO YA, HOMER?

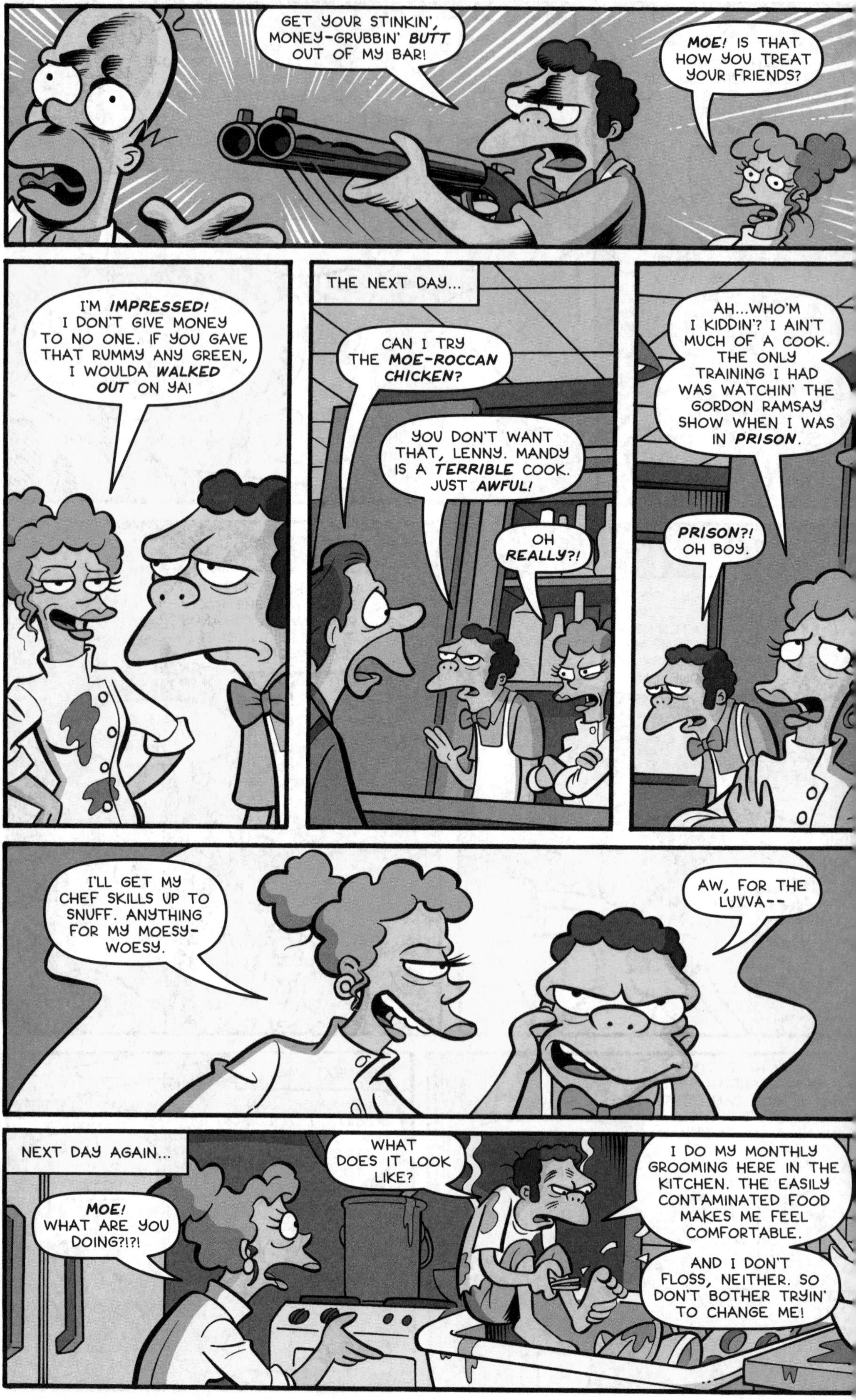
GET YOUR STINKIN', MONEY-GRUBBIN' BUTT OUT OF MY BAR!
MOE! IS THAT HOW YOU TREAT YOUR FRIENDS?
I'M IMPRESSED! I DON'T GIVE MONEY TO NO ONE. IF YOU GAVE THAT RUMMY ANY GREEN, I WOULDA WALKED OUT ON YA!
THE NEXT DAY...
CAN I TRY THE MOE-ROCCAN CHICKEN?
YOU DON'T WANT THAT, LENNY. MANDY IS A TERRIBLE COOK. JUST AWFUL!
OH REALLY?!
AH...WHO'M I KIDDIN'? I AIN'T MUCH OF A COOK. THE ONLY TRAINING I HAD WAS WATCHIN' THE GORDON RAMSAY SHOW WHEN I WAS IN PRISON.
PRISON?! OH BOY.
I'LL GET MY CHEF SKILLS UP TO SNUFF. ANYTHING FOR MY MOESY-WOESY.
AW, FOR THE LUVVA--
NEXT DAY AGAIN...
MOE! WHAT ARE YOU DOING?!?!
WHAT DOES IT LOOK LIKE?
I DO MY MONTHLY GROOMING HERE IN THE KITCHEN. THE EASILY CONTAMINATED FOOD MAKES ME FEEL COMFORTABLE.
AND I DON'T FLOSS, NEITHER. SO DON'T BOTHER TRYIN' TO CHANGE ME!

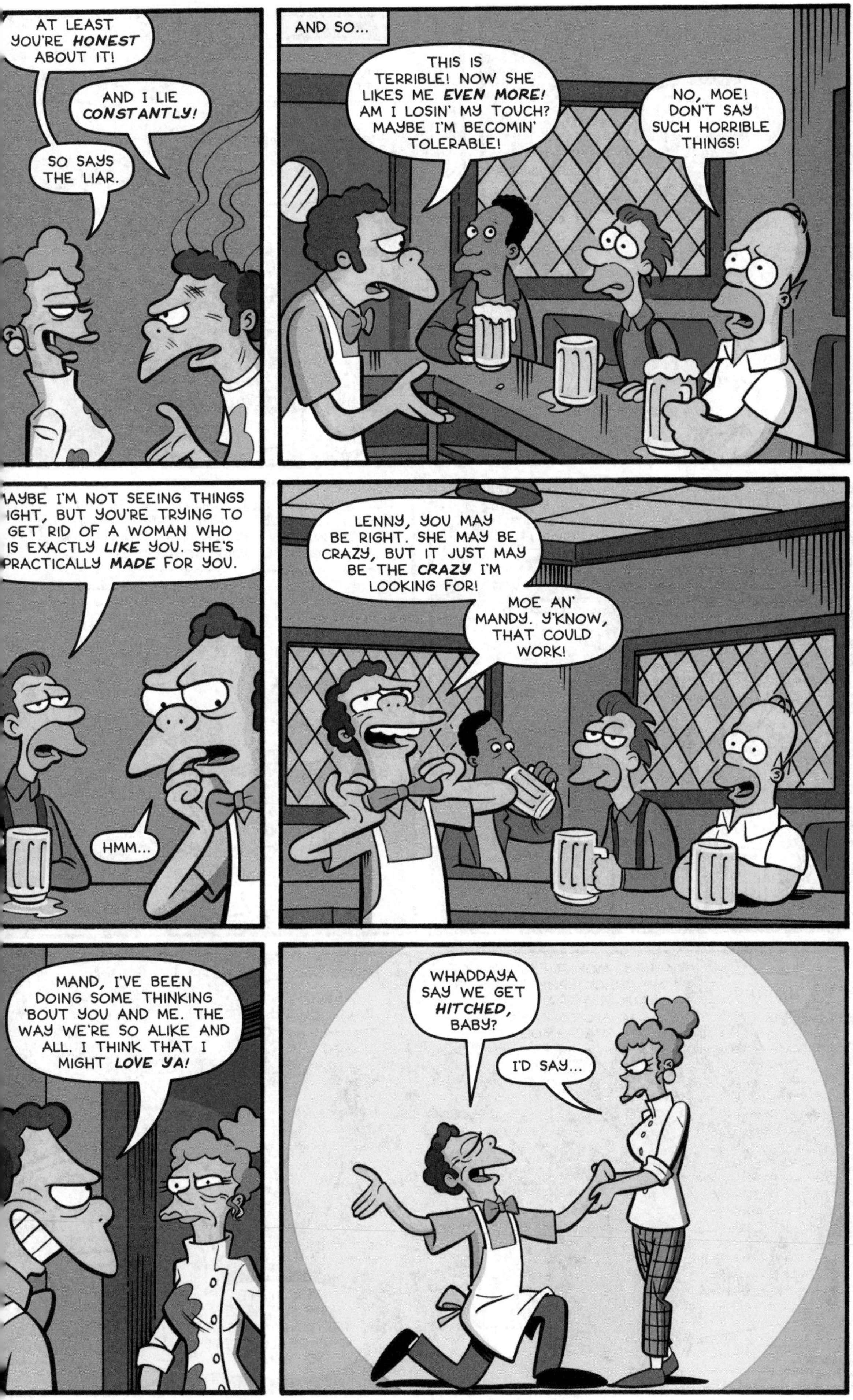
AT LEAST YOU'RE HONEST ABOUT IT!
AND I LIE CONSTANTLY!
SO SAYS THE LIAR.
AND SO...
THIS IS TERRIBLE! NOW SHE LIKES ME EVEN MORE! AM I LOSIN' MY TOUCH? MAYBE I'M BECOMIN' TOLERABLE!
NO, MOE! DON'T SAY SUCH HORRIBLE THINGS!
AYBE I'M NOT SEEING THINGS IGHT, BUT YOU'RE TRYING TO GET RID OF A WOMAN WHO IS EXACTLY LIKE YOU. SHE'S PRACTICALLY MADE FOR YOU.
HMM...
LENNY, YOU MAY BE RIGHT. SHE MAY BE CRAZY, BUT IT JUST MAY BE THE CRAZY I'M LOOKING FOR!
MOE AN' MANDY. Y'KNOW, THAT COULD WORK!
MAND, I'VE BEEN DOING SOME THINKING 'BOUT YOU AND ME. THE WAY WE'RE SO ALIKE AND ALL. I THINK THAT I MIGHT LOVE YA!
WHADDAYA SAY WE GET HITCHED, BABY?
I'D SAY...

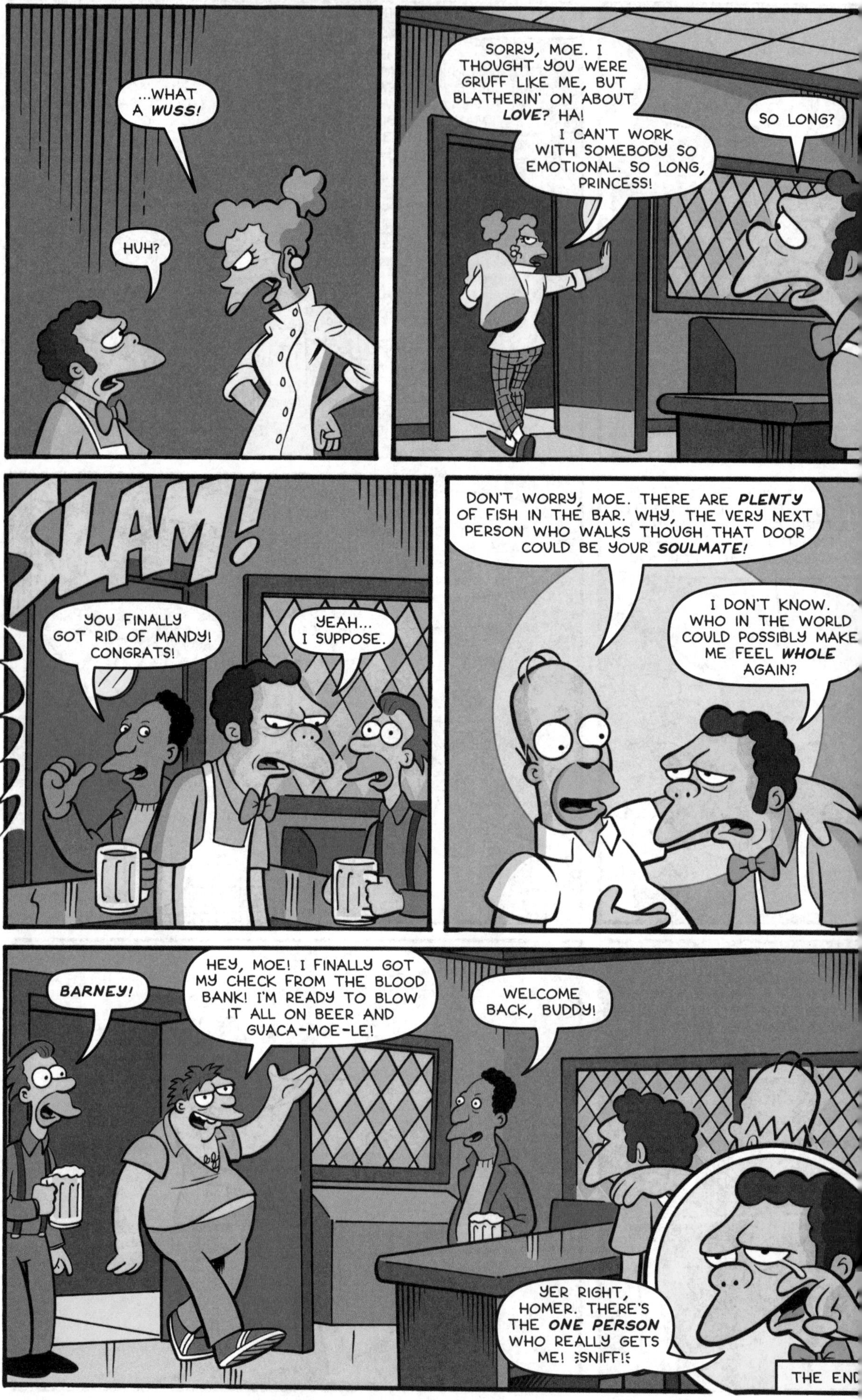

...WHAT A WUSS!
HUH?
SORRY, MOE. I THOUGHT YOU WERE GRUFF LIKE ME, BUT BLATHERIN' ON ABOUT LOVE? HA!
I CAN'T WORK WITH SOMEBODY SO EMOTIONAL. SO LONG, PRINCESS!
SO LONG?
SLAM!
YOU FINALLY GOT RID OF MANDY! CONGRATS!
YEAH... I SUPPOSE.
DON'T WORRY, MOE. THERE ARE PLENTY OF FISH IN THE BAR. WHY, THE VERY NEXT PERSON WHO WALKS THOUGH THAT DOOR COULD BE YOUR SOULMATE!
I DON'T KNOW. WHO IN THE WORLD COULD POSSIBLY MAKE ME FEEL WHOLE AGAIN?
BARNEY!
HEY, MOE! I FINALLY GOT MY CHECK FROM THE BLOOD BANK! I'M READY TO BLOW IT ALL ON BEER AND GUACA-MOE-LE!
WELCOME BACK, BUDDY!
YER RIGHT, HOMER. THERE'S THE ONE PERSON WHO REALLY GETS ME! SNIFF!
THE END

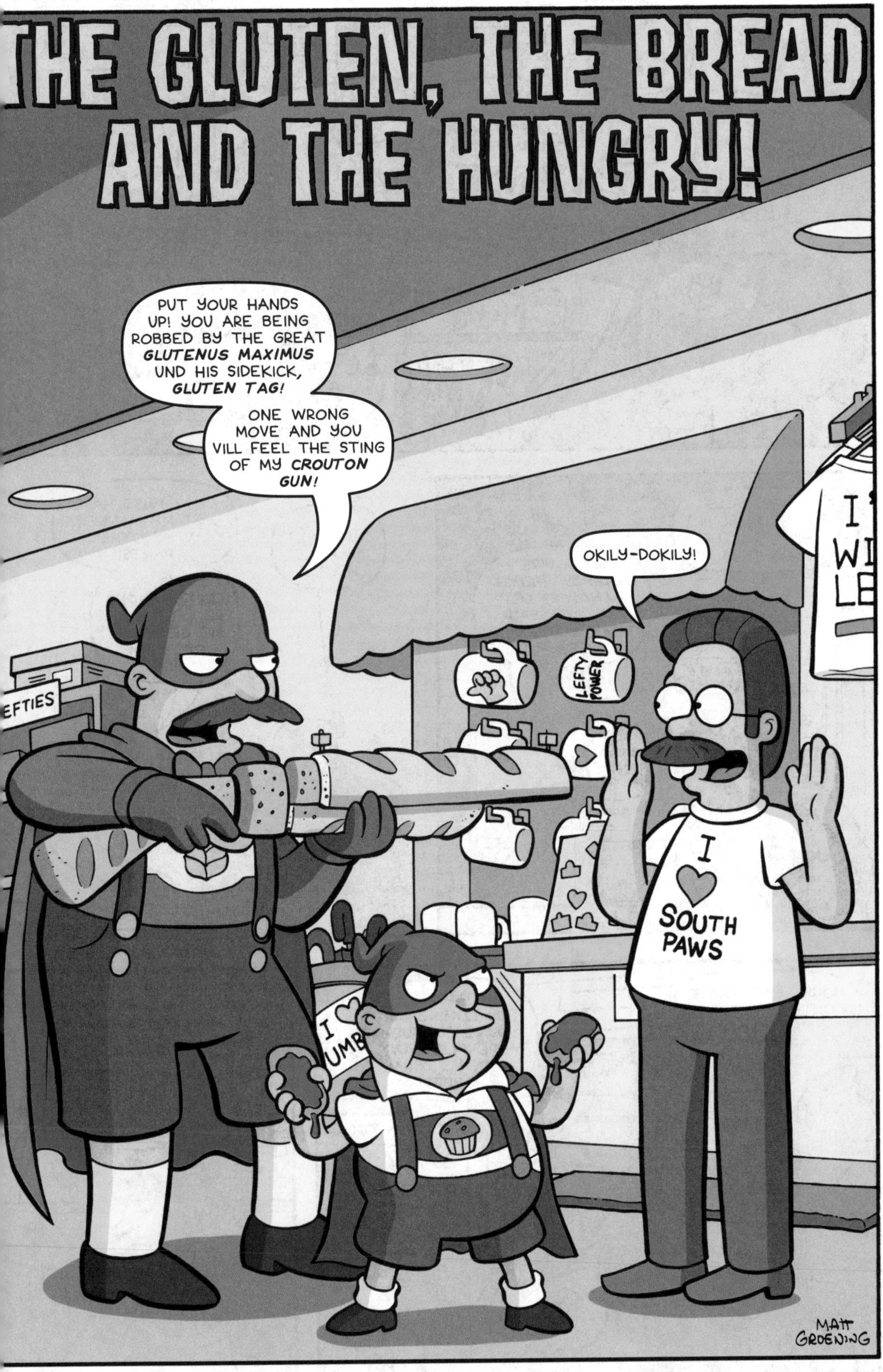
THE GLUTEN, THE BREAD AND THE HUNGRY!
PUT YOUR HANDS UP! YOU ARE BEING ROBBED BY THE GREAT **GLUTENUS MAXIMUS** UND HIS SIDEKICK, **GLUTEN TAG!**
ONE WRONG MOVE AND YOU VILL FEEL THE STING OF MY **CROUTON GUN!**
OKILY-DOKILY!
LEFTY POWER
I ♥ SOUTH PAWS
MATT GROENING

AN BOOTHBY	***NINA MATSUMOTO***	***ANDREW PEPOY***	***NATHAN HAMILL***	***KAREN BATES***	***NATHAN KANE***
WRITER	PENCILS	INKS	COLORS	LETTERS	EDITOR

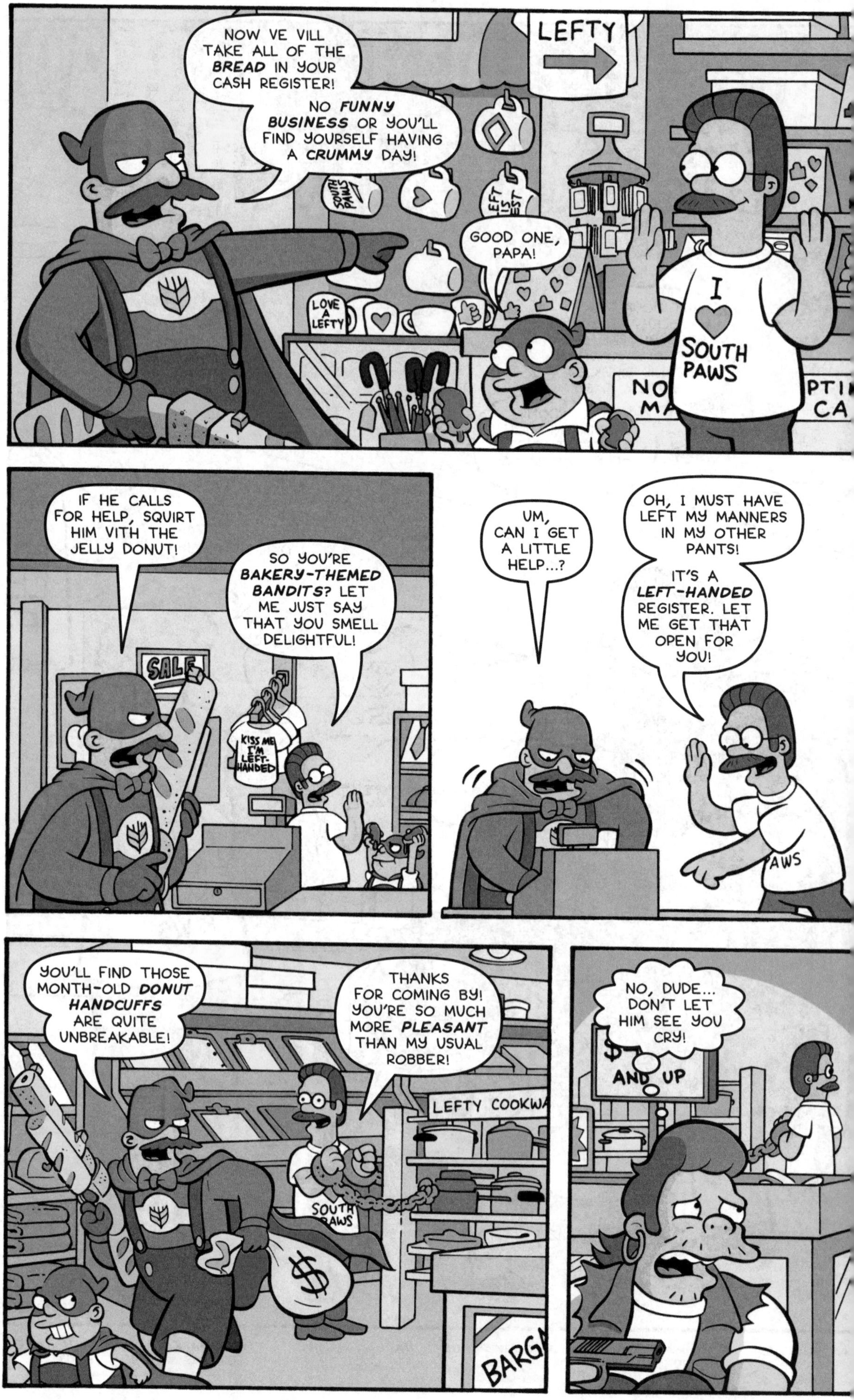
NOW VE VILL TAKE ALL OF THE BREAD IN YOUR CASH REGISTER!
NO FUNNY BUSINESS OR YOU'LL FIND YOURSELF HAVING A CRUMMY DAY!
LEFTY
SOUTH PAWS
LEFT IS BEST
GOOD ONE, PAPA!
LOVE A LEFTY
I ♥ SOUTH PAWS
IF HE CALLS FOR HELP, SQUIRT HIM VITH THE JELLY DONUT!
SO YOU'RE BAKERY-THEMED BANDITS? LET ME JUST SAY THAT YOU SMELL DELIGHTFUL!
SALE
KISS ME I'M LEFT-HANDED
UM, CAN I GET A LITTLE HELP...?
OH, I MUST HAVE LEFT MY MANNERS IN MY OTHER PANTS!
IT'S A LEFT-HANDED REGISTER. LET ME GET THAT OPEN FOR YOU!
YOU'LL FIND THOSE MONTH-OLD DONUT HANDCUFFS ARE QUITE UNBREAKABLE!
THANKS FOR COMING BY! YOU'RE SO MUCH MORE PLEASANT THAN MY USUAL ROBBER!
LEFTY COOKWA
SOUTH PAWS
NO, DUDE... DON'T LET HIM SEE YOU CRY!
AND UP

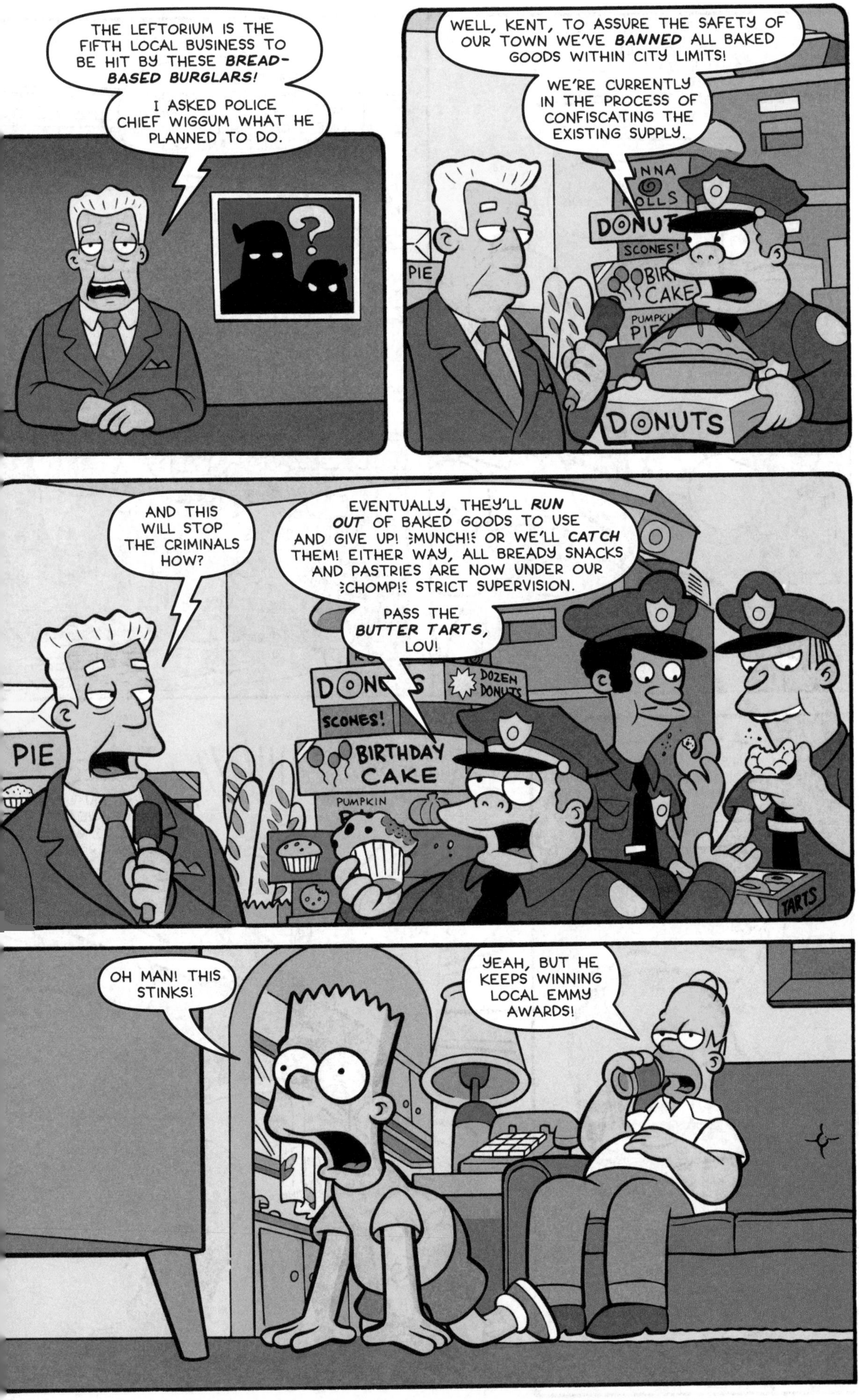

THE LEFTORIUM IS THE FIFTH LOCAL BUSINESS TO BE HIT BY THESE *BREAD-BASED BURGLARS!*
I ASKED POLICE CHIEF WIGGUM WHAT HE PLANNED TO DO.
WELL, KENT, TO ASSURE THE SAFETY OF OUR TOWN WE'VE ***BANNED*** ALL BAKED GOODS WITHIN CITY LIMITS!
WE'RE CURRENTLY IN THE PROCESS OF CONFISCATING THE EXISTING SUPPLY.
DONUT
SCONES!
PIE
CAKE
DONUTS
AND THIS WILL STOP THE CRIMINALS HOW?
EVENTUALLY, THEY'LL ***RUN OUT*** OF BAKED GOODS TO USE AND GIVE UP! ⁝MUNCH!⁝ OR WE'LL ***CATCH*** THEM! EITHER WAY, ALL BREADY SNACKS AND PASTRIES ARE NOW UNDER OUR ⁝CHOMP!⁝ STRICT SUPERVISION.
PASS THE ***BUTTER TARTS,*** LOU!
PIE
SCONES!
DOZEN
BIRTHDAY CAKE
PUMPKIN
TARTS
OH MAN! THIS STINKS!
YEAH, BUT HE KEEPS WINNING LOCAL EMMY AWARDS!

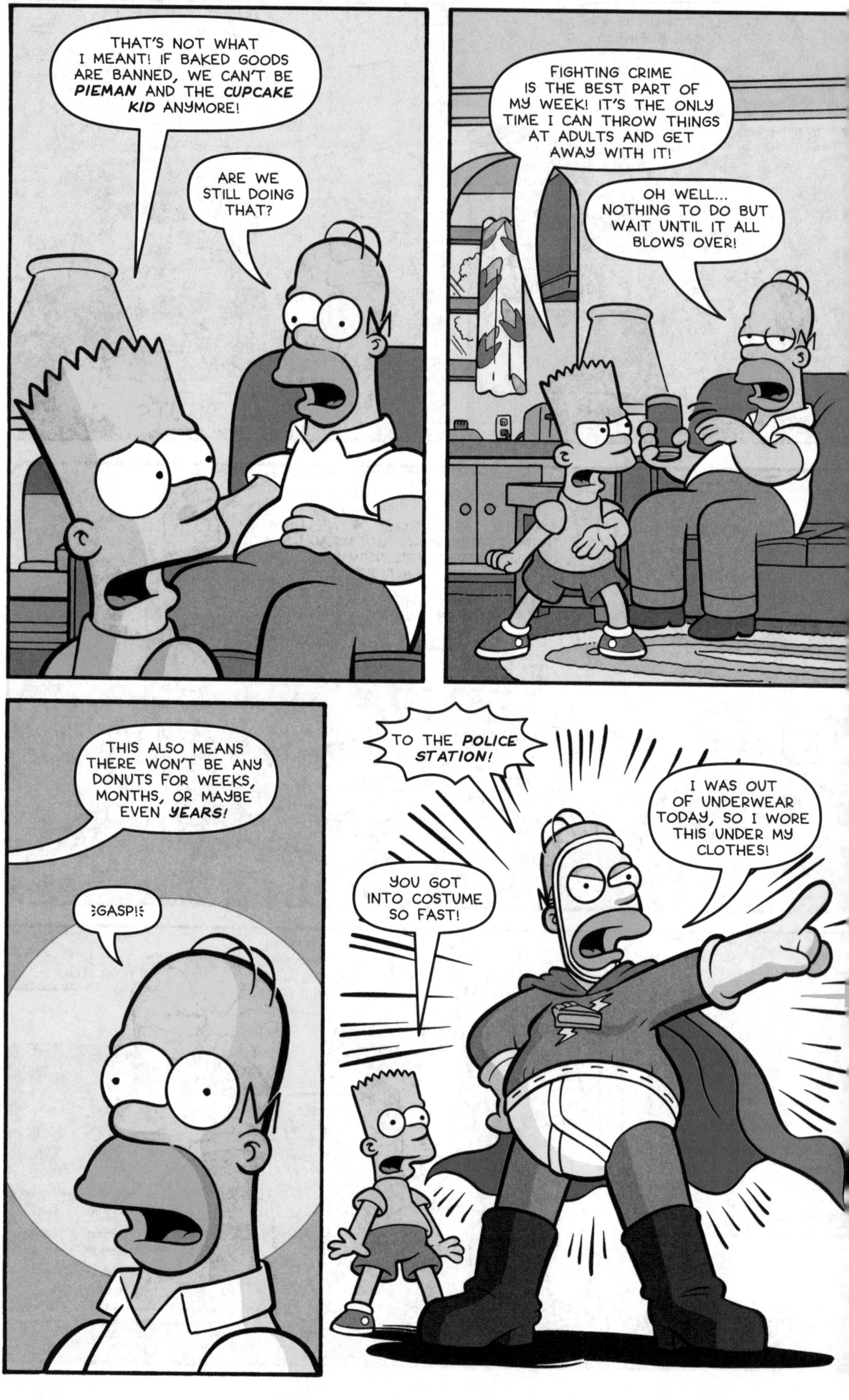
THAT'S NOT WHAT I MEANT! IF BAKED GOODS ARE BANNED, WE CAN'T BE PIEMAN AND THE CUPCAKE KID ANYMORE!
ARE WE STILL DOING THAT?
FIGHTING CRIME IS THE BEST PART OF MY WEEK! IT'S THE ONLY TIME I CAN THROW THINGS AT ADULTS AND GET AWAY WITH IT!
OH WELL... NOTHING TO DO BUT WAIT UNTIL IT ALL BLOWS OVER!
THIS ALSO MEANS THERE WON'T BE ANY DONUTS FOR WEEKS, MONTHS, OR MAYBE EVEN YEARS!
GASP!
TO THE POLICE STATION!
I WAS OUT OF UNDERWEAR TODAY, SO I WORE THIS UNDER MY CLOTHES!
YOU GOT INTO COSTUME SO FAST!

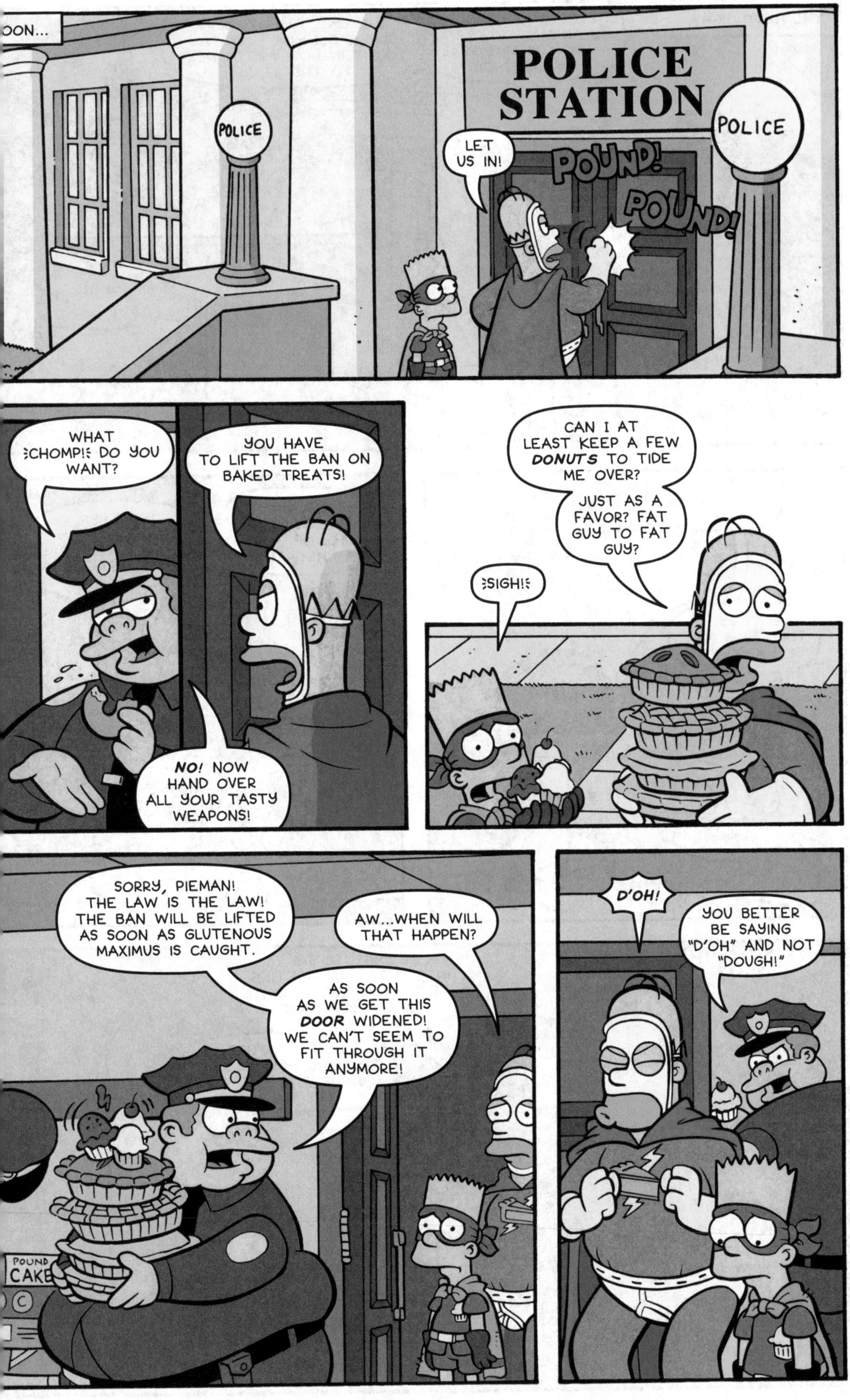

...OON...
POLICE STATION
POLICE
POLICE
LET US IN!
POUND!
POUND!
WHAT ⁝CHOMP!⁝ DO YOU WANT?
YOU HAVE TO LIFT THE BAN ON BAKED TREATS!
NO! NOW HAND OVER ALL YOUR TASTY WEAPONS!
CAN I AT LEAST KEEP A FEW DONUTS TO TIDE ME OVER?
JUST AS A FAVOR? FAT GUY TO FAT GUY?
⁝SIGH!⁝
SORRY, PIEMAN! THE LAW IS THE LAW! THE BAN WILL BE LIFTED AS SOON AS GLUTENOUS MAXIMUS IS CAUGHT.
AW...WHEN WILL THAT HAPPEN?
AS SOON AS WE GET THIS DOOR WIDENED! WE CAN'T SEEM TO FIT THROUGH IT ANYMORE!
POUND CAKE
D'OH!
YOU BETTER BE SAYING "D'OH" AND NOT "DOUGH!"

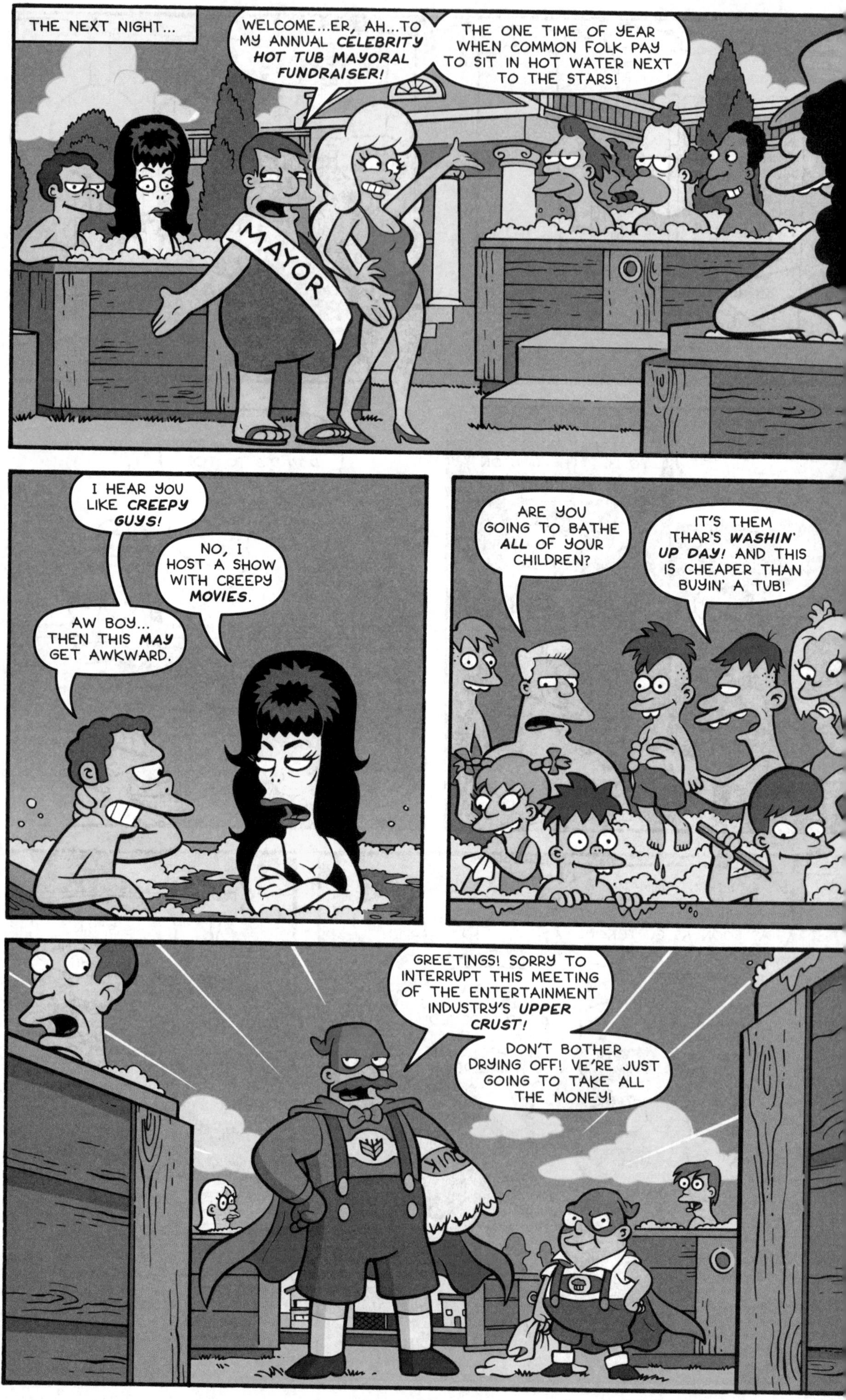
THE NEXT NIGHT...
WELCOME...ER, AH...TO MY ANNUAL CELEBRITY HOT TUB MAYORAL FUNDRAISER!
THE ONE TIME OF YEAR WHEN COMMON FOLK PAY TO SIT IN HOT WATER NEXT TO THE STARS!
MAYOR
I HEAR YOU LIKE CREEPY GUYS!
NO, I HOST A SHOW WITH CREEPY MOVIES.
AW BOY... THEN THIS MAY GET AWKWARD.
ARE YOU GOING TO BATHE ALL OF YOUR CHILDREN?
IT'S THEM THAR'S WASHIN' UP DAY! AND THIS IS CHEAPER THAN BUYIN' A TUB!
GREETINGS! SORRY TO INTERRUPT THIS MEETING OF THE ENTERTAINMENT INDUSTRY'S UPPER CRUST!
DON'T BOTHER DRYING OFF! VE'RE JUST GOING TO TAKE ALL THE MONEY!

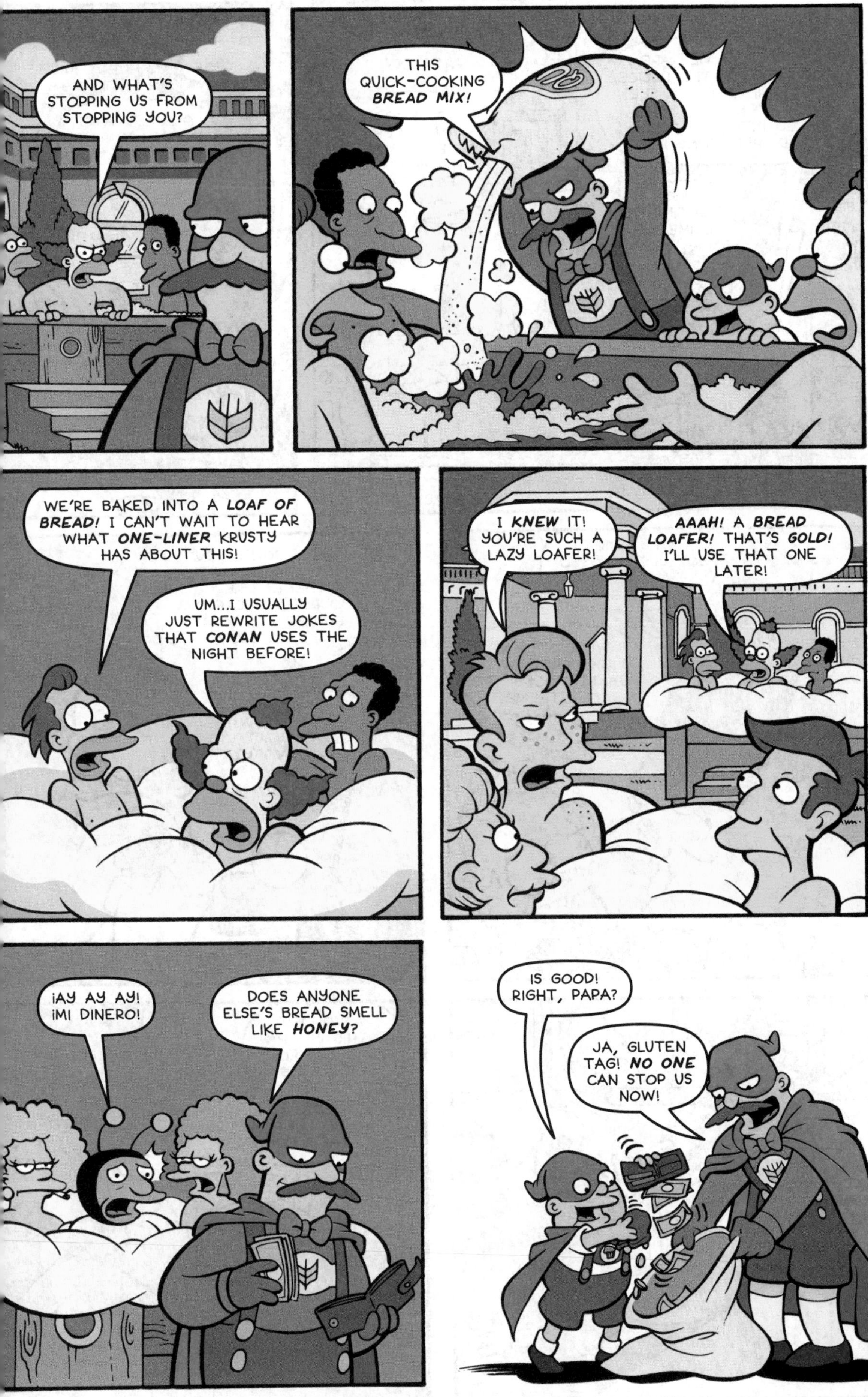

AND WHAT'S STOPPING US FROM STOPPING YOU?
THIS QUICK-COOKING **BREAD MIX!**
WE'RE BAKED INTO A **LOAF OF BREAD!** I CAN'T WAIT TO HEAR WHAT **ONE-LINER** KRUSTY HAS ABOUT THIS!
UM...I USUALLY JUST REWRITE JOKES THAT **CONAN** USES THE NIGHT BEFORE!
I **KNEW** IT! YOU'RE SUCH A LAZY LOAFER!
AAAH! A **BREAD LOAFER!** THAT'S **GOLD!** I'LL USE THAT ONE LATER!
¡AY AY AY! ¡MI DINERO!
DOES ANYONE ELSE'S BREAD SMELL LIKE **HONEY?**
IS GOOD! RIGHT, PAPA?
JA, GLUTEN TAG! **NO ONE** CAN STOP US NOW!

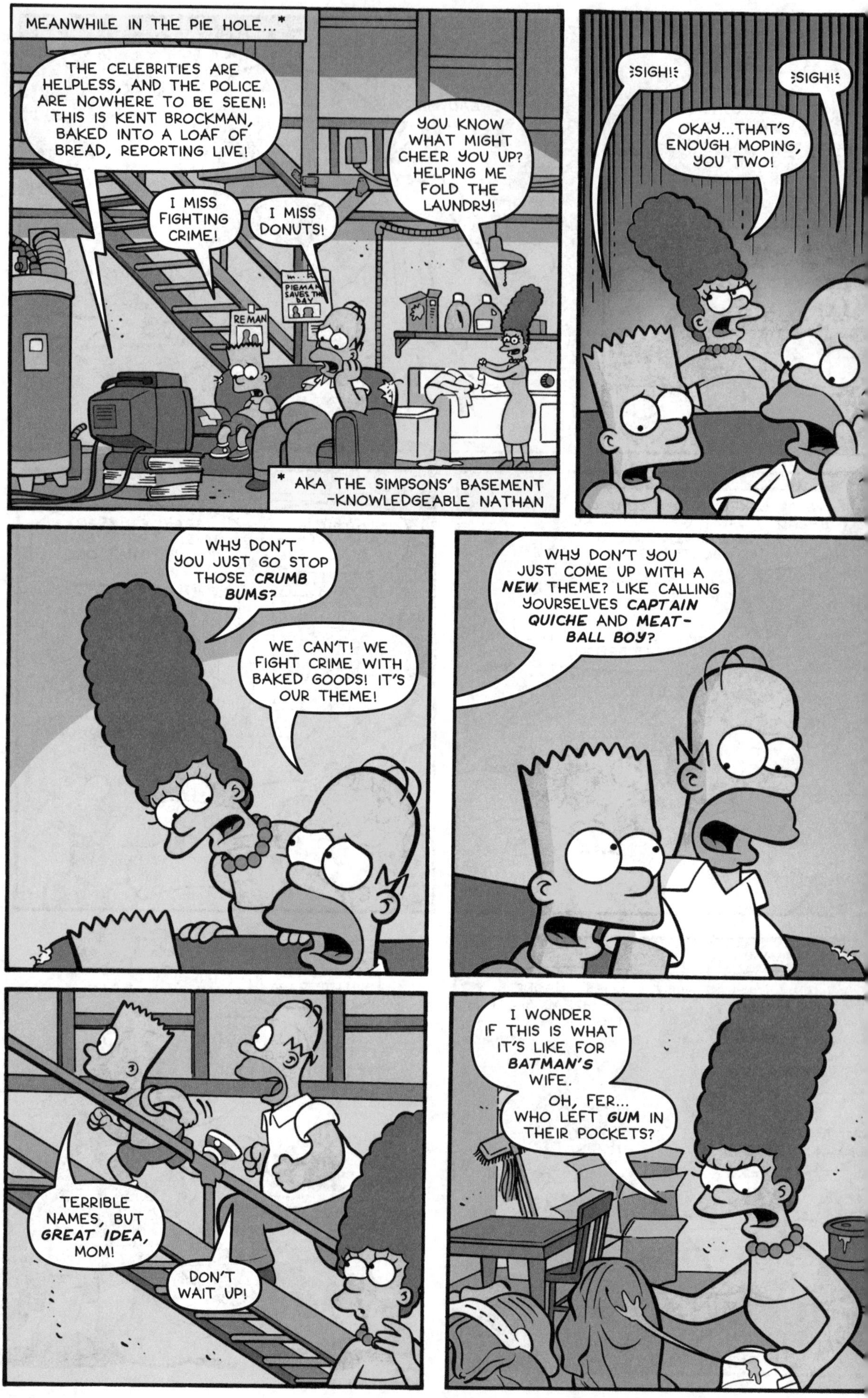
MEANWHILE IN THE PIE HOLE...*
THE CELEBRITIES ARE HELPLESS, AND THE POLICE ARE NOWHERE TO BE SEEN! THIS IS KENT BROCKMAN, BAKED INTO A LOAF OF BREAD, REPORTING LIVE!
I MISS FIGHTING CRIME!
I MISS DONUTS!
YOU KNOW WHAT MIGHT CHEER YOU UP? HELPING ME FOLD THE LAUNDRY!
PIEMAN SAVES THE DAY
* AKA THE SIMPSONS' BASEMENT -KNOWLEDGEABLE NATHAN
SIGH!
SIGH!
OKAY...THAT'S ENOUGH MOPING, YOU TWO!
WHY DON'T YOU JUST GO STOP THOSE CRUMB BUMS?
WE CAN'T! WE FIGHT CRIME WITH BAKED GOODS! IT'S OUR THEME!
WHY DON'T YOU JUST COME UP WITH A NEW THEME? LIKE CALLING YOURSELVES CAPTAIN QUICHE AND MEAT-BALL BOY?
TERRIBLE NAMES, BUT GREAT IDEA, MOM!
DON'T WAIT UP!
I WONDER IF THIS IS WHAT IT'S LIKE FOR BATMAN'S WIFE.
OH, FER... WHO LEFT GUM IN THEIR POCKETS?

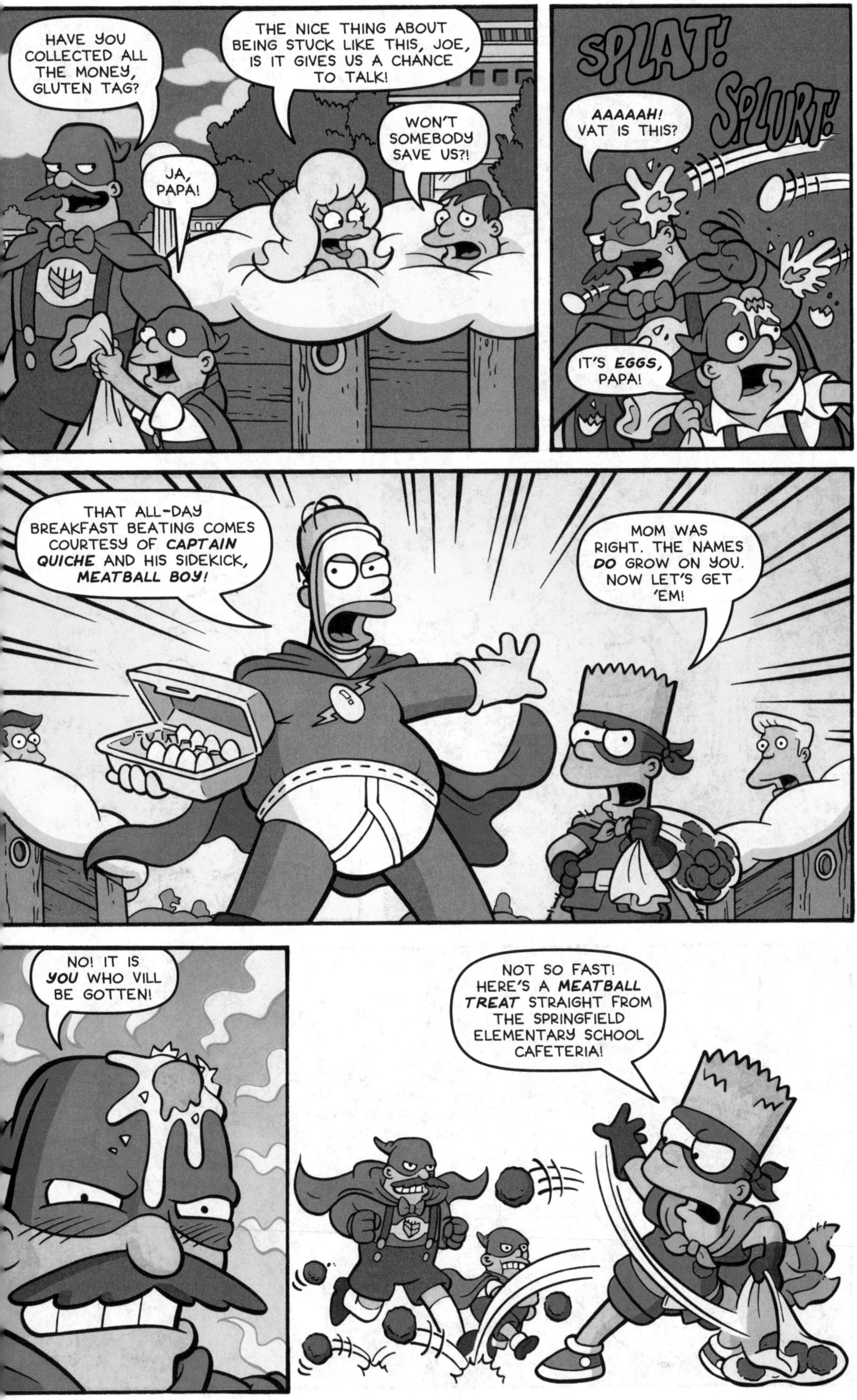
HAVE YOU COLLECTED ALL THE MONEY, GLUTEN TAG?
JA, PAPA!
THE NICE THING ABOUT BEING STUCK LIKE THIS, JOE, IS IT GIVES US A CHANCE TO TALK!
WON'T SOMEBODY SAVE US?!
SPLAT!
SPLURT!
AAAAAH! VAT IS THIS?
IT'S EGGS, PAPA!
THAT ALL-DAY BREAKFAST BEATING COMES COURTESY OF CAPTAIN QUICHE AND HIS SIDEKICK, MEATBALL BOY!
MOM WAS RIGHT. THE NAMES DO GROW ON YOU. NOW LET'S GET 'EM!
NO! IT IS YOU WHO VILL BE GOTTEN!
NOT SO FAST! HERE'S A MEATBALL TREAT STRAIGHT FROM THE SPRINGFIELD ELEMENTARY SCHOOL CAFETERIA!

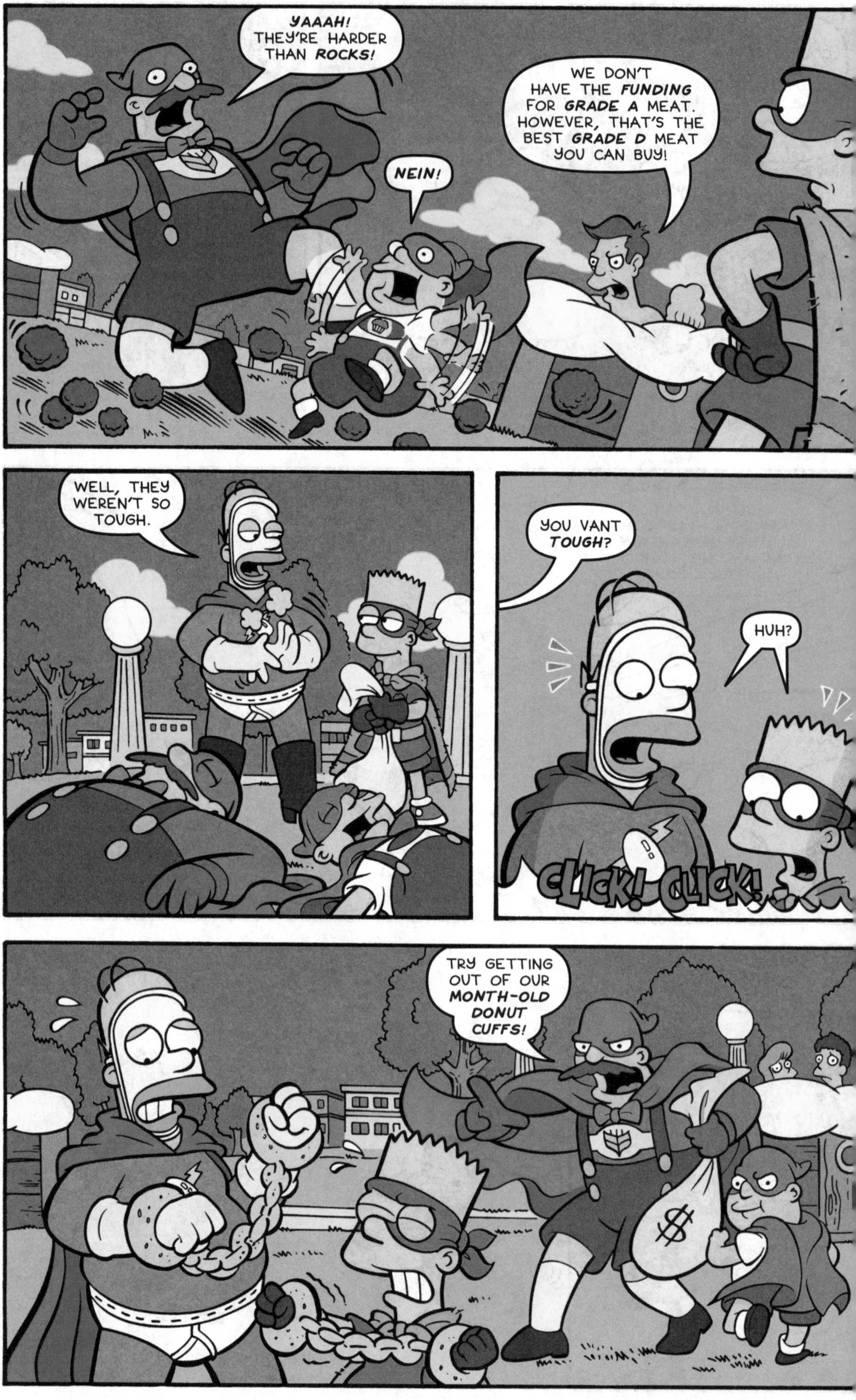
YAAAH! THEY'RE HARDER THAN ROCKS!
NEIN!
WE DON'T HAVE THE FUNDING FOR GRADE A MEAT. HOWEVER, THAT'S THE BEST GRADE D MEAT YOU CAN BUY!
WELL, THEY WEREN'T SO TOUGH.
YOU VANT TOUGH?
HUH?
CLICK! CLICK!
TRY GETTING OUT OF OUR MONTH-OLD DONUT CUFFS!

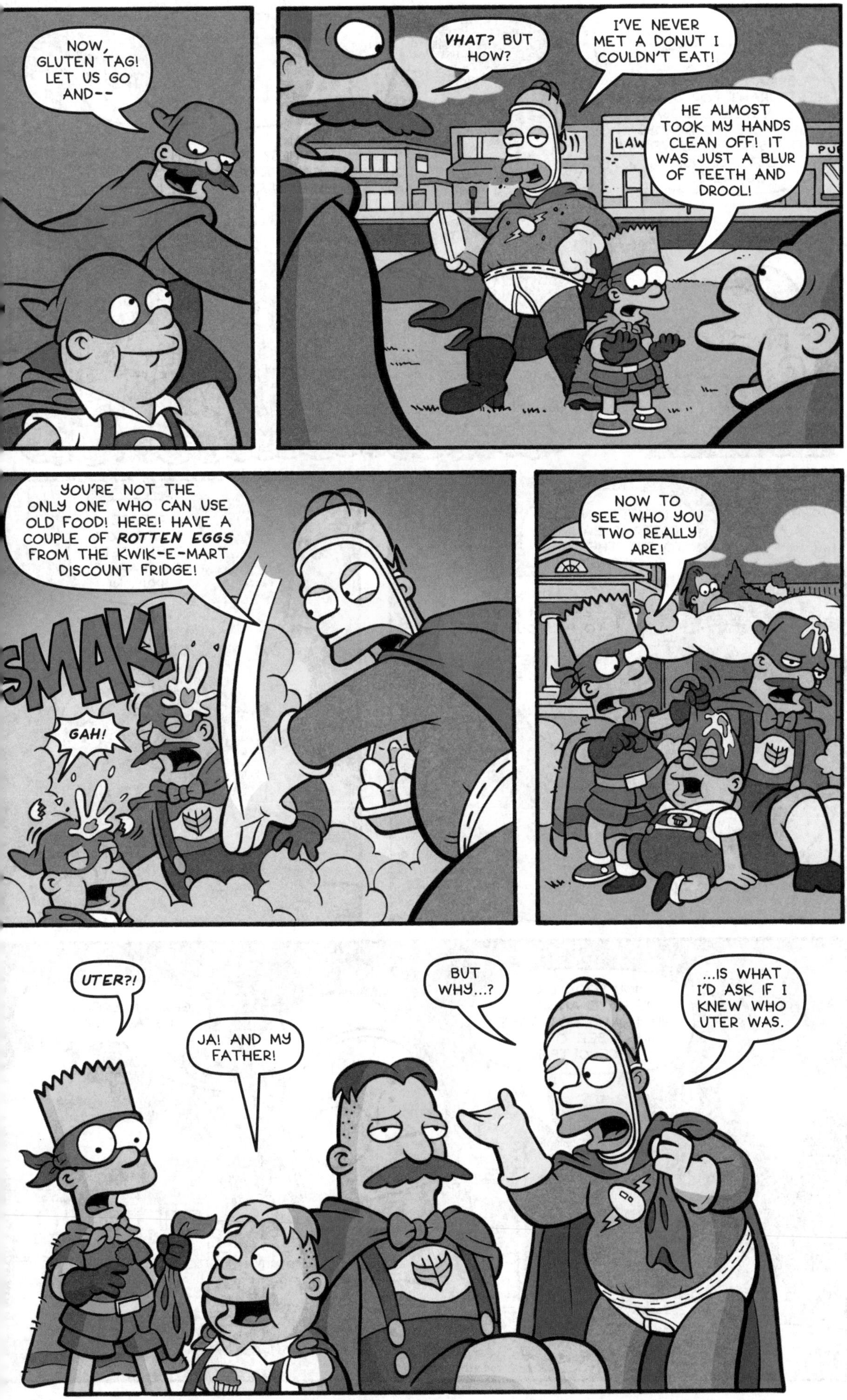
NOW, GLUTEN TAG! LET US GO AND--
VHAT? BUT HOW?
I'VE NEVER MET A DONUT I COULDN'T EAT!
HE ALMOST TOOK MY HANDS CLEAN OFF! IT WAS JUST A BLUR OF TEETH AND DROOL!
YOU'RE NOT THE ONLY ONE WHO CAN USE OLD FOOD! HERE! HAVE A COUPLE OF ROTTEN EGGS FROM THE KWIK-E-MART DISCOUNT FRIDGE!
SMAK!
GAH!
NOW TO SEE WHO YOU TWO REALLY ARE!
UTER?!
JA! AND MY FATHER!
BUT WHY...?
...IS WHAT I'D ASK IF I KNEW WHO UTER WAS.

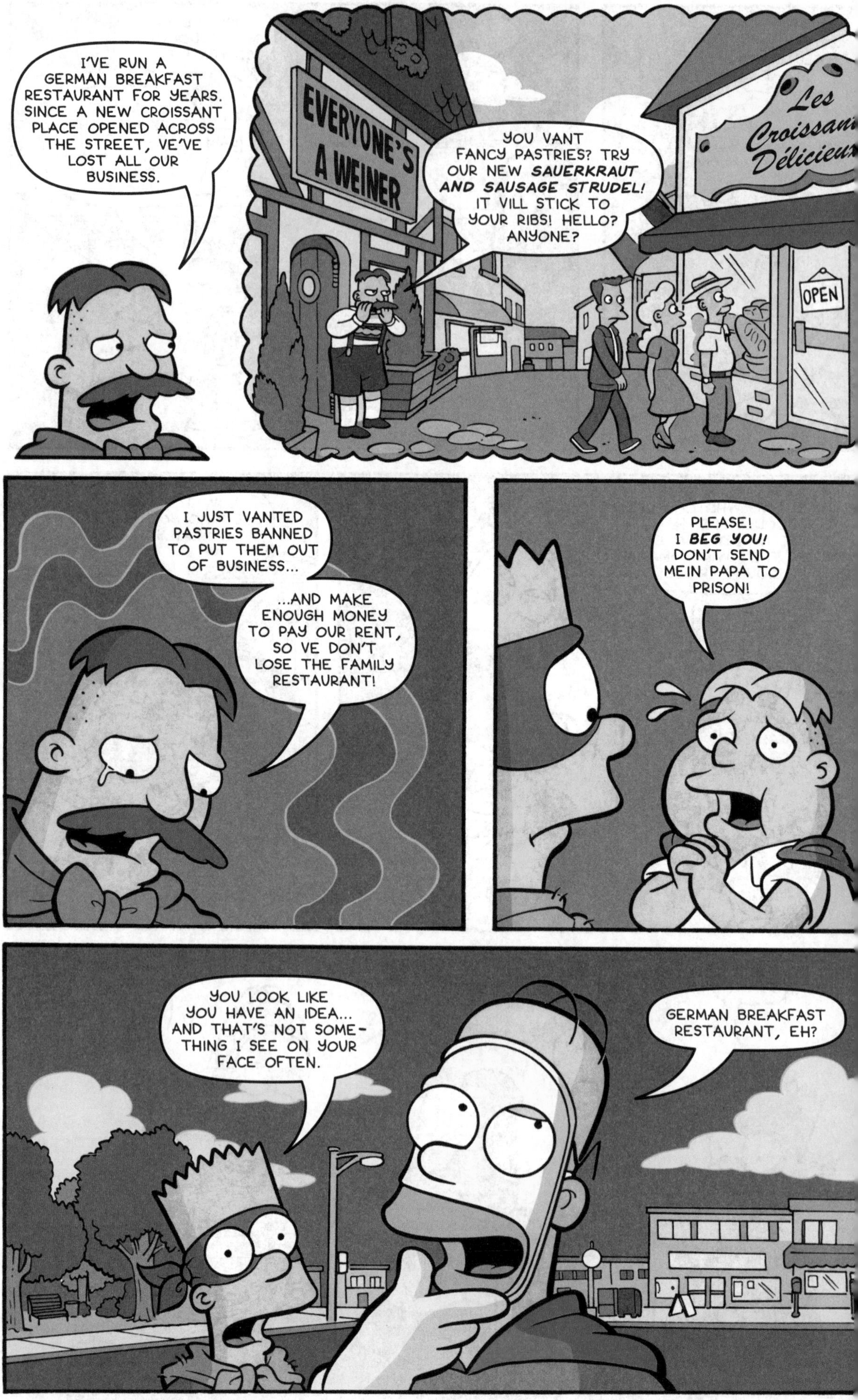
I'VE RUN A GERMAN BREAKFAST RESTAURANT FOR YEARS. SINCE A NEW CROISSANT PLACE OPENED ACROSS THE STREET, VE'VE LOST ALL OUR BUSINESS.
EVERYONE'S A WEINER
Les Croissants Délicieux
YOU VANT FANCY PASTRIES? TRY OUR NEW SAUERKRAUT AND SAUSAGE STRUDEL! IT VILL STICK TO YOUR RIBS! HELLO? ANYONE?
OPEN
I JUST VANTED PASTRIES BANNED TO PUT THEM OUT OF BUSINESS...
...AND MAKE ENOUGH MONEY TO PAY OUR RENT, SO VE DON'T LOSE THE FAMILY RESTAURANT!
PLEASE! I BEG YOU! DON'T SEND MEIN PAPA TO PRISON!
YOU LOOK LIKE YOU HAVE AN IDEA... AND THAT'S NOT SOME-THING I SEE ON YOUR FACE OFTEN.
GERMAN BREAKFAST RESTAURANT, EH?

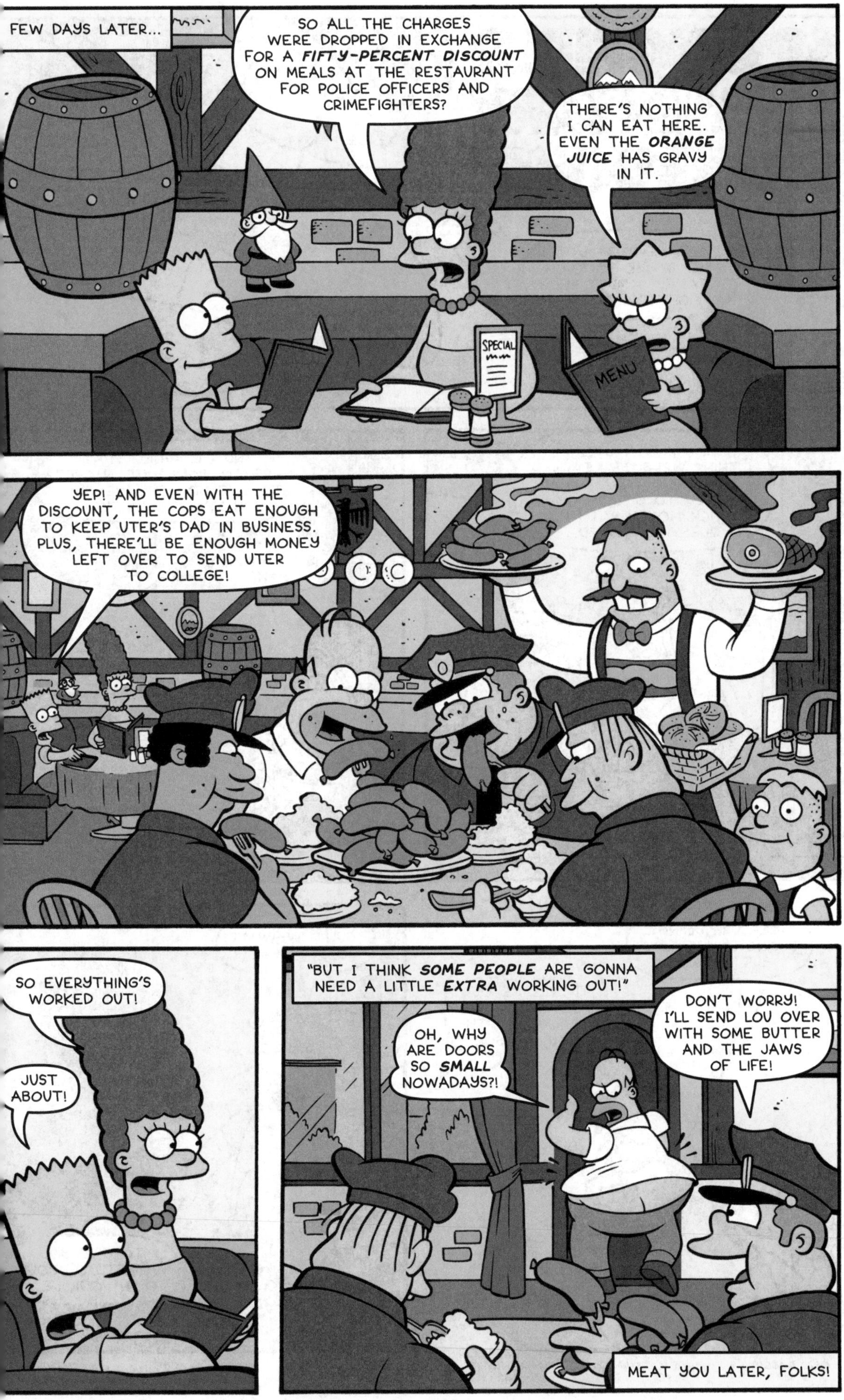
FEW DAYS LATER...
SO ALL THE CHARGES WERE DROPPED IN EXCHANGE FOR A FIFTY-PERCENT DISCOUNT ON MEALS AT THE RESTAURANT FOR POLICE OFFICERS AND CRIMEFIGHTERS?
THERE'S NOTHING I CAN EAT HERE. EVEN THE ORANGE JUICE HAS GRAVY IN IT.
SPECIAL
MENU
YEP! AND EVEN WITH THE DISCOUNT, THE COPS EAT ENOUGH TO KEEP UTER'S DAD IN BUSINESS. PLUS, THERE'LL BE ENOUGH MONEY LEFT OVER TO SEND UTER TO COLLEGE!
SO EVERYTHING'S WORKED OUT!
JUST ABOUT!
"BUT I THINK SOME PEOPLE ARE GONNA NEED A LITTLE EXTRA WORKING OUT!"
OH, WHY ARE DOORS SO SMALL NOWADAYS?!
DON'T WORRY! I'LL SEND LOU OVER WITH SOME BUTTER AND THE JAWS OF LIFE!
MEAT YOU LATER, FOLKS!

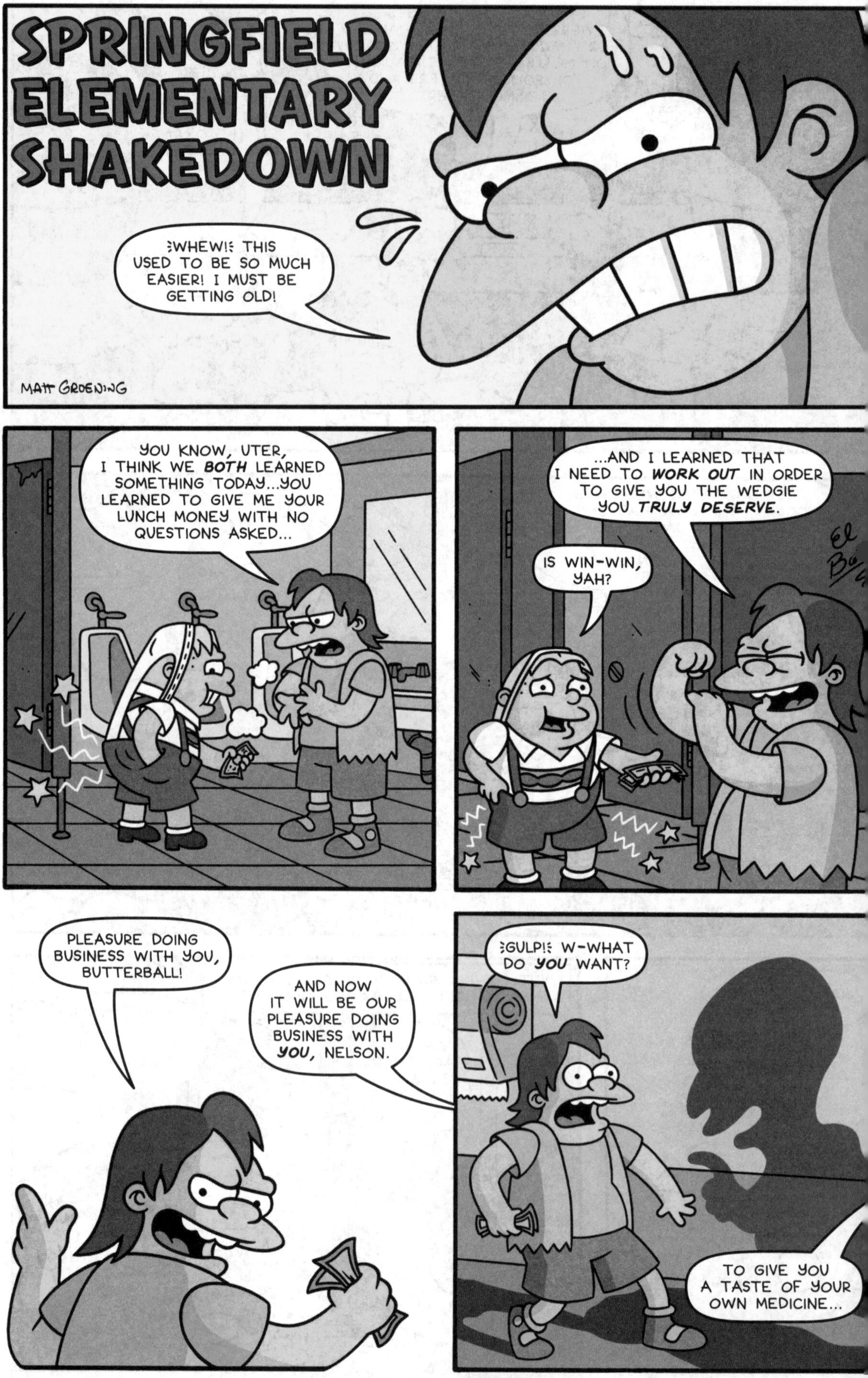
SPRINGFIELD ELEMENTARY SHAKEDOWN
ːWHEW!ː THIS USED TO BE SO MUCH EASIER! I MUST BE GETTING OLD!
MATT GROENING
YOU KNOW, UTER, I THINK WE BOTH LEARNED SOMETHING TODAY...YOU LEARNED TO GIVE ME YOUR LUNCH MONEY WITH NO QUESTIONS ASKED...
...AND I LEARNED THAT I NEED TO WORK OUT IN ORDER TO GIVE YOU THE WEDGIE YOU TRULY DESERVE.
IS WIN-WIN, YAH?
PLEASURE DOING BUSINESS WITH YOU, BUTTERBALL!
AND NOW IT WILL BE OUR PLEASURE DOING BUSINESS WITH YOU, NELSON.
ːGULP!ː W-WHAT DO YOU WANT?
TO GIVE YOU A TASTE OF YOUR OWN MEDICINE...

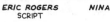

ERIC ROGERS SCRIPT
NINA MATSUMOTO PENCILS
MIKE ROTE INKS
NATHAN HAMILL COLORS
KAREN BATES LETTERS
NATHAN KANE EDITOR

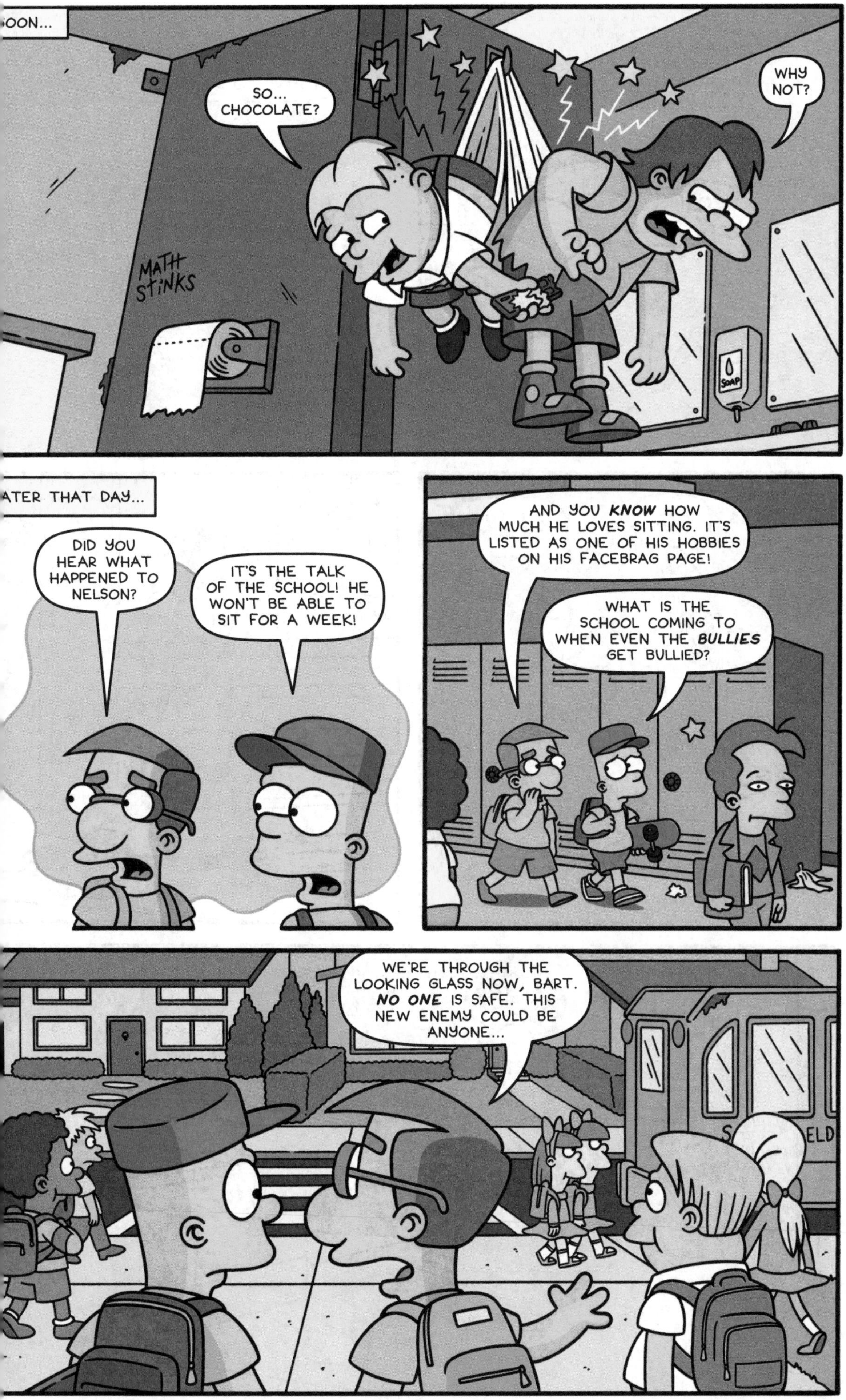

SOON...
SO... CHOCOLATE?
WHY NOT?
MATH STINKS
SOAP
LATER THAT DAY...
DID YOU HEAR WHAT HAPPENED TO NELSON?
IT'S THE TALK OF THE SCHOOL! HE WON'T BE ABLE TO SIT FOR A WEEK!
AND YOU KNOW HOW MUCH HE LOVES SITTING. IT'S LISTED AS ONE OF HIS HOBBIES ON HIS FACEBRAG PAGE!
WHAT IS THE SCHOOL COMING TO WHEN EVEN THE BULLIES GET BULLIED?
WE'RE THROUGH THE LOOKING GLASS NOW, BART. NO ONE IS SAFE. THIS NEW ENEMY COULD BE ANYONE...

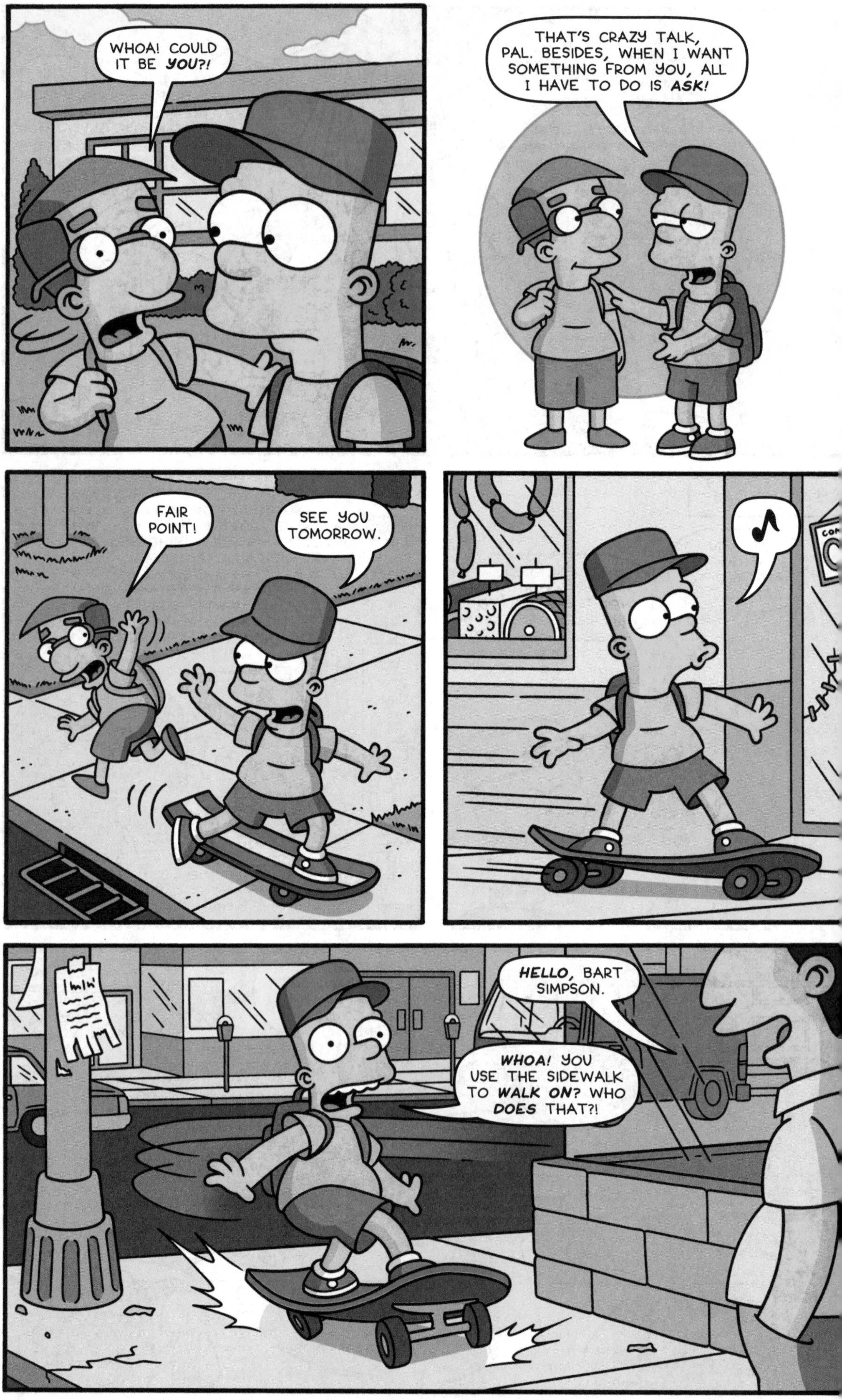
WHOA! COULD IT BE *YOU*?!
THAT'S CRAZY TALK, PAL. BESIDES, WHEN I WANT SOMETHING FROM YOU, ALL I HAVE TO DO IS *ASK*!
FAIR POINT!
SEE YOU TOMORROW.
HELLO, BART SIMPSON.
WHOA! YOU USE THE SIDEWALK TO *WALK ON*? WHO *DOES* THAT?!

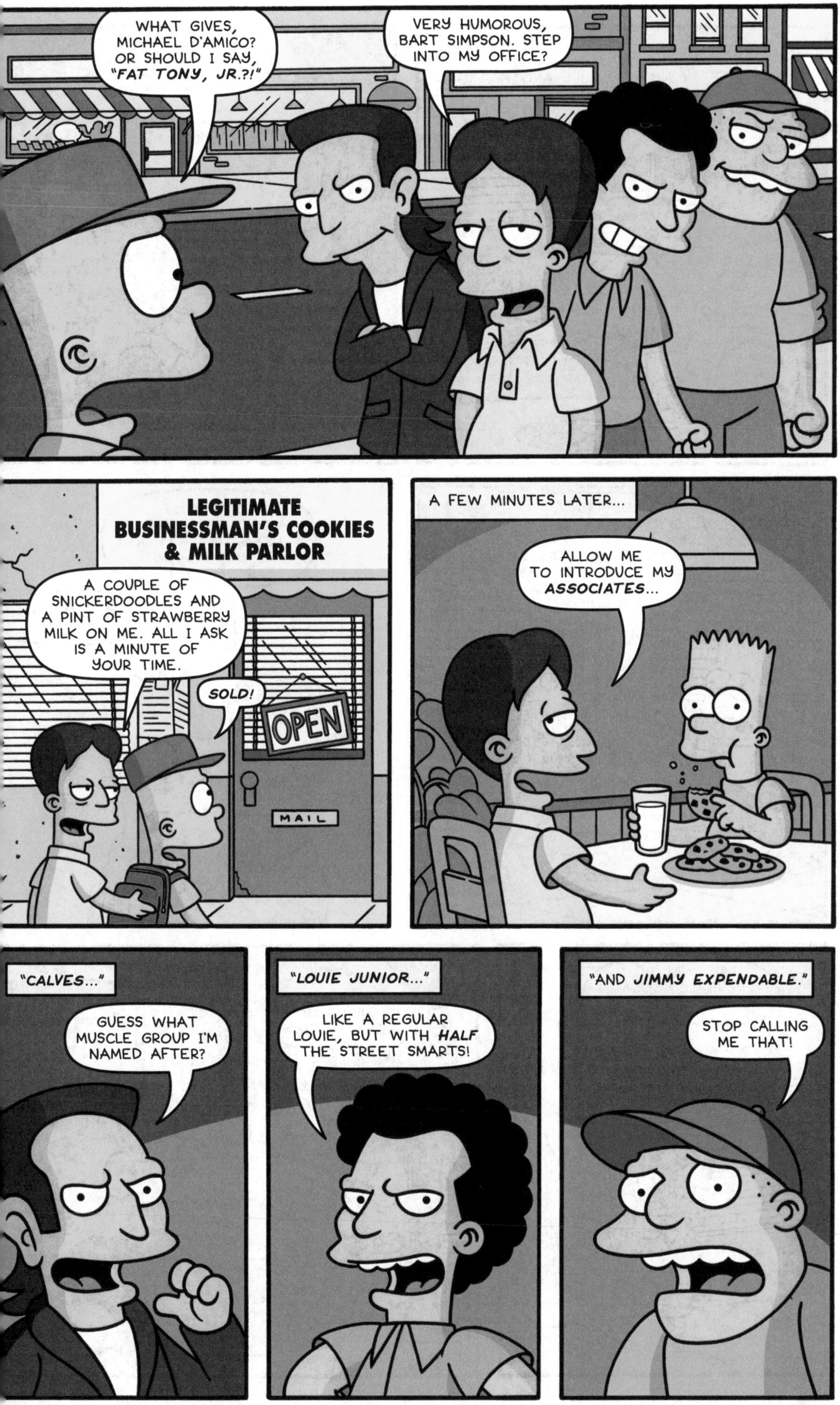
WHAT GIVES, MICHAEL D'AMICO? OR SHOULD I SAY, "*FAT TONY, JR.?!*"
VERY HUMOROUS, BART SIMPSON. STEP INTO MY OFFICE?
LEGITIMATE BUSINESSMAN'S COOKIES & MILK PARLOR
A COUPLE OF SNICKERDOODLES AND A PINT OF STRAWBERRY MILK ON ME. ALL I ASK IS A MINUTE OF YOUR TIME.
SOLD!
OPEN
MAIL
A FEW MINUTES LATER...
ALLOW ME TO INTRODUCE MY *ASSOCIATES*...
"*CALVES*..."
GUESS WHAT MUSCLE GROUP I'M NAMED AFTER?
"*LOUIE JUNIOR*..."
LIKE A REGULAR LOUIE, BUT WITH *HALF* THE STREET SMARTS!
"AND *JIMMY EXPENDABLE*."
STOP CALLING ME THAT!

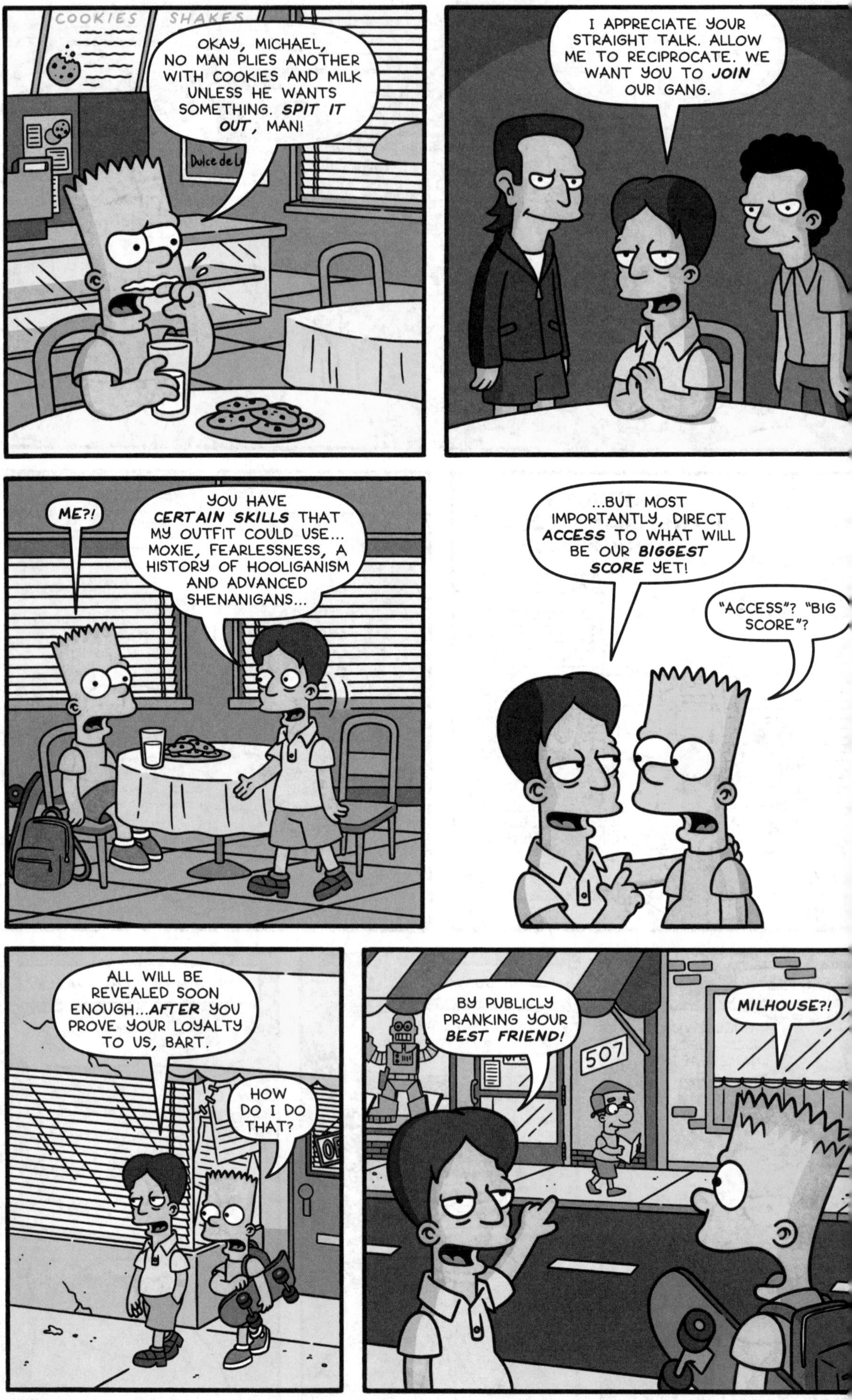

COOKIES
SHAKES
OKAY, MICHAEL, NO MAN PLIES ANOTHER WITH COOKIES AND MILK UNLESS HE WANTS SOMETHING. *SPIT IT OUT*, MAN!
I APPRECIATE YOUR STRAIGHT TALK. ALLOW ME TO RECIPROCATE. WE WANT YOU TO *JOIN* OUR GANG.
ME?!
YOU HAVE *CERTAIN SKILLS* THAT MY OUTFIT COULD USE... MOXIE, FEARLESSNESS, A HISTORY OF HOOLIGANISM AND ADVANCED SHENANIGANS...
...BUT MOST IMPORTANTLY, DIRECT *ACCESS* TO WHAT WILL BE OUR *BIGGEST SCORE* YET!
"ACCESS"? "BIG SCORE"?
ALL WILL BE REVEALED SOON ENOUGH...*AFTER* YOU PROVE YOUR LOYALTY TO US, BART.
HOW DO I DO THAT?
BY PUBLICLY PRANKING YOUR *BEST FRIEND!*
507
MILHOUSE?!

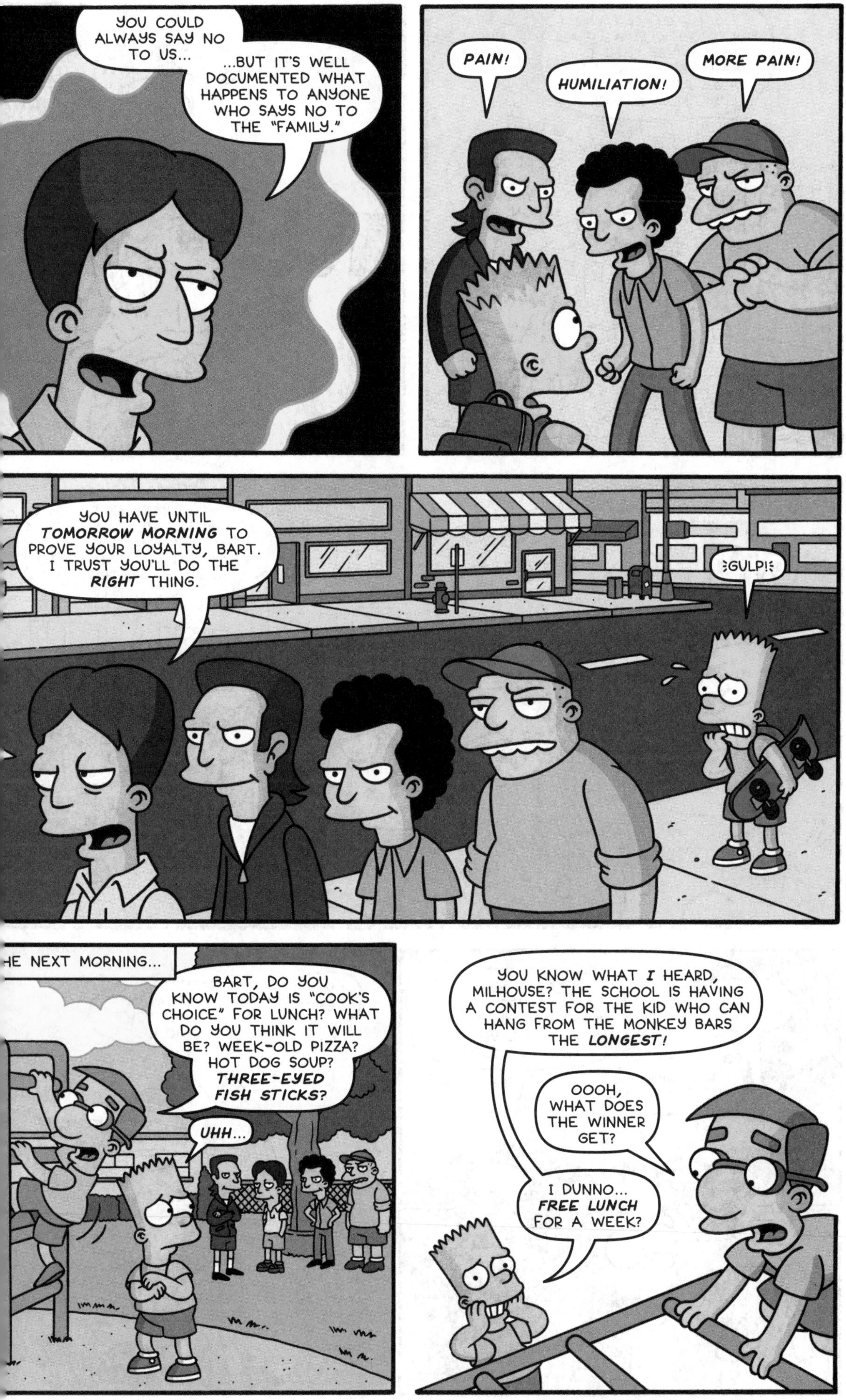
YOU COULD ALWAYS SAY NO TO US...
...BUT IT'S WELL DOCUMENTED WHAT HAPPENS TO ANYONE WHO SAYS NO TO THE "FAMILY."
PAIN!
HUMILIATION!
MORE PAIN!
YOU HAVE UNTIL TOMORROW MORNING TO PROVE YOUR LOYALTY, BART. I TRUST YOU'LL DO THE RIGHT THING.
GULP!
HE NEXT MORNING...
BART, DO YOU KNOW TODAY IS "COOK'S CHOICE" FOR LUNCH? WHAT DO YOU THINK IT WILL BE? WEEK-OLD PIZZA? HOT DOG SOUP? THREE-EYED FISH STICKS?
UHH...
YOU KNOW WHAT I HEARD, MILHOUSE? THE SCHOOL IS HAVING A CONTEST FOR THE KID WHO CAN HANG FROM THE MONKEY BARS THE LONGEST!
OOOH, WHAT DOES THE WINNER GET?
I DUNNO... FREE LUNCH FOR A WEEK?

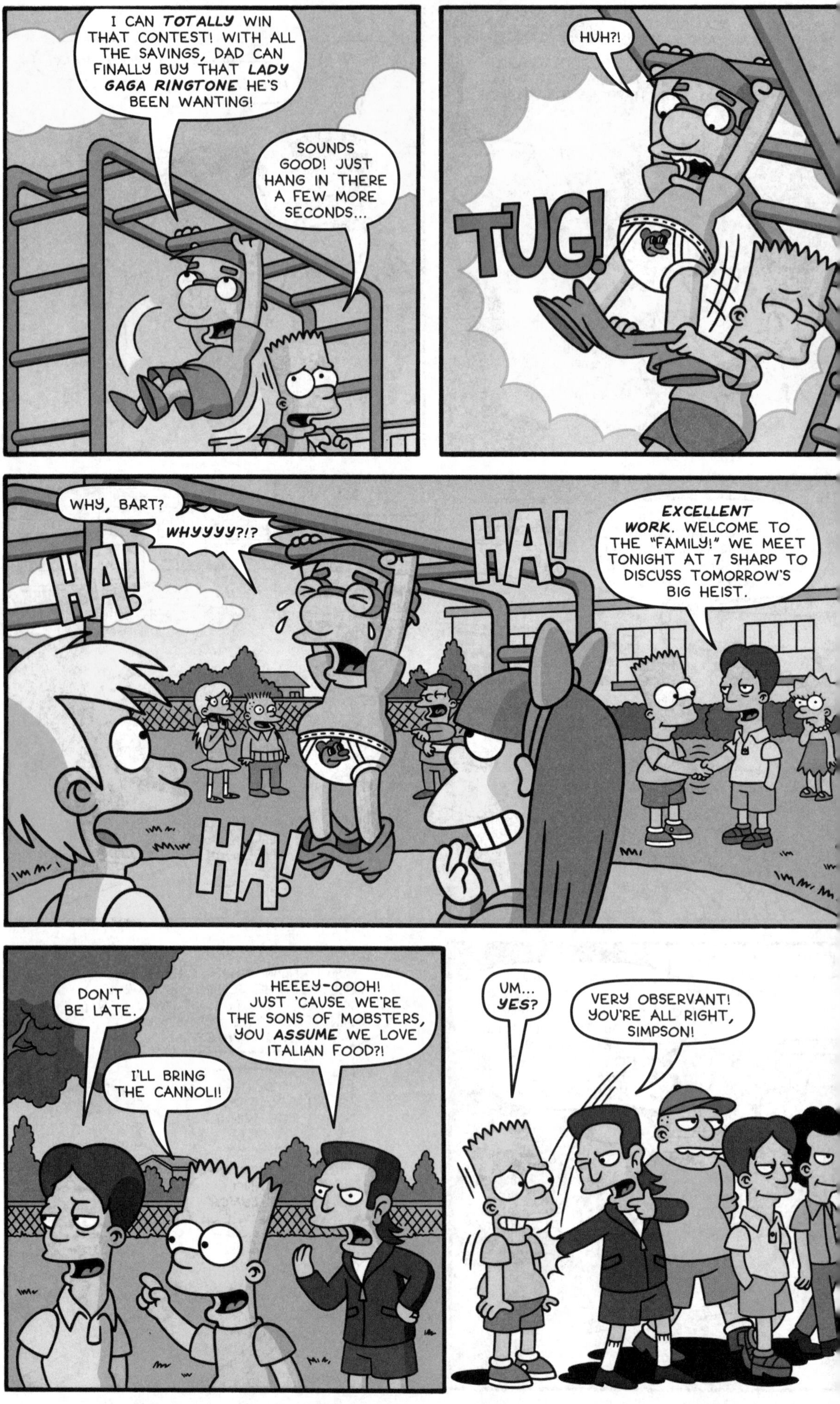
I CAN *TOTALLY* WIN THAT CONTEST! WITH ALL THE SAVINGS, DAD CAN FINALLY BUY THAT *LADY GAGA RINGTONE* HE'S BEEN WANTING!
SOUNDS GOOD! JUST HANG IN THERE A FEW MORE SECONDS...
HUH?!
TUG!
WHY, BART?
WHYYYY?!?
HA!
HA!
HA!
EXCELLENT WORK. WELCOME TO THE "FAMILY!" WE MEET TONIGHT AT 7 SHARP TO DISCUSS TOMORROW'S BIG HEIST.
DON'T BE LATE.
I'LL BRING THE CANNOLI!
HEEEY-OOOH! JUST 'CAUSE WE'RE THE SONS OF MOBSTERS, YOU *ASSUME* WE LOVE ITALIAN FOOD?!
UM... *YES*?
VERY OBSERVANT! YOU'RE ALL RIGHT, SIMPSON!

¦AHEM!¦

LISA?!

WHY ARE YOU EVEN TALKING TO MICHAEL D'AMICO, LET ALONE TRYING TO JOIN HIS *JUNIOR MAFIA*?

BELIEVE ME, THE LESS YOU KNOW, THE *BETTER*.

THEY'RE GOING TO GET YOU IN *BIG TROUBLE,* BART! THE KIND THAT LEADS TO LIVING IN A CELL AND PRAYING FOR CAKES WITH FILES HIDDEN INSIDE!

I DON'T HAVE TO EXPLAIN MYSELF TO YOU!

OH, BART... WHAT HAVE YOU GOTTEN YOURSELF *INTO*?

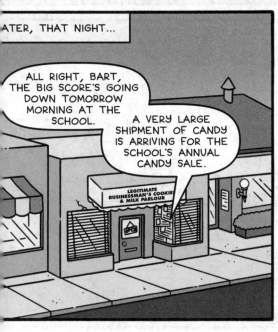

ATER, THAT NIGHT...

ALL RIGHT, BART, THE BIG SCORE'S GOING DOWN TOMORROW MORNING AT THE SCHOOL.

A VERY LARGE SHIPMENT OF CANDY IS ARRIVING FOR THE SCHOOL'S ANNUAL CANDY SALE.

LEGITIMATE BUSINESSMAN'S COOKIES & MILK PARLOUR

YOUR SISTER LISA IS IN CHARGE OF DISTRIBUTING THE CANDY TO THE STUDENT BODY. BUT BEFORE SHE GETS THE CHANCE TO DO THAT...

...*WE* ARE GOING TO STEAL THAT CANDY. AND THIS IS WHERE *YOU* COME IN.

¦GULP!¦

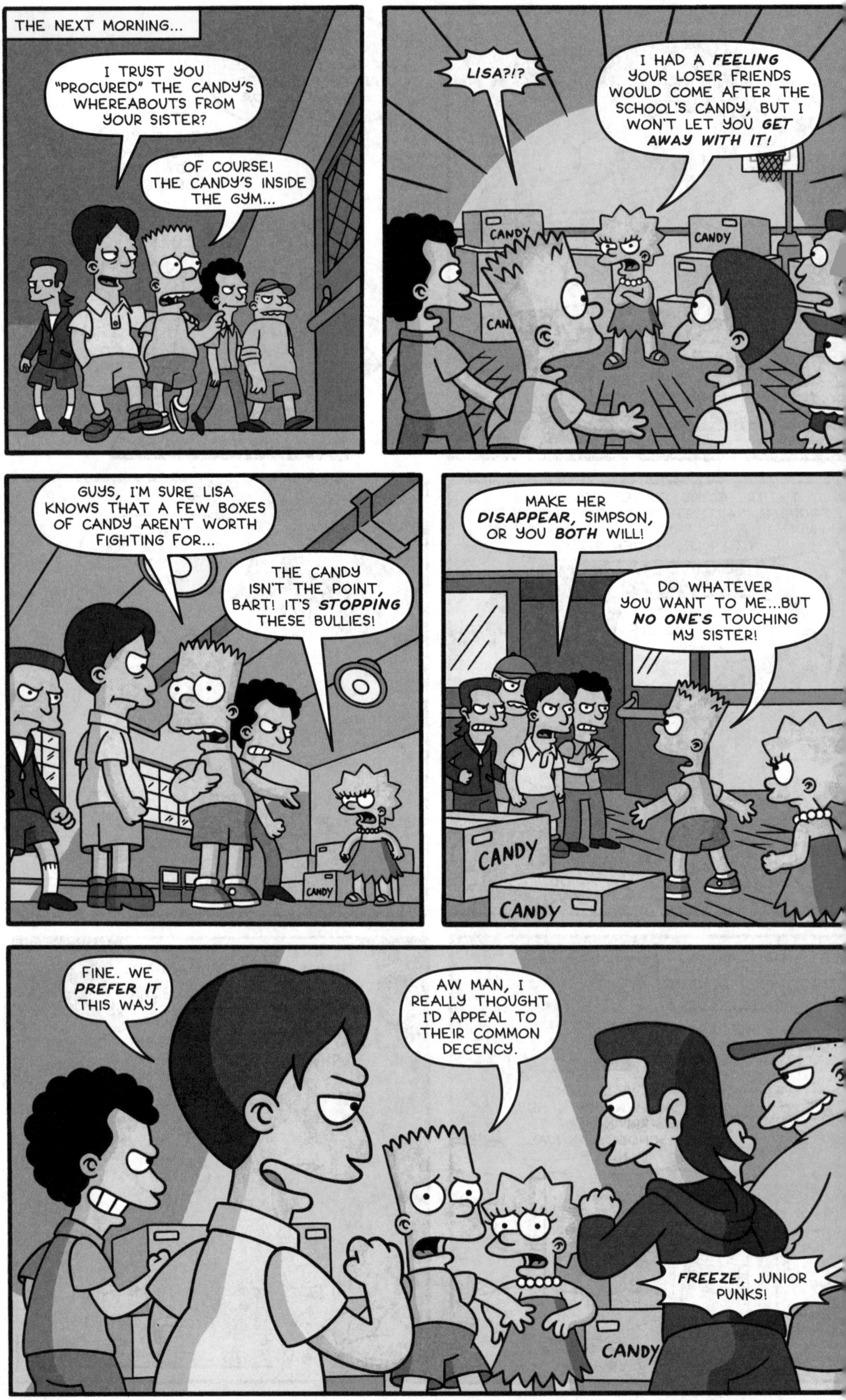

THE NEXT MORNING...
I TRUST YOU "PROCURED" THE CANDY'S WHEREABOUTS FROM YOUR SISTER?
OF COURSE! THE CANDY'S INSIDE THE GYM...
LISA?!?
I HAD A **FEELING** YOUR LOSER FRIENDS WOULD COME AFTER THE SCHOOL'S CANDY, BUT I WON'T LET YOU **GET AWAY WITH IT!**
CANDY
GUYS, I'M SURE LISA KNOWS THAT A FEW BOXES OF CANDY AREN'T WORTH FIGHTING FOR...
THE CANDY ISN'T THE POINT, BART! IT'S **STOPPING** THESE BULLIES!
MAKE HER **DISAPPEAR,** SIMPSON, OR YOU **BOTH** WILL!
DO WHATEVER YOU WANT TO ME...BUT **NO ONE'S** TOUCHING MY SISTER!
CANDY
FINE. WE **PREFER IT** THIS WAY.
AW MAN, I REALLY THOUGHT I'D APPEAL TO THEIR COMMON DECENCY.
FREEZE, JUNIOR PUNKS!
CANDY

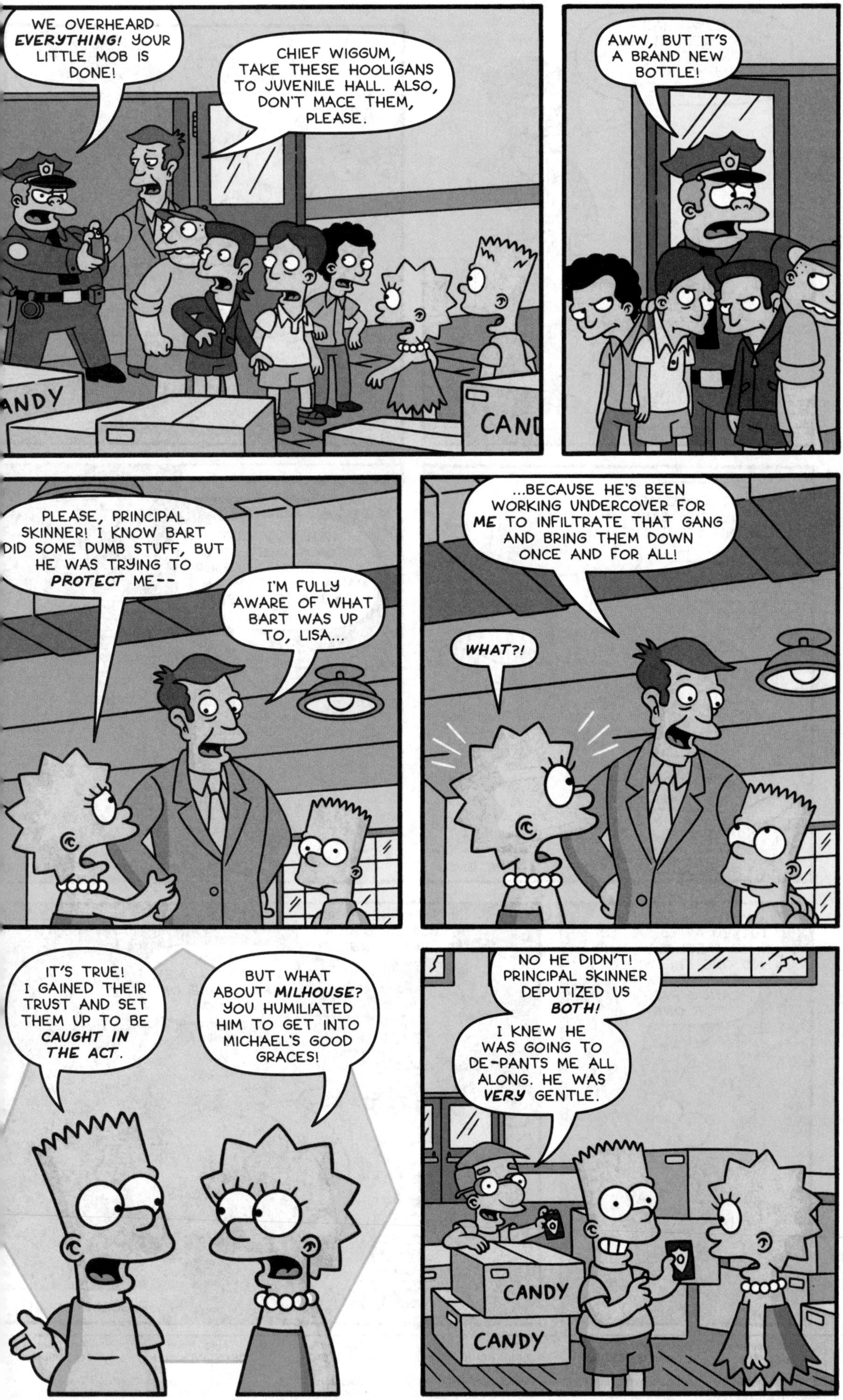
WE OVERHEARD EVERYTHING! YOUR LITTLE MOB IS DONE!
CHIEF WIGGUM, TAKE THESE HOOLIGANS TO JUVENILE HALL. ALSO, DON'T MACE THEM, PLEASE.
ANDY
CAND
AWW, BUT IT'S A BRAND NEW BOTTLE!
PLEASE, PRINCIPAL SKINNER! I KNOW BART DID SOME DUMB STUFF, BUT HE WAS TRYING TO PROTECT ME--
I'M FULLY AWARE OF WHAT BART WAS UP TO, LISA...
...BECAUSE HE'S BEEN WORKING UNDERCOVER FOR ME TO INFILTRATE THAT GANG AND BRING THEM DOWN ONCE AND FOR ALL!
WHAT?!
IT'S TRUE! I GAINED THEIR TRUST AND SET THEM UP TO BE CAUGHT IN THE ACT.
BUT WHAT ABOUT MILHOUSE? YOU HUMILIATED HIM TO GET INTO MICHAEL'S GOOD GRACES!
NO HE DIDN'T! PRINCIPAL SKINNER DEPUTIZED US BOTH!
I KNEW HE WAS GOING TO DE-PANTS ME ALL ALONG. HE WAS VERY GENTLE.
CANDY
CANDY

NOW THAT THAT'S SETTLED, LET'S TAKE INVENTORY OF THE CANDY WE HAVE TO SELL THIS YEAR!

‡GASP!‡ IT'S *EMPTY!!!*

IT CAN'T BE!!

BUT IF MICHAEL D'AMICO'S GANG DIDN'T STEAL THE CANDY...

...WHO DID?

THE END?

EPILOGUE: THAT NIGHT...

HEH HEH! JUST BECAUSE I STOPPED THE SCHOOL'S JUNIOR MAFIA DOESN'T MEAN I CAN'T *WET MY BEAK* A LITTLE...

WITH THE CANDY TUCKED AWAY SAFELY IN MY TREEHOUSE, AND NO ONE THE WISER, IT'S TIME FOR A *CANDY PARTY FOR ONE!*

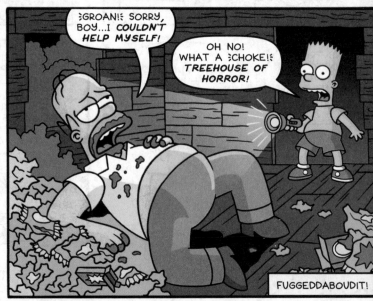

‡GROAN!‡ SORRY, BOY...I *COULDN'T HELP MYSELF!*

OH NO! WHAT A ‡CHOKE!‡ *TREEHOUSE OF HORROR!*

FUGGEDDABOUDIT!

| Matt Groening PUBLISHER | Terry Delegeane MANAGING EDITOR | Christopher Ungar PRODUCTION MGR. | Jason Ho ART DIRECTOR | Karen Bates ASSISTANT EDITOR | Pete Benson COORDINATOR |
| Nathan Kane CREATIVE DIRECTOR | Robert Zaugh OPERATIONS | Serban Cristescu SPECIAL PROJECTS | Mike Rote ASST. ART DIRECTOR | Art Villanueva COLORS | Ruth Waytz ADMINISTRATION |